Taking the MYP Forward

Edited by
Mary Hayden and Jeff Thompson

John Catt Educational Ltd

First Published 2011

by John Catt Educational Ltd,
12 Deben Mill Business Centre, Old Maltings Approach,
Melton, Woodbridge IP12 1BL

Tel: +44 (0) 1394 389850 Fax: +44 (0) 1394 386893
Email: enquiries@johncatt.com
Website: www.johncatt.com

ISBN: 978 1 908095 17 6

eISBN: 978 1 908095 18 3

Set and designed by John Catt Educational Limited

Printed and bound in Great Britain by Bell & Bain, Glasgow, Scotland

Acknowledgements and notes

The authors, editors and publishers are grateful to the International Baccaulaureate Organization for permission to reproduce its intellecutal property, specifically the IB learner profile and the MYP model; to Ian Fox of FoxEd Education Consultants Ltd, New Zealand, for permission to use the 'Learning to Learn Portfolio Model'; and for permission to use 'The Key Elements for Responsible Global Citizenship' on page 105, which is reproduced from *Education for Global Citizenship*, 2006, and is used with the permission of Oxfam GB, Oxfam House, John Smith Drive, Cowley, Oxford OB4 2JY, UK (www.oxfam.org.uk/education).

Oxfam GB does not necessarily endorse any text or activities that accompany the materials, nor has it approved the adapted text.

This material has been developed independently by the publisher and the content is in no way connected with nor endorsed by the International Baccalaureate Organization.

In 2008 the IB dropped the 'O' from their acronym – IBO became IB. The latter style has been used throughout.

Contents

Part D: Futures for Middle Years Schooling

Taking the MYP Forward

About the Contributors

Matthew Albrighton, after graduating from Cambridge with a degree in geography and management, entered the field of advertising. Following teacher training (PGCE) at the University of Birmingham, he taught at King Edward's School Birmingham and Warwick School before moving to Wellington College, as head of geography. More recently he was appointed as the MYP coordinator at Wellington, where he is also tutor in a boarding house as well as a coach of rugby and athletics.

David Batten has worked in nine international schools in four continents over the past 35 years. His guiding inspiration remains true to a singular philosophy presented in the very early years of the IB – to help create a better and more peaceful world by promoting education as a force for good. David is currently a trustee of the Kindred Project, a member of the senior leadership team and the MYP coordinator at Sotogrande International School, Spain.

Adam Brown has taught MYP English for many years at the International School of Milan, combining teaching with the role of MYP coordinator and, more recently, middle school Principal. Adam recently completed a Masters degree in education with the UK Open University, a course which provided much useful material for his contribution to this book, taking particular inspiration from the work of Neil Mercer and Jerome Bruner.

Michael Chapman is Headmaster of St Gilgen International School, Austria. He is entering his 21st year of school leadership, having been designated as a 'National Leader of Education' in the UK in 2008. This highest accolade for school leaders is reserved for those with a proven track record of outstanding learner achievement, success and innovation over an extended period. His specialist areas are in leadership of change, curriculum innovation, performance management and teacher pedagogical development.

Chris Charleson has worked in IB schools and organisations for over 25 years, involving a variety of roles in a wide diversity of locations. He continues to be passionate about helping young people find their unique talent through authentic learning and global citizenship experiences. He is currently chair of the IB Heads Council and Head of Sotogrande International School, Spain. He is also a trustee of the Kindred Project, organised from his school, providing activities in four communities worldwide.

Dominic Currer is Director of the International School of Zug and Luzern. After degrees from the University of Southampton, he taught a range of subjects at A level, AP and IB. He has held posts as assistant principal, Principal and curriculum coordinator. He has worked with middle school students for 20 years, and has also designed middle school curricula. He has served on international school accreditation teams, orchestrated a school merger, and been most recently involved in the construction of new school buildings.

Maggie Dickson has taught English language and literature, EAL and art in international education for many years, before which she worked in comprehensive schools in London. She is an active presenter of language-related matters at European conferences and within the European School system. She has recently been appointed MYP coordinator at the International School of Milan, having previously been responsible for EAL and language support coordination.

Erika Elkady worked from 1996 to 2007 at the International Secondary School of Eindhoven in The Netherlands, where she taught MYP and DP history before becoming acting MYP coordinator. After moving to Uptown School in Dubai as MYP coordinator she subsequently became deputy head. In September 2011 she will become Head of secondary at Jumeira Baccalaureate School, a Dubai-based IB school in the Taaleem group. Experience in MYP has included being a consultant and team member on various pre-authorization, authorization and evaluation visits.

Janet Field has taught music and English in MYP schools since 1998, and has coordinated the MYP in two schools for ten years in total. She is now the Head of the primary and middle school at Skagerak International School in Sandefjord, Norway. Over the past decade she has participated in the development of the MYP through curriculum review, assessment moderation, the development of teacher support material and online courses, school visits and leading teacher workshops.

Dr John Hare is head of chemistry at Graveney School, London, having previously taught in the UK, USA and Switzerland. He was a school governor and science teacher at the International School of the Basel Region, where he first became interested in the holistic approach to education through MYP. This led to an MPhil at the University of Bath. John's interest continues in developing holistic education programmes within both international and national schools. Before entering education, John was a human resources professional with several multinational organisations.

Dr Mary Hayden is Director of the Centre for the study of Education in an International Context (CEIC) at the University of Bath, and editor of the *Journal of Research in International Education*. Her teaching, publishing and research supervision focus particularly on international schools and international education. She is a trustee of the Alliance for International Education, a member of the International Primary Curriculum (IPC) Advisory Board and academic advisor to the International Leadership Management Programme (ILMP).

Tracy Moxley has worked in both international and UK education for over 20 years and has also been a trainer for UK-based educational organisations. As a curriculum developer she is committed to interdisciplinary, global citizenship education. Currently she is head of pastoral care and a member of the senior leadership team at Sotogrande International School in Spain, where she continues to be inspired by her students.

Éanna O'Boyle left teaching in Ireland nearly 20 years ago and has worked ever since in a variety of international schools located in Spain, Turkey, and Uzbekistan. He is currently based in Tanzania, where he is the MYP coordinator and Head of the Arusha campus at the International School Moshi. He has contributed to the development of the MYP as a consultant and also as a workshop leader.

Eif Phillips has been at Munich International School (MIS) since 1986 and is currently the middle school Principal. MIS was authorised to implement the MYP in 1998 and since then it has hosted two subsequent evaluation visits. Working on the self-studies prior to these visits and the action plans following them, along with participating in 19 MYP team visits, have been essential aspects of his own professional development.

J Eric Robertson is coordinator of curriculum and professional development at Toronto French School, which is currently implementing both the PYP and MYP to complement its well-established IB Diploma Programme. Eric previously coordinated the MYP at The York School in Toronto, Canada, and the International School of Basel in Switzerland. He recently completed his work for a doctoral thesis on MYP coordination at the University of Bath.

Sally Smitheram has been coordinating and teaching MYP language A English at the International School of Milan since 2007. Prior to this she was a head of department at a specialist English state school, having coordinated Key Stage 3 and literacy across the curriculum in two other schools. Sally is a strong advocate of the national literacy strategy, believing that students must be given the necessary tools to express themselves appropriately.

Dr Lesley Snowball is an experienced special education, language and curriculum specialist. For ten years she worked with the International School of Amsterdam, the first school in the world to offer all three IB programmes, and she now runs her own organization, Putting it into Practice, supporting the implementation of PYP and MYP in schools worldwide. With Pearson Education, she and her husband, Kenneth, have recently published the *Primary Inquirer* series.

Wilf Stout has been an educationalist for over 40 years as a biology teacher, curriculum developer at the University of Cambridge and founding Director of the International School of South Africa and the four campuses of the International School of Cape Town. He was involved in developing and pioneering the Cambridge IGCSE in the 1980s and is currently Head of School at the International School of London in Qatar.

Professor Jeff Thompson teaches, supervises, researches and publishes through the Centre for the study of Education in an International Context (CEIC) of the

University of Bath, in areas relating specifically to international schools and international education. He has worked closely for many years with the International Baccalaureate organization and, more recently, the International Primary Curriculum (IPC) for which he is chair of the Advisory Board. He was founding editor for the *Journal of Research in International Education* and founding chair of the Alliance for International Education.

Foreword

The middle years phase of schooling, whether in national or international systems, seems to present both challenge and opportunity in equal measure to those responsible for arrangements relating to curricular and resource (human and other) provision. It follows on from the primary or elementary phase, which in most contexts sets foundations within the compulsory period of education based upon clearly defined pedagogic approaches. It is succeeded by an upper secondary education that is hardly less targeted in its goals and intentions, particularly in respect of progression to higher education or employment. It can therefore suffer from the multiple requirements it is called upon to satisfy both by precedent and as antecedent. Consequently, across the wide range of provision throughout the world, there exists a high degree of diversity of programme design for the middle years. For some educators freedom of curricular exploration and implementation will be welcomed. For others, it will represent a challenge in securing the role of the middle years as part of the curricular continuity that underpins the planned and supported progression in learning and development that should be the right of each individual student.

The middle years also constitute a period of rapid change and development in all aspects of the life of adolescents, as they leave childhood behind and move towards adulthood. It is during this phase that they progress from experiencing significant scaffolding of their learning at the primary level to becoming increasingly responsible for their own learning. The transition from elementary to secondary schooling is therefore influenced by a wide range of cognitive, affective, social and emotional factors, often within a changing school environment, which can present challenges both to the students themselves and to those with whom they live and study.

The addition in 1994 of the MYP to the existing and well established Diploma Programme (DP) of the International Baccalaureate organisation (IB), together with the acquisition in 1997 of the Primary Years Programme (PYP), gave the IB a continuum of curricular provision for the entire school age range for the first time in its history. Since 1997 each of the three programmes has undergone significant development in responding to the rapidly changing contexts in which they are placed, and to an increase in our understanding of how children learn. That development will surely continue, as will the effort to weld the three separately originated programmes into a homogeneous continuum, a great deal of which is expended by those in the schools authorised by the IB to teach its programmes. In agreeing to edit a collection of views, perceptions and opinions concerning possible ways in which the MYP may be taken forward in future, we have drawn heavily upon the experience of teachers, coordinators, administrators, workshop leaders, researchers and curriculum developers who are not only familiar with the current MYP but who, reflecting upon their work in school and programme improvement in the middle years, are also prepared to share their experience and their thinking more widely.

The manner in which we have structured this book is a response to the notion – embedded in its title – that the experience of those involved in the MYP should be drawn upon in identifying aspects of current practice that could contribute to the development of the programme. Material is organised in four distinct parts. The first (Part A) sets out the context of the MYP, in terms of a description of the programme (enabling reference to be made throughout the reading of the book to the design features of the MYP model) and a consideration of the nature of adolescence and the ways in which student needs may be met through the pedagogy of middle years schooling. Part B comprises a series of chapters grounded in MYP practice in schools, and the ways in which experienced practitioners have interpreted the essential elements of the programme in responding to the current learning needs of their students and anticipating how those needs may change in the future. Part C widens the scope of the discussion by considering a range of factors affecting the implementation of the MYP, including the crucial role of the MYP coordinator in that process. For the final part (Part D) we have invited two experienced Heads to speculate about the likely nature of middle years schooling in the future, which the IB may wish to consider in the long-term development of the MYP programme.

As editors and commissioners of the contributions to this collection, we have attempted to encourage in the writing of chapters a blend of personal reflection on selected aspects of current practice with ideas arising from experiences of making it happen in schools. By so doing we hope that the issues raised will be of interest and relevance to those with responsibility for MYP teaching, learning and organisation in schools and that they will provoke interest in the programme amongst those who may consider its adoption in future.

We wish to thank everyone who has been involved in the production of this book. In particular, our appreciation for their efforts is extended to our chapter authors – all of whom have been prepared to share their views, based upon impressively wide experience, and who have thereby made such a valuable contribution to this collection. We pay tribute to them for their patience, their expertise and their willingness to find time in their busy schedules to work with us in this way. We also acknowledge the support and guidance we have received from colleagues at John Catt Educational Limited, with whom it has been a pleasure to work.

Mary Hayden

Jeff Thompson

Part A

The Middle Years Context

Chapter 1

The Middle Years Programme

Mary Hayden and Jeff Thompson

Background

Anyone new to the International Baccalaureate (IB) Middle Years Programme (MYP), who sees that in 2011 it is offered in over 850 schools worldwide (IB, 2011), might well be surprised to learn that the programme has only been in existence since 1994. Though that may have been the date of its formal creation as an IB programme, the MYP has its roots in ideas and discussions dating back some two decades previously. As is documented in the excellent, recently-published, history of the MYP produced by Malcolm Nicolson and Lister Hannah (IB, 2010b), the origins of the MYP were arguably in the need expressed by a number of international schools in the 1970s for a middle school curriculum that would act as an appropriate preparation for the Diploma Programme (DP) offered by the IB for the first time in 1970. The development of the IB diploma as the first international curriculum offered for the 16-19 age range, which would not be affiliated to any one national system, would encourage an international rather than national outlook, and would be recognised by universities worldwide, is documented in a number of publications including Peterson's seminal account based on his own first hand involvement in its development (Peterson, 1987). As the IB diploma grew in popularity, the perceived mismatch with nationally-focused middle years programmes became more marked, leading to an initiative by the International Schools Association (ISA) to develop what became the ISA Curriculum (ISAC) in the late 1980s, and subsequently the 11-16 IB Middle Years Programme in 1994. The addition of the 3-12 Primary Years Programme (PYP) in 1997 resulted in a continuum of IB programmes available across the school age range in the form that – notwithstanding relatively minor developments and modifications – we know it today.

Each of the three IB programmes merits extensive research in terms of the role it plays in encouraging the development of suitable skills and knowledge for the global future of the adults of tomorrow. And the research and literature database is indeed growing – if not perhaps as quickly as we may wish. This book, as a contribution to that growing literature base, has as its focus the IB Middle Years Programme – sitting as it does in the middle of the IB continuum, with interfaces to the other two programmes. The various chapters in this book focus on different aspects of middle years education and the MYP and require on the part of the reader, to differing extents, an understanding of the structure and philosophy of the programme. This chapter has as its aim to include sufficient information about that structure and philosophy to enable the 'new reader' to the MYP to understand the discussion that arises. It does not claim to be a comprehensive source of information, and for those who wish to access more detailed information a number of IB publications are the definitive source that should be consulted. These include *MYP: From Principles into Practice* (IB, 2008a) and the *MYP Guide to Interdisciplinary Teaching and Learning* (Boix-Mansilla, 2010), in addition to a number of publications relating to particular aspects of the programme as well as those with a focus on its place in the three programme IB continuum. In this chapter will be found, we intend, sufficient information to be used as support for the reading of other chapters and, perhaps, to whet the appetite of new readers to find out more about the MYP.

The IB context

The MYP shares with the PYP and Diploma Programme a mission that makes clear the location of all IB programmes in a context of international education, and an aim to develop inquiring, knowledgeable and caring young people who demonstrate intercultural understanding and respect, and who become active, compassionate and lifelong learners (IB, 2008a). The attributes it is intended will be exemplified by the internationally-minded learners who emerge from the IB's programmes are made explicit in the IB learner profile, which is meant to apply across the PYP, MYP and DP and which is included in detail in Appendix 1. In summary, IB learners strive to be:

Inquirers
Knowledgeable
Thinkers
Communicators
Principled
Open-minded
Caring
Risk-takers
Balanced
Reflective

(IB, 2008b)

Also common to all three programmes is a set of standards and practices, which are translated into programme-specific requirements for each programme's implementation (IB, 2010a).

The MYP structure

Within that overall context, the MYP is guided by three fundamental concepts that are rooted in the IB mission statement: communication, intercultural awareness and holistic learning (in the context of the last of which a recently published IB position paper (Hare, 2010) makes interesting reading).

Structurally, the MYP has arranged subjects into eight groups, from each of which schools are required to teach at least one subject, ensuring that a broad and balanced choice of subjects is offered in every year of the programme. Subjects are intended to be linked both with each other and with 'real-world issues', through an approach to teaching and learning that encourages students to understand that dealing with issues in the real world generally requires 'insights gained from a variety of disciplines' (IB, 2008a), the development of skills of inquiry, and the ability to apply knowledge and skills acquired in one context to other different contexts. With an emphasis not only on acquiring a body of knowledge but also on the understanding of concepts, the mastery of skills and the development of attitudes that can lead to considered and appropriate action, the contexts for learning through the MYP are provided by its five areas of interaction as follows:

Approaches to learning
Community and service
Health and social education
Environments
Human ingenuity (formerly known as *homo faber*)

The MYP model (Figure 1) shows the relationships between the eight subject groups, the five areas of interaction and the IB learner profile, with the student at its centre.

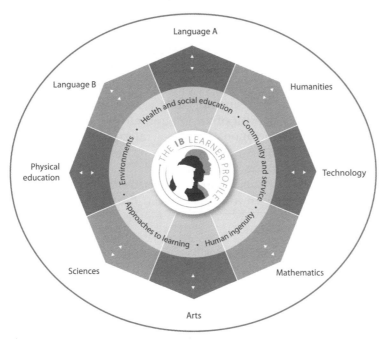

Figure 1: MYP model. Extracted with permission from the IB World Schools Yearbook 2011 © *International Baccalaureate Organization (2011)*

MYP curriculum and assessment

The IB makes clear that schools should not expect to be supplied with detailed curriculum documents that specify how precisely each element of the MYP is to be implemented. Rather, the MYP provides a framework within which each school develops its own written curriculum, with teachers encouraged by IB to provide opportunities for students to build meaning and refine understanding through structured inquiry (IB, 2008a). Aims and objectives are provided for each subject group as well as for the personal project (a significant piece of work completed during the student's fifth year of the programme). As a support for teachers when designing MYP units of work, the IB provides an optional planning tool known as the MYP unit planner.

Assessment of the MYP is internal, and no external examinations or other forms of external assessment are set. All assessment tasks, strategies and tools 'are designed, developed and applied by teachers working with students in their schools' (IB, 2008a). Based on the objectives provided for each subject group, the IB identifies a set of assessment criteria against which students' success is measured in terms of levels of achievement. Objectives (making clear what a student should know, understand and be able to do and feel at the end of the programme (IB, 2008a)) are aligned with criteria (Objective A aligned with Criterion A; Objective B aligned with Criterion B, and so on). General information about the criteria is provided as guidance for teachers in designing suitable tasks and assessing student performance. In Years 1-4 of the MYP, schools develop their own assessment criteria, while in Year 5 they must use MYP assessment criteria as published in subject-group guides. On the basis of these published criteria and achievement level descriptors, schools determine students' final MYP grades for the different subjects they have studied, as well as for the personal project.

For those schools that wish it (and not all do), grades awarded by the school to MYP students in their final year of the programme may be validated by the IB. A process of external moderation of teachers' internal assessment provides the basis for this official validation. Following the process of external moderation, students who satisfy a number of conditions relating to achievement across the programme and have participated in the programme for at least the final two years may be issued by the IB with an MYP certificate.

Summary

The MYP, acting as a framework for a school-designed curriculum, has many challenges to face. It is the only one of the three IB programmes to interface two others. In that respect, it bears a heavy responsibility for delivering the continuum of the IB programmes in providing smooth linkage on the one hand from the primary years and, on the other hand, to the immediately pre-university years with their high-stakes assessment and backwash effect from the demands of the university sector. But the MYP may also be completed by students who do not intend to go on to university or to further study of programmes such as the IB diploma. It thus acts not only as a middle years curriculum and as a preparation for pre-university studies, but also as school-leaving certification for those who do not aspire to post-16 study. Not least among the challenges faced by the MYP are those that arise from the fact that it is internally assessed, with the possibility of external moderation. For those familiar with some national education systems, there is nothing unusual about the arrangements for internal assessment as the culmination of middle years schooling. For others, the absence of external examination leading to an externally-awarded certificate at age 16 is anathema. Resolving tensions arising from such differing expectations, together with the organisation and successful integration of the areas of interaction, form part of the responsibilities of each school's MYP coordinator.

The MYP was initially designed principally as a precursor to the IB Diploma Programme. Since then, not only has the MYP been placed at the centre of an IB continuum by the addition of the PYP, it has also been adopted in a more diverse range of national and school contexts than may originally have been envisaged. Each has its own reason for offering the programme: some in conjunction with the PYP and DP; some in conjunction with one or neither of the other IB programmes, and some in conjunction with another middle years curriculum. The diversity of the context in which the MYP operates has brought with it both demands on those responsible for its ongoing design and development, and challenges in terms of the extent to which those demands can be met while maintaining the integrity of the programme and, indeed, the requirements of the other IB programmes with which the MYP interfaces. This book takes up a number of points arising from those challenges, relating to different aspects of the MYP and from the various perspectives of the authors. In the context of a still relatively new programme, and an as yet little-researched field, we hope it will make a positive contribution to the ongoing development of this innovative curriculum.

References

Boix-Mansilla V (2010): *MYP Guide to Interdisciplinary Teaching and Learning*, Cardiff: International Baccalaureate.

Hare J (2010): *Holistic Education: an interpretation for teachers in the IB programmes*, Cardiff: International Baccalaureate.

IB (2008a): *MYP: From Principles into Practice*, Cardiff: International Baccalaureate.

IB (2008b): *IB Learner Profile booklet*, Cardiff: International Baccalaureate.

IB (2010a): *Programme Standards and Practices*, Cardiff: International Baccalaureate.

IB (2010b): *The History of the Middle Years Programme*, Cardiff: International Baccalaureate.

IB (2011): www.ibo.org [Accessed 8 February 2011]

Peterson A D C (1987): *Schools Across Frontiers: the Story of the International Baccalaureate and the United World Colleges*, La Salle Illinois: Open Court.

The IB Learner Profile

The aim of all IB programmes is to develop internationally minded people who, recognizing their common humanity and shared guardianship of the planet, help to create a better and more peaceful world.

IB learners strive to be:

Inquirers	They develop their natural curiosity. They acquire the skills necessary to conduct inquiry and research and show independence in learning. They actively enjoy learning and this love of learning will be sustained throughout their lives.
Knowledgeable	They explore concepts, ideas and issues that have local and global significance. In so doing, they acquire in-depth knowledge and develop understanding across a broad and balanced range of disciplines.
Thinkers	They exercise initiative in applying thinking skills critically and creatively to recognize and approach complex problems, and make reasoned, ethical decisions.
Communicators	They understand and express ideas and information confidently and creatively in more than one language and in a variety of modes of communication. They work effectively and willingly in collaboration with others.
Principled	They act with integrity and honesty, with a strong sense of fairness, justice and respect for the dignity of the individual, groups and communities. They take responsibility for their own actions and the consequences that accompany them.
Open-minded	They understand and appreciate their own cultures and personal histories, and are open to the perspectives, values and traditions of other individuals and communities. They are accustomed to seeking and evaluating a range of points of view, and are willing to grow from the experience.
Caring	They show empathy, compassion and respect towards the needs and feelings of others. They have a personal commitment to service, and act to make a positive difference to the lives of others and to the environment.
Risk-takers	They approach unfamiliar situations and uncertainty with courage and forethought, and have the independence of spirit to explore new roles, ideas and strategies. They are brave and articulate in defending their beliefs.
Balanced	They understand the importance of intellectual, physical and emotional balance to achieve personal well-being for themselves and others.
Reflective	They give thoughtful consideration to their own learning and experience. They are able to assess and understand their strengths and limitations in order to support their learning and personal development.

Used with permission from the IB Learner Profile *booklet* © *International Baccalaureate Organization.*

Chapter 2

The development of the middle years student

Wilf Stout

Introduction

I never cease to be amazed at the diversity and heterogeneity demonstrated, in terms of maturity and behaviour, and of attitude and aptitude to learning, by children in the 11–14 age group. This is the cohort of children usually educated in Years 6-9 in K-12 schools, Years 7-10 in K-13 schools: the 'middle years'. It has been my experience as a teacher for over 40 years that the learning experienced by my students in this age group was of relatively little value. Interestingly though, at a personal level, the influence of two of my teachers when I was 12 years-old shaped my career and influenced the lives of my family. John Marshall taught me biology and sparked in me an interest for the subject, which I subsequently studied and taught. June Reed, a music teacher, identified within me a latent talent that subsequently influenced my choice of wife and the very successful careers of our two sons.

Daily in the media we are reminded that there is a huge gap between the knowledge and skills that students are acquiring in schools and the skills they need in typical 21st century communities and workplaces. We are told that in order for our students to survive the career challenges in a globally competitive workforce:

> Schools must align classroom atmosphere with real world environment by infusing 21st century skills into their teaching and learning process. Skills such as problem solving, innovation and creativity have become critical in today's global economy. One needs to understand that the knowledge-based economy cannot flourish without a proper education system (Gates, 2005).

To paraphrase the media, if we wish to succeed in life we need not only the traditional academic subjects that framed the curriculum of the 19th century, but also to include 21st century subjects such as global awareness, civics, health and wellness, business and entrepreneurship. The media picture schools as cul-de-sacs, where teachers teach and students learn by rote. Learning theory is seen as focusing on an individual quest for meaning and relevance, and calls are made for more emphasis in the areas of creativity, problem-solving, analysis and evaluation. Students, we are told, learn more when they are involved actively in learning than when they are passive recipients of instruction. Employers, too, have their view as to the attributes required of their workforce:

The modern employee must be more highly educated, better informed, more flexible than ever before. He or she must, because that's what we're paying for, have the ability to think, to solve problems, to make informed judgments, to distinguish between right and wrong, to discern the proper course of action in situations and circumstances that are necessarily ambiguous (Kearns, 2005).

It is against this background that I attempt a brief review of current practices and suggest some ideas for the future of middle years pedagogy. As a biologist I recognize that *evolutionary processes* occur over long periods of time in order to ensure best fit between the genotype and environmental pressures, but I sometimes think the historian with his/her *revolutions* has effected most of the great major societal changes.

Nature of adolescence and developmental characteristics

It is essential that teachers recognize and be knowledgeable about the unique developmental characteristics of early adolescence and the impact these have on children. It has been my experience that children coming into secondary school after six or more years of primary education, be it the International Baccalaureate Primary Years Programme (PYP), the International Primary Curriculum (IPC), Key Stages 1 and 2 in the National Curriculum of England or whatever national system prevails, bring with them a spontaneity, sparkle and sheer delight in learning. Eleven-year-old children have a remarkable capacity to acquire knowledge and skills, which seems to resonate with the pedagogy of the primary school. Within six months of exposure to the 'middle years' and to its pedagogy, much of the passion for learning has gone for many children, and for the next two to three years the situation often gets bleaker. Why? I suspect the reason has to do with our failure to develop programmes and to structure the school day and the learning milieu with due regard for the biology of adolescence.

This is nothing new. Donald Eichhorn, considered to be the founding father of the middle school movement in the USA, as far back as the early 1960s called upon teachers to consider the developmental characteristics of emergent adolescents 'when planning curriculum, instruction, and assessment and when structuring the environment of the middle school' (Eichhorn, 1966). These characteristics encompass physical, intellectual, emotional/psychological, moral/ethical and social domains. Further, the characteristics are inter-related and overlapping.

I believe we need to fine tune the educational programme of the middle school to take into account adolescent developmental characteristics. The 'curriculum', methods of instruction and assessment, and spatial and temporal organisation of the middle school (flexible scheduling, team teaching, use of technology and resources, and space and time) need to be modified radically in order to effect an improvement in learning in middle schools.

Physical, hormonal and brain development

During early adolescence, the body undergoes more development than at any other stage in life apart from the first two years. Research has shown that developmental growth spurts begin to occur about two years earlier in girls than in boys (Tanner, 1973) and that girls tend to mature one to two years earlier than do boys (Caissy, 1994). Adolescent growth sees significant increases in height, weight and internal organ size, as well as changes in skeletal and muscular systems (Kellough and Kellough, 2008). Bone tissue grows faster than muscle and tendon tissue, so young adolescents may experience coordination issues and growing pains when muscles and tendons do not adequately protect bones (Wiles *et al*, 2006). Fluctuations in basal metabolism resulting from imbalances between the rates of growth of endocrine glands and the utilization of their hormones by target tissues cause adolescents to experience periods of restlessness, irritability, frustration and lassitude. For this reason, adolescents tend to 'have ravenous appetites and peculiar tastes' (Kellough and Kellough, 2008) and conversely, by way of overcompensating, may exhibit addictive eating disorders. During this period brain size remains relatively unchanged, but advances in neuro-imaging technology have revealed significant internal development taking place within specific areas of the brain, particularly the pre-frontal cortex, which processes the ability to plan, reason, anticipate consequences, sustain attention, and make decisions (Blakemore and Choudhury, 2006; Casey *et al*, 2000; Dahl, 2004).

Teachers need to help adolescents through this time by providing them with accurate information about adolescent development, encouraging them to talk about how they feel and encouraging them to consult credible resources on how to 'master' adolescence (Scales, 2003). Collaborative activities within student groups focusing on diet, healthy lifestyles, physical movement and exercise, role play, sensitivity to appearance and self-awareness can all be helpful in supporting students through this challenging period.

Intellectual development

Whilst intellectual development may not be as evident as physical development, it is just as intense (Stevenson, 2002). Students begin to progress from concrete logical operations and problem solving and become able to test hypotheses, analyze and synthesize data, and think reflectively (Manning, 2002). Metacognition (the ability to think about one's own thinking) and abstract and independent thought begin to emerge, and these need to be nurtured in class. Students tend to be highly curious and they become interested in new activities, though interest may be short-lived. Not surprisingly, they are keen to learn about topics they find interesting and useful in their daily lives and reject the study of what they consider to be 'academic subjects'. They prefer active over passive learning experiences, and value opportunities for interactions with peers during class.

This increasing cognitive maturity enables students to begin to understand more of the world around them, to understand the nuances of metaphors, to make sense of traditional wisdom, to have insight into the nature of hypothesis and to conjecture and appreciate depth of meaning through art and music. They also develop an improved ability to think about the future, anticipate needs, and develop personal goals (Kellough and Kellough, 2008). Similarly, they are increasingly able to consider ideological topics, argue a position, question adult authority, and appreciate sophisticated levels of humour (Stevenson, 2002).

What implication has this for teachers? I suggest that we need to plan our learning experiences in a new way. We need a wide variety of educational approaches and materials that will be appropriate for the range of learners (in terms of physical and cognitive maturity) we have in class. Whilst concrete thinkers require more structured learning experiences, abstract thinkers need more challenging activities (Manning and Butcher, 2005). We need to make sure that we understand and know how, and about what, our students think (Stevenson, 2002).

It is vital that the curriculum is based around real-world concepts and daily world events as portrayed by the media, with authentic educational activities (such as experimentation, analysis and synthesis of data) to which our students can relate. Our students need stimuli for intellectual development, through direct interaction with their world and with peers and adults. Time spent daily watching international news, looking at a range of local and international newspapers, and surfing the web have relevance for them.

At all times we need to recognize that the interest spans of these students are shorter than those of adults. Meeting with students from other local schools during the school day in forum situations, meeting adults in workplaces, meeting young children in crèches and senior citizens in retirement homes can provide wonderful opportunities for students to take themselves 'out of themselves' and become more focused on others and their problems than on themselves and their own problems. These are the times for our students to explore the rationales behind rules and responsibility at home, in school and within society and to realize the causal relationship between action and consequence.

Moral and ethical development

Idealism and a strong sense of fairness in human relations is reported to be a feature of the developing adolescent. (Scales, 2003; Roney, 2005) As students progress through the middle years of school they develop an increased capacity for analytical thought, reflection, and introspection that continues throughout life. Starting from the early teens students begin to recognize increasingly their own egocentricity. (Knowles and Brown, 2000) Young adolescents are particularly critical of others (especially teachers) and vocal about the weaknesses and imperfections of others (especially parents), but are often reluctant to acknowledge their own imperfections, particularly when pointed out by anyone older than themselves. Gradually they begin to appreciate that a self-centred perspective is at odds with the rights and feelings of others. They begin to pose questions about the nature of life, often rejecting the views of others in the process, even though they lack an answer of their own. Having started life broadly embracing the values of their parents, our students start to view moral issues initially in black and white. There are no shades of grey. If complex moral and ethical temptations arise at this stage in life they often do not have the moral and ethical maturity to resist. It is for this reason that many teenagers are at risk, particularly if they have not had exposure to the love and care of responsible adults in early life.

One of the ways in which teachers can help in these situations is to use case studies arising from literature where moral vulnerability is exposed, to focus students' thoughts and to encourage them to express their thoughts and judgements freely in creative writing. Developing an understanding of the causal links between actions and consequences helps students to prepare for such eventualities in their own lives and to develop their own standards and codes of behaviour. The 'responsible adult' who will be a 'credit to society' in the future should be in training during these middle years. This is a perfect time to begin to expose students to the great societal issues of discrimination, racism, gender issues, war and peace, love and compassion.

Emotional and psychological development

The development of identity formation, which began way back in primary school, now accelerates along with a growing sense of independence, a sense of individuality and a sense of self-worth (White, 1959). For this reason, the period of early adolescence can be one of intensity of feelings, emotion, unpredictability, frustration and fear. Laughter and, more often, tears are not far from the surface. Loneliness, alienation and the 'no one loves me' syndrome are all common. These are the times of moodiness, unwillingness to volunteer for anything, withdrawal, anger, restlessness, inconsistency, regression to childish outbursts and infantile behaviour, and lack of self-esteem. The list goes on. It is for these reasons that I often wished that the human species had a pupal [*sic*] stage in its life cycle. This would be a stage when the hungry and busy caterpillar we know as the primary school child could crawl away to a cool spot for three to four years of intense adolescence, only to emerge aged 15 years as a mature teenager ready for some serious learning before the IB diploma, A levels or equivalent. If only!

As teachers, planning and designing a curriculum and a learning experience for our students, there is much to think about here. We can be the change agents for that successful transition through early adolescence. It is the *way* we choose our programme of work, *what* our students study, *when* they study it, for *how long* they study it, in *what surroundings* they study and with *what resources and techniques* that hold the key to that metamorphosis of which I dream. It is also my hope that every student will find at least one adult kindred spirit on the school staff to whom he or she can relate and who will be, for that student, the perfect role model. Amongst peers there is often safety in numbers, and generally speaking the more positive relationships a student has amongst peers, the more smooth will be his/her transition through adolescence.

Social development

Emotional development is inextricably linked to social development. This is the process by which mature relationships and interactions build up within society. The human race is gregarious and productive; effective relationships based on good communication, understanding, tolerance and love are key elements in forging a mature society. Belonging to a social group is an important characteristic of most animal species, not least ours. Tribes, troops, gaggles, clans, swarms, gangs, clubs, teams, sects, religious groupings – all are united by common needs, expectations and rewards. Membership of groups is important and it is not unusual for adolescents to wish to gain entry to them. To do this, conformity is required to the group expectations in terms of behaviour and acceptance of its codes. This may have positive or negative connotations, depending upon the social mores of the group. The rites of passage for an adolescent joining a narcotic gang on the Cape Flats of South Africa, for instance, may be different from those for joining the Young Conservatives in rural England. Conformity with or rejection of parental or school values may play a role in decisions to join particular groups. In most cases adolescents will test the limits of acceptable behaviour. As teachers, and as parents, we need to prepare our charges for such eventualities. Failure to support adolescents and to prevent them from feeling rejected at school and at home, worthless, second rate, written off, may inevitably drive youngsters to seek comfort from illegal or immoral activities.

There can be many signals of potential danger amongst adolescents such as occurrences of 'cutting', body piercing, tattooing, eating disorders, binge drinking, drug abuse and inappropriate sexual activity. Adolescents will look for comfort from someone or somewhere if rejected elsewhere. For many students, particularly girls, social and moral development lags behind physical development, which enhances their vulnerability to negative influences. Pop culture, in terms of videos, movies and the media, makes life attractive when there is otherwise a vacuum in one's life resulting from a lack of self-esteem, positive relationships and the respect and love of others.

The availability of positive peer groups fostering relationships within school is important. Extracurricular activities can be a help here with interest groups such as clubs, societies, Model United Nations, debating groups, drama groups, choirs, bands, dance groups and sports teams providing opportunities to develop effective relationships, a group identity, a positive sense of self and a distraction from negative influences. For many adolescents, school may be the only 'safe' environment they experience. Within the school day collaborative experience and cooperative learning opportunities foster that sense of belonging.

In conclusion, the way in which the middle school curriculum is presented, how the school is organised and how students are treated and respected by teachers must be based on a thorough understanding, and recognition, of the processes by which children transition through adolescence. Developmentally appropriate learning experiences within a developmentally appropriate environment are essential. To treat middle school students as primary children or as 12th graders/sixth-formers is totally inappropriate. Supporting middle school students in the most appropriate way is a huge responsibility.

What do adolescents want from school?

Typically, education systems around the world are driven by political expediency. What is taught, to whom, and at what stage has traditionally been determined by the need to maintain a balance between generating sufficient professional expertise to run the country and provide essential social services, and having enough 'workers' to generate adequate GNP. Added to this is the covert need to control the masses. This may sound cynical, but it conjures up a model for the organisation of education based on the social organisation of a beehive and set in the world of Orwell's *1984*.

Government control of education has been pervasive, but increasingly teachers are generating curricula, teaching styles and learning situations focused on student needs rather than on political needs. Instead of telling students what is good for them, we are asking them: 'What do you want from education and what is the best way to get what you want?' I recently asked groups of middle school students what they expected from the middle school experience. I asked them what was important in school and they gave me: friends, socializing, sports, how they were perceived, extracurricular activities and lunch. I asked them what motivated them to work at school and they gave me: fun activities, being with friends, how interesting was [sic] the subject, how relevant the subject was to them, competitions and getting good grades.

From these results I was intrigued to notice the references to the relevance and level of interest of the topics that they studied, the context of relationships and self-esteem, the need for fun, food and activity and, surprisingly, the elements of competition and achievement. I then set about comparing these 'adolescent primary needs' with what we are told from motivational theory and cognitive theory, as a means of generating guidelines for a futuristic model curriculum and model for school organisation for the middle years.

How do we help students to meet their needs?

With a vague notion of what seems relevant to adolescent expectations in school, we must look to motivational theory and to cognitive theory for the means of providing the appropriate pedagogy to meet these perceived needs.

Relevance and interest

We know that students engage in activities that are relevant and interesting to them personally, because they are enjoyable and rewarding. If so motivated, we can expect students to engage in activities with greater energy and enthusiasm, to set goals for themselves, to spend more time on task, to initiate activities that they design, to persist in the task despite difficulties and interruptions, and to be cognitively engaged: *ie* actually thinking about what they are doing. Students who are intrinsically motivated are more likely to begin a task on their own, pay attention, learn material in a meaningful way, show creativity, be persistent despite failures, enjoy the activity, evaluate their own progress and achieve at high levels.

Motivational theory informs us that students work best if what they study has direct and immediate relevance to their own lives, if the task is linked to external approval and if they intrinsically link what they do to personal satisfaction. In terms of cognitive theory we know that learning involves an internal change in neuronal activity, that knowledge is organised by association and interconnectedness, that new knowledge is related to previously learned information, and that students are more actively involved in the learning they organize and over which they have control. Cognitive theory also informs us that students have a number of physiological and psychological needs that need to be met to maximise the effectiveness of the learning situation and process. These can be summarized as: physiological needs, the needs to achieve competence and self-worth, relatedness, affiliation, approval and achievement. In developing a futuristic model of curriculum we need also to consider the implications of 'forms of intelligence' for the way we design our learning activities.

In terms of the need to achieve competence and self-worth, White (1959) suggested that humans have a basic need for competence: 'a belief that they can deal effectively with their environment', while Ormrod (2004) and Covington (1992) suggested that self-worth (defending one's competency) is a primary need for humans. Paradoxically, if individuals fail to achieve the higher levels of self-worth they compensate by setting themselves lower levels that they then strive to attain. This, White believes, can be done either by consistently succeeding, or by avoiding failure by setting low expectations, refusing to participate in an activity or to complete an assignment, making excuses, cheating and procrastinating. Such traits may ring bells among those familiar with the adolescent student.

In terms of the need for *relatedness*, middle school students want to be connected socially to others. They feel this may give them an assurance that they are wanted and respected, and it may be manifested by them prioritizing socializing over completing school work, trying to gain popularity, look smart, foolish, *etc.* and, more positively, by showing concern and helping others. With respect to the need for *affiliation*, middle school students desire friendly relationships. Students with a *high need for affiliation* need to communicate frequently, are more interested in relationships than in tasks, generally earn lower grades than their peers and thrive in a classroom with a nurturing teacher. Where the need for *approval* is concerned, some middle school students have a strong desire to look good in front of others, which might be manifested by seeking or avoiding teacher recognition/approval and seeking or avoiding peer recognition/approval.

Relational

Current practice suggests that most creative thinking is driven by group activities. We have 'think tanks' and 'brainstorming sessions'; we 'caucus', we have 'Boards' and 'Cabinets' (even senior management teams in schools), and the reason is because the way in which groups interact models the way in which the human brain makes decisions. Neuroimagery of the brain shows us that during any given cognitive activity, various regions of the brain 'light up' due to the accumulation of tracers carried in the blood stream to those areas which are actively metabolizing, therefore needing increased oxygen supplies as they function in response to that specific stimulus. Few cognitive activities involving higher order skills such as creativity and problem solving occur in only one region of the brain. The cumulative effects of primary and middle school learning lead to the build-up of long-term memory stored in '*networks of association*'. The more 'associations' or connections a student builds up with respect to a particular fact or concept, the more easily that information can be recalled. Experience shows that learning is facilitated through social interaction and that creating a *variety* of flexible group contexts engages students in a way that maximizes individual learning. The cognitive basis of collaborative and cooperative learning within groups is constructivist theory. Self-realized knowledge, recognised and relevant as personally important to students, can be successfully stored in the brain. It is then available for reconstruction and expansion through new learning experiences.

High performing groups are dynamic. Members of groups bring different experiences, have points of view, have different 'takes', have different value systems, and have different 'agendas'. If appropriately chaired and motivated they will fire each other's imaginations and in turn respond to the creative impulses and ideas generated by others. Consensus is achieved, decisions are made which can then be implemented, and everyone goes home happy.

Self-esteem

By providing a learning environment where students perceive that they are safe from physical, verbal, or psychological harm, where they are encouraged to experiment and to take risks when learning, to work alongside a teacher within a group in which relationships have been developed, and are repeatedly informed that they are valued members of the class, we have ideal opportunities for students to become more confident in their ability to learn. If students feel safe and cared for, if teachers and others are responsive to their needs, their ability to focus and learn will be enhanced.

'Other' intelligences

The published works of Gardner (1984), Payne (1985) and Goleman (1995) have to a greater or lesser extent impacted upon the way we think of learning. Each one of us is biologically unique. Our brains are unique. The underlying anatomy, biochemistry and electrophysiology of the brain are pretty similar for all of us, but put the whole thing together and expose it to 12 years of diverse experiences and we have a class full of adolescents totally different from each other. Is it therefore surprising that we will differ in the way we view the world and what and how we choose to learn? In learning to meet basic physiological needs, as per Maslow (1954), and in the art of survival we are hard-wired, we have default positions. Give a three hour old baby a breast and it will suckle. Not so when it comes to learning in the middle years.

In developing the curriculum we need to be aware of the need to involve students in active learning experiences that engage a variety of learning channels: auditory, visual, kinaesthetic. We need to provide opportunities and access to activities so that students may have an opportunity to use a variety of 'intelligences' (visual-spatial, mathematical-logical, verbal-linguistic, musical, bodily kinaesthetic, interpersonal, intrapersonal, naturalist and emotional). Active involvement will focus student attention and facilitate the likelihood that our students will have learned what they have experienced.

Summary

This chapter has attempted to outline the major features of adolescent development that tend to be experienced during the middle years of schooling, and to point to some of the implications that those whose responsibility it is for designing and implementing the programmes of learning for such students should bear in mind. There can be no unique solutions in curricular terms – the diverse nature of the wide range of specific educational contexts across national and international schools alike demands that – but the central feature in programme design and development must surely remain the characteristics of the young person and, through those characteristics, an awareness of the opportunities that present themselves to those of us who have the privilege of guiding and supporting their learning whilst in school.

References

Blakemore, S and Choudhury, S (2006): Development of the adolescent brain: Implications for executive function and social cognition, in *Journal of Child Psychology and Psychiatry*, 47(3/4) pp296-312.

Caissy, G A (1994): *Early adolescence: understanding the 10 to 15 year old*, Reading, MA: Perseus Books.

Casey, B J, Giedd, J N and Thomas, K M (2000): Structural and functional brain development and its relation to cognitive development, in *Biological Psychology,* 54, pp241-257.

Covington, M V (1992): *Making the grade: A self worth perspective on motivation and school reform.* Cambridge: Cambridge University Press.

Dahl, R E (2004): Adolescent Brain Development: A period of vulnerabilities and opportunities, in *Annals of the New York Academy of Sciences,* 1021: pp1-22.

Eichhorn, D (1966): *The middle school.* New York: Centre for Applied Research in Education.

Gates, B (2005): Speech given at the National Education Summit on High Schools. New York, 26 February 2005.

Gardner, H (1984): *Frames of Mind: The Theory of Multiple Intelligences,* London: Heinemann.

Goleman, D (1995): *Emotional Intelligence.* London: Bloomsbury Publishing Plc.

Kearns, D (2005): editorial, *The Guardian.* July/August 2005.

Kellough, R D and Kellough, N G (2008): *Teaching young adolescents: methods and resources for middle grades teaching* (5th ed.). Upper Saddle River, NJ: Pearson Merrill Prentice Hall.

Knowles, T and Brown, D F (2000): *What every middle school teacher should know.* London: Heinemann.

Manning, M L (2002): *Developmentally appropriate middle level schools* (2nd ed.). Olney, MD: Association for Childhood Education International.

Manning, M L and Butcher, K T (2005): *Teaching in the Middle School.* Upper Saddle River. NJ: Merrill/Prentice Hall.

Maslow, A (1954): *Motivation and Personality,* New York: Harper and Row.

Ormrod, J E (2004): *Human learning* (4th ed.) Upper Saddle River, NJ: Pearson.

Payne, W (1985): *A Study of Emotion: Developing Emotional Intelligence,* Dissertation submitted for the degree of Doctor of Philosophy.

Roney, K (2005): Young Adolescent Development, in V A Anfara Jr, G Andrews and S B Mertens (eds.) *The encyclopedia of middle grades education* (pp397-401). Greenwich, CT: Information Age Publishing and National Middle School Association.

Scales, P C (2003): Characteristics of young adolescents, in National Middle School Association, *This we believe: Successful schools for young adolescents* (pp43-51). Westerville, OH: National Middle School Association.

Stevenson, C (2002): *Teaching ten to fourteen year olds* (3rd ed.) Boston: Allyn and Bacon.

Tanner, J M (1973): Growing up, in *Scientific American,* 229(3), pp35-43.

White, R W (1959): Motivation Reconsidered: The Concept of Competence, in *Psychological Review,* 66 (5), pp297-333.

Wiles, J, Bondi, J and Wiles, M T (2006): *The essential middle school.* (4th ed.) Upper Saddle River, NJ: Pearson Prentice Hall.

Part B

Exploring Characteristics of the MYP

Chapter 3

International-mindedness and intercultural awareness in the MYP: a relationship reviewed

Eif Phillips

This chapter affirms the importance of international-mindedness and intercultural awareness to the MYP. It considers the prominence given to the areas of interaction: in the model, in planning units, in making interdisciplinary and real world connections, in defining the personal project, and in the programme evaluation process. It then goes on to suggest that intercultural awareness should itself be given a higher level of prominence.

MYP: the genesis

The MYP has deep roots in international schools. The International Schools Association (ISA) was founded in 1951 and, amongst other things, was involved in the development of the IB in the 1960s. The ISA 'works to promote international and intercultural understanding' and 'is supportive of all organizations which share its conviction about internationalism, international-mindedness and international education in all its forms and wherever it may be found' (ISA, 2010a). Accordingly, the organization does not limit its remit to international schools and two of its six mission objectives are 'to nurture interest in national schools of international matters as a means of improving international understanding' and 'to publicize the aims and principles of international schools and promote international understanding among national schools' (ISA, 2010b). Developed in the 1980s, the International Schools Association Curriculum (ISAC) for 11-16 year-old students was the prototype 'which with further development by the IB became the IBMYP' (ISA, 2010b).

Significant numbers of national schools are adopting one or more of the International Baccalaureate (IB) programmes, and 'although the first IB schools were predominantly private international schools, today over half of all IB World Schools are state schools' (IB, 2010a). Nicolson and Hannah indicate that, when the IB adopted the MYP in 1994, the number of schools authorised to deliver the programme was 15, (IB, 2010h: 24) They trace the growth in the IB regions until 2009, when the number of authorised schools in North America alone was 466 and the worldwide total was 747 (2010: 36). The head of MYP development, Malcolm Nicolson, indicated in November 2010 that there were then 856 schools offering the MYP and that as many as 555 of the 856 were state schools (Nicolson, 2010). There are several good reasons for national schools to apply for candidate status and I believe that the 'international' aspect of the programme is one of the, if not the, most important of these reasons.

So how does the international aspect of the MYP relate to the wider context? In discussing what might be meant by the term international education, Cambridge and Thompson note that it 'has been used to denote an ideology of education oriented towards "internationalism" and "international-mindedness" and the education offered by international schools' (2004: 161). More generally, education has been argued to be 'a carrier of the values of the culture of a society [through which] these values are transmitted from teacher to students, from school to teacher and educational system to school' and through which 'culture is maintained' (Brown, 2002: 70). Such a definition of education then gives rise, when considering the international context, to the questions: 'From which society's culture(s) is an international school to select? What sort of society or culture is the school aiming to promote?' (Hayden, 2006: 131) It is reasonable to expect that schools with the word 'international' in their titles would want to offer an 'international education', but what does this mean? Hayden suggests that 'international education as a concept is inclusive, with many interpretations within different contexts. Within schools, international education has a number of facets including, though not exclusively, the formal curriculum', before going on to say that 'international education may be experienced in national schools, where suitable opportunities are built in to facilitate this experience for students' (2006: 7). As one form of international education, the MYP has relevance both for international schools and for state schools in which an international dimension to the curriculum is valued. It is in this context that the concepts of international-mindedness and intercultural awareness are relevant, as will be discussed further in this chapter.

Why we are here

Mission statements and 'Philosophy and Objectives' statements are meant to be the beacon that guides a school's strategic plan. For MYP schools, these statements should resonate with the IB mission statement (IB, 2010b) – which emphasises 'intercultural understanding', 'international education', and appreciating and respecting differences – as well as with the attributes of the IB learner profile. The preamble to the learner profile refers to the development of internationally-minded people and the recognition of 'our common humanity and shared guardianship of the planet' (IB, 2008: 8). The knowledgeable and open-minded attributes refer to students exploring 'concepts, ideas and issues that have local and global significance', appreciating and understanding 'their own cultures and personal histories' and being 'open to the perspectives, values and traditions of other individuals and communities' (IB, 2008: 8).

At Munich International School (MIS), our review cycle dictates that we look again periodically at our mission, philosophy, and educational values and goals.

The current iteration – though somewhat verbose – encapsulates the attributes that we wish our students to develop. There is significant overlap with the IB learner profile and congruence with the IB mission statement. It is too long for students, teachers and parents to remember, but it is widely displayed and is evident in inter-personal interactions and the feeling of community amongst the students. It includes many key phrases that are paraphrased in schools all over the world, and the main link to international-mindedness can be found in the statement that MIS 'fosters an appreciation in its students of their cultural heritage and the cultural richness of the global community' and that 'learning is explicitly focused on intercultural awareness' (MIS, 2005).

What we teach

Broadly speaking, the curriculum is the whole range of a student's experiences at a school. Both by design and practice, these experiences have a cultural context. Skelton postulates that 'Any definition of an international curriculum implicitly suggests that such a curriculum is significantly different from a national curriculum' but goes on to say that 'it can be argued that an international curriculum shares (or should share) many of the aims, targets and procedures of national curricula. Perhaps it might be better to think of an "internationally-minded" curriculum than of an "international" one' (2002: 42). If we accept Hayden's suggestion that international education as a concept is inclusive, it follows that the curriculum offered should also be inclusive. Coelho envisages an inclusive curriculum as one in which 'teachers help students to explore many perspectives on issues, themes and concepts, and encourage their students to articulate the beliefs and values that are part of their family and cultural background'. Coelho goes on to state that 'All students and teachers need opportunities to learn about other points of view' and that we gain a better understanding of 'what our own values are when we articulate them and compare them with others' (1998: 234). As with the term 'international education', Haywood contends that there is no simple, generic definition of international-mindedness. He discusses international-mindedness under seven headings but does not profess that his typology is all-encompassing. He suggests that there are essential components but recognises that 'there can be many distinct ways of educating for international-mindedness' (2007: 88).

Is it not incumbent upon us as international school educators to be eclectic in our approach to acquiring best practice from a wide range of educational systems? The MYP is designed to facilitate this inclusion – even to operate in tandem with national curricula and prescribed 16+ examinations. In delivering a programme that enables students to achieve their potential, it is important to recognise that potential is achieved through good test scores but not exclusively so. The programme is intended to transition from the transdisciplinary, mostly single classroom, environment of the Primary Years Programme (PYP);

through encouraging respect for, an understanding of, and making connections between the ways of knowing in different disciplines in the MYP; to, eventually, preparing students for the rigours of the externally examined Diploma Programme – the gold card for entrance into tertiary education. The common threads running through the three programmes are the learner profile and international-mindedness.

The fundamental concepts

The fundamental concepts of the MYP are holistic learning, communication and intercultural awareness. MYP values the various disciplines but does not keep them in separate silos: an inter-disciplinary approach is preferred. Using the areas of interaction (see below) to inform unit questions and provide the context for teaching units facilitates holistic learning. Communication is fundamental to all educational programmes and is enhanced in the MYP by the following requirements: a language policy, all students studying at least one language A and one language B (or two languages A), a support programme in the school's language of instruction for second language learners who need it, and a mother tongue programme. Schools are encouraged to develop policies and procedures that facilitate a climate of intercultural awareness. Staff are encouraged to model intercultural awareness and to select content/learning experiences that facilitate its development. Students are encouraged to be interculturally aware, to develop international-mindedness by considering issues from a variety of perspectives, and to benefit from membership of a diverse community of learners by learning about the cultures represented – including their own. The MYP requires that schools facilitate intercultural awareness by:

- 'embedding in the curriculum examples drawn from a variety of cultural, social, religious and national perspectives, as well as implementing activities and practices that celebrate a range of cultural identities;

- 'allowing students to consider different perspectives so that they develop an understanding of what is common as well as what is different;

- 'helping students develop their own cultural identity and understanding of their present environment through the study of the traditional subjects and the Areas of Interaction;

- 'ensuring time for staff to identify and teach the skills and knowledge necessary for students to appreciate different points of view.'

(IB, 2008: 10-11)

These requirements emphasise that intercultural awareness is fundamental to the programme. That said, in my experience the option of learning about and through different cultural perspectives is not one that is chosen often enough.

The areas of interaction

There are aspects of the MYP that some feel could be improved. In my experience some mathematics teachers, for instance, have a problem with the weighting of the assessment criteria, feeling that placing more emphasis on criterion A would be a better preparation for the Diploma Programme. Some parents struggle with the variety of number scales for the criteria within and across subjects. That said, the majority of teachers and parents I have worked with or met over the last decade or so see criterion-referenced assessment as one of the programme's true strengths. The 'MYPophobic' teachers I have worked with or met focus their discontent on the areas of interaction: viewing them as artificial and unnecessary constructs that take time away from their day jobs.

The areas of interaction were designed as bridges between disciplines but became the lenses through which the disciplines were viewed. They are now 'the contexts through which the curriculum content interacts with the real world' and 'have an integrative function: they bring diverse subjects together under common contexts … demonstrating the interdisciplinary potential of the MYP' (IB, 2008: 14). Personally, I preferred bridges to lenses and feel that the term context is far better than either bridge or lens as a descriptor for the function of the areas of interaction.

The MYP is conceptually and pedagogically constructivist: students are encouraged to reflect continuously upon their learning and to make meaning of what they learn. Central to this process is the acquisition of knowledge and skills within a context provided by one or more area(s) of interaction. This context enables the learner to connect the learning in one subject with what is learned in other subjects and to envisage real world applications.

The IB document *MYP: From principles into practice* (IB, 2008) describes the five areas of interaction and outlines how recommended student learning expectations can be developed for each. Approaches to learning (ATL) relates to learning how to learn and is broken down into the skills of 'organization, collaboration, communication, information literacy, reflection, thinking and transfer'. In my experience, even 'MYPophobes' appreciate ATL; seeing it as a skill set fundamental to good pedagogy and student learning. At MIS we had developed a set of 'Grade 8 exit skills' before the MYP came into existence. These were not prerequisites for being promoted to Grade 9: they were a range of skills that we wanted students to have by the end of middle school, and the document indicated in which subjects and grade levels the skills were taught or reinforced. In the early days of development, we came to realise that we had made many assumptions with regard to the skills that students should have, and that some of these skills were not in fact being taught. At authorisation by the IB in 1998, we had asked to be authorised to deliver the programme in Grade 6 (MYP Year 1) and we moved the programme forward with this cohort. When the students got to Grade 9, there was a head-on collision with the International General Certificate of Secondary Education (IGCSE) and teachers were concerned about having to cover a lot of prescribed content without the time needed for inquiry, as well as having to apply two very different forms of assessment. It was by design and not by accident that we used ATL as the 'foot in the door' and this worked – for a while!

Community and service (C&S) is broken down into 'community awareness and understanding, reflection, and involvement through service'. Schools have a tendency to focus on service and reflection upon it. Usually they do a good job, with this aspect often functioning as a co-curricular activity. The IB encourages schools to place less emphasis on the amount of time spent doing C&S activities and more on the quality of the activities – 'making a difference'. I am in full agreement with this. It would be sad to liken any C&S programme to a poorly developed strategic plan: one that measures what is easy to measure, as opposed to what is worth measuring. Satisfactory completion of the service aspect is required of students but summative assessment is discouraged. Schools can use formative assessment to decide whether a student has met the service requirements – which sounds pretty summative to me! At the start of each MYP unit in any subject, it is made clear to students on which criteria they are being assessed and what they need to be able to do to reach the highest levels. I would argue that the service element of C&S deserves the same clarity. Compared to service, the awareness aspect arising from the curriculum is often an area for growth.

Health and Social Education (HSE) relates to sensible choices leading to the healthy development of the individual and constructive interaction with others. It can be considered as 'ourselves in the wider society, ourselves and others, understanding ourselves, and looking after ourselves'. In many schools, as well as linking the discipline to others and the learning to the real world, this area provides the context for linking the pastoral care programme to the rest of the curriculum.

Environments relates to interdependence and taking responsibility. It can be considered as 'awareness and understanding, reflection, and taking action'. The development of this area is only as good as the area leader. This is probably true of all areas, but the importance of the area leader has come to my attention most often with environments. It may sound like a job for a science teacher, but understanding and awareness must also translate into lifestyle choices and action.

Back in the last millennium, 'Human Ingenuity' was known as *homo faber* and was something of an enigma. When asked what it was, people 'in the know' responded with examples instead of providing a definition: it was all a bit fuzzy. I once witnessed an inconclusive discussion/argument on whether or not a well known crime against humanity was an example of *homo faber*, and this was during a session at an MYP conference. Much has happened since then and, as well as getting a new name, *homo faber* has been more clearly described in terms of how and why we create, and the consequences – both positive and negative. The aforementioned crime against humanity was a form of human ingenuity that we could have done without. By encouraging students to reflect upon how we create at the different points of the MYP octagon – for instance the creative cycle in the arts and the design cycle in technology – human ingenuity can serve as a lead-in to the theory of knowledge (ToK) in the IB diploma. Human ingenuity encourages students to be aware of and to understand systems, processes, solutions and products: to make responsible choices and to be creative.

Interim expectations should be developed for the areas of interaction, for each year of the programme. These may simply involve modified wording, applying the same wording to age-appropriate tasks, or conscious decisions on the readiness of students to process/apply a given aspect of the expectations (IB, 2008: 20-33).

The unit planner and interdisciplinary learning

If we do not know where we are going, there is a good chance that we will end up somewhere else! Wiggins and McTighe (2005: 17-28) elaborate upon this old adage by emphasising the importance of clarifying the 'Desired Results' as the first stage of curriculum planning by backward design. This includes establishing goals and what the students will understand in terms of 'big ideas', and what they will know and be able to do at the end of the unit, as well as generating essential questions that require divergent, as opposed to convergent, thinking. The second stage includes establishing assessment criteria and how students will show evidence of understanding. Only then does the teacher consider content and methodology.

Accordingly, the first stage of the MYP unit planner (IB, 2008: 69-70) is designed around the integration of the area of interaction focus, the significant concept(s) and the MYP unit question, followed by a clarification of assessment in terms of tasks, evidence of understanding, specifying MYP objectives, and establishing which MYP criteria will be used. The area of interaction sets the context for the unit, and the significant concepts 'are the big ideas of the unit that the student needs to retain for the long-term future' (IB, 2008: 74). Both afford opportunities for interdisciplinary planning. The unit question relates to the significant concepts, is informed by the area of interaction and requires divergent thinking. All units have an ATL focus but this is more the 'how' than the 'what' and is specified in the second stage of the planner. As a rule, the unit question is informed by one of the other areas of interaction: C&S, HSE, environments or human ingenuity. Would it not be a strong statement in support of international-mindedness if intercultural awareness were to be added to this list as an option? Intercultural awareness setting the context for big ideas and informing the unit question – I believe that this has mileage.

In *MYP: From principles into practice*, there are many references to the use of the areas of interaction for facilitating interdisciplinary planning and teaching, as well as some references to the use of significant concepts for the same purpose. The coordinator's handbook (IB, 2010c: 5) makes many references to *From principles into practice*, which attest to the interdisciplinary role of the areas of interaction, and a PowerPoint presentation used for workshop leader training states that the areas of interaction 'contribute to an interdisciplinary approach to learning' (IB, 2010d: 5).

Based on the outcomes of the Project Zero research conducted by the Harvard Graduate School of Education and in collaboration with the researchers, the IB has produced a guide to interdisciplinary teaching and learning in the MYP. The guide recognises that there are multiple ways of fostering interdisciplinary learning and deepening student understanding. A whole chapter is dedicated to the importance of using the areas of interaction to design multi-faceted unit questions that facilitate interdisciplinary learning. The in-depth investigation of topics related to intercultural awareness can be enhanced by an interdisciplinary approach, and intercultural awareness could be a rich source of multi-faceted unit questions (Boix-Mansilla, 2010: 42-53).

The personal project

The personal project is rightly perceived as an essential element of the final year of the programme. It is the opportunity for students to choose something that they wish to work on in-depth, as well as being a chance to apply the ATL skills they have acquired and to use one of the other areas of interaction as the context for the project. Apart from the generic introduction and the glossary that were standard at the time of publication, there is no reference to intercultural awareness in the current personal project guide (IB, 2004) and no opportunity for it to be the context for the project. There are many references to the importance of the areas of interaction; they are also included in the assessment criteria. The update heralding changes to objectives and criteria that appear in the new guide (published January 2011) also makes no mention of it (IB, 2010e). I do not believe that intercultural awareness has been excluded intentionally: could it be time for a re-think?

Quality assurance

How can parents and students be assured that the quality of education delivered by a given school is of a sufficiently high standard? State schools implementing the MYP are tied into their national systems: they offer national examinations and/or host inspection-style visits that should assure quality. This may be the case for some international schools but it is not a given. For international schools in general, Hayden suggests that the 'growing emphasis on aspects of quality assurance such as authorisation and accreditation ... seems likely to help to ensure that the students who attend such schools, and their parents, are assured of the quality of the educational experience upon which they are embarking' (2006: 158). Relative to defined standards, accrediting bodies such as the Council of International Schools (CIS) and the New England Association of Schools and Colleges (NEASC) evaluate all aspects of a school's operation, from the essence of the school's philosophy and objectives and curriculum delivery through the practicalities of finances, facilities, safety procedures, and much more. CIS and NEASC affirm that 'The guiding principles of the accreditation programme are that a school will be evaluated against prescribed standards but in terms of its own Philosophy and Objectives, and that the school's programmes are appropriate to its unique demography.' (CIS, 2006: 6) As my focus is the MYP I will not go into the details of accreditation procedures, but it is important to note that, if a school applying for MYP authorisation by the IB is already accredited, a general assurance of quality already exists. This allows the MYP process really to focus on the school's philosophy, leadership and structure, and curriculum.

All schools interested in adopting the MYP apply to their regional office – the IB office that manages the region in which the school is located – for candidate status. The candidate school trials the programme and is involved in a process of consultation that includes a visit to the school by an IB-appointed consultant. Staff may attend IB workshops, and on-site MYP-related professional development is an option that can be combined with the consultant's visit. A verification visit is followed by the decision on authorisation (IB, 2010f: 1). Authorised schools complete an evaluation self-study in preparation for hosting a team visit, every five years. Not all visitors are IB employees, but all receive training from the IB before they participate in visits. As visitors, they are acting on behalf of the IB regional manager and there is open communication between the team leader and the regional office, especially after the team leader has submitted the draft report. As an experienced team leader, I have found this communication to be invaluable. The regional manager is responsible for the final report that is sent to the school; highlighting commendations, recommendations to be responded to prior to the next evaluation visit, and perhaps matters to be addressed more immediately. Evaluation team members are neither consultants nor are they meant to pontificate on how things are done at their own school. However, they are experienced educators and may be able to facilitate the development of specific aspects of the programme by connecting the school to another school, in order that they may learn from the good practice there. I believe that this balance of responsibility between practitioner and IB official facilitates collegiality between schools, as well as quality assurance across the region.

The previous 'Guide to programme evaluation' and 'Programme evaluation self-study' (IB, 2005) have been reviewed and replaced by the *Programme evaluation guide and self-study questionnaire: Middle Years Programme* (IB, 2010g). This became available in December 2010 and is activated for schools hosting their team visits in January 2012 or later. It is more concise and, in my opinion, less prescriptive than its predecessors. It nonetheless facilitates an analysis of the essential features of the MYP at a school and the degree of implementation relative to the programme standards, and more emphasis is placed upon gathering evidence to inform judgements. The previous guide asks for 'further information where necessary' (IB, 2005: 2), whereas the new guide stresses that 'the self study should be evidence based' (IB, 2010g: 5). Another significant difference is that the current guide is a composite of the three programmes, each section having a generic set of practices followed by programme-specific practices. The new guide focuses specifically on the MYP. I find the latter more user-friendly.

It is important to envisage the implementation of the programme as a continuous cycle of development. It is easy to focus on the visit, and it would be foolish for a school not to do its best in completing the self-study, in preparation for the visit. The new guide stresses the importance of the use of the evaluation report to inform the school's action plan, with the self-study and the visit being next steps in the cycle (IB, 2010g: 2).

Along with related practices, standard A2 from the current tool (international-mindedness) has been subsumed under A1 (educational beliefs and values) to make the new standard A: 'The school's educational beliefs and values reflect IB philosophy.' (IB, 2010g:14) There are practices related to the fundamental concepts and international-mindedness. Some could see the loss of specificity embodied in A2 as collateral damage in the effort to streamline the evaluation process and make it more user-friendly for schools. I believe that this is balanced in other sections of the self-study by practices such as 'The school ensures access to information on global issues and diverse perspectives', 'The written curriculum promotes students' awareness of individual, local, national and world issues' and 'Teaching and learning addresses human commonality, diversity and multiple perspectives' (IB, 2010g: 23, 27 and 29). As expected, the areas of interaction are prominent and feature in each section of the self-study.

Schools must ensure that at least one teacher from each subject group attends an MYP workshop between evaluation visits. Beyond the 'beginners' stage, an essential feature of MYP workshops is that participants are not just passive recipients of information. Instead, they are encouraged to bring and share examples of good practice from their schools. As well as keeping participants informed of developments and assuring quality, these workshops provide a feedback loop to the IB and thus influence the future development of the programme. Following the workshops there is a significant amount of networking amongst participants and with presenters.

Schools that wish their students to receive MYP certificates must have the students' grades validated by the IB. They submit samples of each Year 5 student's work for each subject group, for moderation. Feedback to schools relates to the appropriateness of set tasks for assessment using the criteria chosen, and standardises the awarding of descriptor levels for each criterion. Moderation can result in grades changing. The IB offers the monitoring of assessment service for advisory purposes. This process does not involve work from all students, but samples of work from the subject groups for which feedback is required. This feedback provides support and guidance for the future development of assessment procedures. Schools that do not have students' grades validated by the IB are required, in the year prior to the evaluation visit, to participate in the monitoring of assessment for each subject group and the personal project. The self-study, moderation/monitoring of assessment feedback and the ensuing evaluation report highlight what a school should keep doing, stop doing and start doing. This forms the basis of the school's action plan for the continued implementation of the programme.

MIS is accredited by CIS and NEASC and we value the quality assurance that this status brings. However, in terms of international-mindedness, adding MYP evaluation brings another dimension. We now have joint ten-year accreditation/evaluation visits whereby the curriculum section is the IB continuum and international-mindedness is prioritised.

Summary

Schools using the curriculum framework of the MYP have certainly not cornered the market in international-mindedness or intercultural awareness. That said, the MYP's focus on international-mindedness and intercultural awareness is intentional, and there are vehicles for the development and sharing of good practice within and amongst international and national schools that have adopted the programme.

The three fundamental concepts – holistic learning, intercultural awareness and communication – have pride of place in the MYP, but no place in the MYP model. As a visiting team member, I have met a significant number of students, parents and educators who could not name all three of the fundamental concepts but who had no problem remembering the five areas of interaction. Could this be because the latter are displayed in the MYP model? Could it be because they are required elements in the development of curriculum units – and feature in the first stage of the unit planner? Could it be because the IB has specified student learning expectations for them? Could it be because schools are expected to show their development over the five years of the programme? Could it be that they are integral to the personal project? Could it be 'all of the above'?

I suggest addition not subtraction. I do not mean to suggest that intercultural awareness should be made less fundamental to the programme by limiting it to providing the context for some units. However, I feel that it should be more explicit. Could it have a dual role: remaining a fundamental concept and sitting alongside the areas of interaction? Could it become an area of interaction, and international-mindedness be the fundamental concept? In the very early days of the MYP the model was most of what we had and there were educators who were very much against changing it in any way. However, over time, *homo faber* has been re-named and in some ways re-defined, the original 'stick person' of the early model is no longer its central image, colour has been added, colours have changed, the personal project satellite has come and gone, and the IB learner profile is prominent. Can we now find a place for intercultural awareness?

Can we help our students to benefit from the wealth inherent in exposure to a variety of viewpoints and cultures, and assessing their own values in the context of this diversity? Most of us are, at a minimum, educating tomorrow's voters. I believe that I am helping to educate tomorrow's leaders: people who will be able to make a difference and who will want to do so. With respect to intercultural awareness and international-mindedness, I believe that the MYP, and the systems designed to share good practice and assure quality, facilitate that growth and help schools offering the programme to be 'more equal than others'. I think the MYP is the best that is out there, and that we can work together to make it even better. Across the world, the growing number of 'national' schools adopting the MYP suggests that there are going to be more and more internationally-minded citizens who are 'open to the perspectives, values and traditions of other individuals and communities' (IB, 2008: 8). This bodes well for future inter-religious, inter-ethnic and international relations.

References

Boix-Mansilla, V (2010): *MYP guide to interdisciplinary teaching and learning.* Cardiff: International Baccalaureate.

Brown, R (2002): Cultural dimensions of national and international educational assessment, in M Hayden, J Thompson and G Walker (eds), *International Education in Practice: Dimensions for National and International Schools.* (pp66-79) London: Routledge.

Cambridge, J and Thompson, J (2004): Internationalism and Globalisation as contexts for international education, in *Compare,* 34 (2), pp161-175.

CIS (2006): *The Guide to School Evaluation and Accreditation Seventh Edition* (Version 7.02). Petersfield: CIS/NEASC.

Coelho, E (1998): *Teaching and Learning in Multilingual Schools.* Clevedon: Multilingual Matters Ltd.

Hayden, M (2006): *Introduction to International Education: International Schools and their Communities.* London: SAGE.

Haywood, T (2007): A Simple Typology of International-Mindedness and Its Implications for Education, in M Hayden, J Levy and J Thompson (eds), *The SAGE Handbook of Research in International Education.* (pp79-89) London: SAGE.

IB (2004): *MYP: Personal project guide.* Cardiff: International Baccalaureate.

IB (2005): *IBO Programme evaluation self-study questionnaire.* Cardiff: International Baccalaureate.

IB (2008): *MYP: From principles into practice.* Cardiff: International Baccalaureate.

IB (2010a): *History of the International Baccalaureate.* Available from: http://ibo.org/history/ [Accessed 28 November 2010]

IB (2010b): *Mission statement.* Available from: www.ibo.org/mission/index.cfm [Accessed 24 August 2010]

IB (2010c): *MYP: Coordinator's handbook 2010-2011.* Cardiff: International Baccalaureate.

IB (2010d): *MYP Areas of Interaction* PowerPoint, 3.1.10. Workshop leaders training. Available from: http://occ.ibo.org

IB (2010e): *Personal project: Changes to objectives and criteria.* Cardiff: International Baccalaureate.

IB (2010f): *Guide to school authorization: Middle Years Programme.* Cardiff: International Baccalaureate.

IB (2010g): *Programme evaluation guide and self-study questionnaire: Middle Years Programme.* Cardiff: International Baccalaureate.

IB (2010h): *History of the Middle Years Programme.* Cardiff: International Baccalaureate.

ISA (2010a): *Mission Statement.* Available from: www.isaschools.org/ [Accessed 28 November 2010]

ISA (2010b): *Mission Objectives & Practical Activities.* Available from: www.isaschools.org/ [Accessed 28 November 2010]

MIS (2005): *Mission and Philosophy.* Available from: www.mis-munich.de [Accessed 24 August 2010]

Nicolson M (2010): Personal communication about MYP, 29 November 2010.

Skelton, M (2002): Defining 'international' in an international curriculum, in M Hayden, J Thompson and G Walker (eds), *International Education in Practice: Dimensions for National and International Schools.* (pp39-54) London: Routledge.

Wiggins, G and McTighe, J (2005): *Understanding by Design* (2nd ed) Alexandria, VA: ASCD.

Chapter 4

Holistic education and the MYP

John Hare

Identifying holistic education

Many educators are familiar with the term 'holistic education' but when asked to reflect on what this means, the interpretations offered would likely be inconsistent. Responses may include reference to the education of the whole student but, when pressed, agreement would vary on what this actually means, what educational interventions would be needed or what the outcomes would look like.

This is not surprising. Holistic education does not exist as a single entity or form. There is no core text telling us what holistic education means. Indeed, Forbes describes holistic education as a group of beliefs, feelings, principles and general ideas – a broad range of initiatives – that share family resemblances (Forbes; 2003: 2, 11). It has as its goal the fullest possible human development (Forbes 2003: 3) and, as such, it is more than the education of the whole student. It goes beyond intellectual growth and addresses the broad development of the individual at the cognitive and affective levels, enabling him/her to become the very best they can be as active and compassionate members of society.

The lack of clarity over holistic education has consequences. It is difficult for educational practitioners, parents or students to appreciate fully what holistic education represents and what it offers. Such an inadequacy makes detailed comparison with other educational approaches difficult and discussion of the advantages of holistic education challenging. Moreover, the points of difference and advantage offered through the MYP as a programme of holistic education, as compared with other programmes, cannot be leveraged.

The characteristics of holistic education: how does the MYP compare?

The MYP places considerable emphasis on the importance of holistic learning and holistic education (IB, 2008), but a description of what this represents as an educational approach is not developed. Furthermore, in none of the MYP documentation is there a detailed interpretation of holistic education. The reader must know what is meant by holistic education before it can be identified within the MYP literature. Reference is made to subject interconnections and their relationships with the world around them (IB, 2008), but this is only a small element of a holistic approach to education. The question emerges as to whether the MYP reflects a programme of holistic education and, if it does, then what are the outcomes this leads to for the student? For this reason a review of the holistic credentials of the MYP is appropriate, as discussed below.

The Characteristics of Holistic Education

Whilst a definition of holistic education remains elusive, Miller (1991:3) has proposed that education may be described as holistic when it demonstrates the following four characteristics:

'1 Holistic education nurtures the development of the whole person; it is concerned with intellectual as well as emotional, social, physical, creative/intuitive, aesthetic, and spiritual potentials.

'2 Holistic education revolves around *relationships* between learners, between young people and adults. The teacher-student relationship tends to be egalitarian, open, dynamic in holistic settings, rather than bound by bureaucratic roles or authoritarian rules. A sense of community is essential.

'3 Holistic education is concerned with life experience, not with narrowly defined 'basic skills'. Education is growth, discovery, and a widening of horizons; it is an engagement with the world, a quest for understanding and meaning. This quest goes far beyond the limited horizons of conventional curricula, textbooks, and standardised exams.

'4 Holistic education enables learners to critically approach the cultural, moral, and political contexts of their lives. It recognises that cultures are created by people and can be changed by people if they fail to serve important human needs. In contrast, conventional education aims only to replicate the established culture in the next generation. Holistic education, then, is a radical endeavour.'

In the following sections, it is these characteristics that will be used as reference points in examining the holistic credentials of the MYP.

The Development of the Whole Person

Miller describes the first characteristic of holistic education as nurturing 'the development of the whole person; it is concerned with intellectual as well as emotional, social, physical, creative/intuitive, aesthetic, and spiritual potentials' (Miller, 1991:3).

Peterson described the overall educational aims of the International Baccalaureate (IB) in similar terms, stating that the aim of the IB (at that time the IB Diploma Programme only) was 'to develop to their fullest potential the powers of each individual to understand, to modify and to enjoy his or her environment, both inner and outer, in its physical, social, moral, aesthetic and spiritual aspects' (Peterson, 1987: 33). The education and *development of the whole person* in its broadest sense is at the core of IB philosophy.

47

Furthermore, the MYP 'promotes the education of the whole person, emphasising intellectual, personal, emotional, and social growth, through all domains of knowledge, involving the major traditions of learning in languages, humanities, sciences, mathematics, and the arts' (IB, 2002d: 1). This statement indicates that the education of the whole person is facilitated through all areas of knowledge. The emphasis on the role of the subject areas and their interrelatedness is maintained by 'insisting upon thorough study of the various disciplines', through which the MYP 'accentuates the interrelatedness of them and so advances a *holistic* view of learning' (IB, 2002b: 4). Moreover, it is through this interrelatedness that students 'learn to see knowledge as an interrelated whole' (IB, 2008) and 'explore the disciplines in increasing depth (realising) how they are linked to each other and to local and global issues', (IB, 2008) confirming that holistic learning within the MYP gives due regard to the interrelationships of the subject disciplines. These statements alone, however, are inadequate to confirm the holistic nature of the MYP; holistic education demands a broader consideration of interrelationships and interconnections.

This breadth is evident. The MYP addresses features beyond the intellectual domain, recognising that students are entering a time of transition in their lives. They are seeking meaning and relevance, a sense of their worth and value, as well as developing social awareness and their relationships with others. The student-centred approach of the MYP recognises this and addresses Miller's first characteristic. Students 'are entering a phase where their social and cultural experiences in and outside school have a determining impact on their perception of themselves, their self-esteem, their sense of identity and their capacity to relate to others [and the MYP seeks to develop in students] a sense of personal and cultural identity and a respect for themselves and for others' (IB, 2002a: 4).

Further reference to the development of social potential has been made elsewhere through arguing that the focus of holistic learning includes the discovery of relationships between the individual, communities and the world, and furthermore that:

> Integrating health and social education throughout the curriculum and school life aims to prepare students for life by developing their ability to make choices from alternatives and to evaluate and make decisions about health hazards which they may face. Students also become aware of related social issues and their effects on communities. (IB, 2002c: 42)

Collectively, these statements confirm a focus on the development of the emotional, social and physical potentials of the student within the MYP, and align with Miller's first characteristic of holistic education.

Holistic education promotes the aesthetic potential of the student and within the area of interaction known as human ingenuity (previously known as *homo faber*), students are encouraged 'to explore the relationships between science, aesthetics, technology and ethics' (IB, 2002c: 8), Development of the aesthetic potential of the student requires further emphasis within the MYP literature. At present it is under-represented and receives inadequate reference as an element of holistic education.

Development of the whole person is referred to within the community and service area of interaction element of the MYP in which students are required to participate actively within communities, be they at school or elsewhere (IB, 2011a). The outputs of community and service involvement include a heightened awareness of students' social roles and responsibilities in their communities and a clearer understanding of the world around them. Furthermore, they are in a position to start to 'discover the social reality of self, others and community. In so doing, the [community and service] area of interaction encourages the affective, creative, ethical and cognitive development of the adolescent' (IB, 2008). These aspects of the area of interaction further reflect Miller's first characteristic of holistic education.

Miller (1991: 3) identifies the development of the spiritual potential of the student as an element of holistic education as did Peterson (1987: 33), though not in so many words. The spiritual development of the student is not identified within the MYP and this is understandable. Perceptions of spirituality will differ between students, between communities and between cultures; spirituality represents an area of development that is very personal to the student. Connotations of spiritual development are best left as a highly personal agenda that will be influenced by knowledge and experience gained from personal encounters and experiences. There can be little doubt that the MYP can offer such opportunities. For example, in developing a sense of community concern and awareness students are involved in a process of discovery of self and community. Consequently, there is no reason to believe that some style of personal spiritual development is not taking place.

It is made clear in MYP documentation that schools promote the connections between the subject areas and, significantly, their place within the outside world (IB, 2008). The areas of interaction are the vehicles through which not only the subject connections but also the broader thinking skills and processes are developed and a firm grasp of principles and practices are accessed. Thereby, students will learn to view knowledge as an interrelated, coherent whole (IB, 2008) and understand the relevance and application of what they learn and experience.

In summary, there is evidence in the MYP literature that the programme is designed to support the development of the whole person at the intellectual, emotional, social, creative, and aesthetic levels. Spiritual development is not addressed but, if spiritual development represents encouragement and guidance to achieve the very best that students can become, with a realisation of their place in the world and with a caring attitude to those around them, then the programme can claim to develop spiritual potential. Holistic education is, indeed, 'a radical endeavour' (Miller, 1991: 3).

Relationships

Miller's second characteristic describes holistic education revolving

> ... around relationships between learners, between young people and adults. The teacher-student relationship tends to be egalitarian, open, dynamic in holistic settings, rather than bound by bureaucratic roles or authoritarian rules. A sense of community is essential. (Miller, 1991: 3)

This characteristic emphasises the role of relationships at a number of levels but also emphasises the importance of the quality of these relationships. It can best be evaluated by reviewing the learning environment encouraged by the MYP.

The emphasis within the MYP is to develop students as independent learners and to encourage them to question and evaluate information critically, developing an awareness of their own place in the world. Moreover, within the community and service area of interaction teachers are encouraged to share personal experiences with students, facilitating discussion and reflection. Such a pedagogical approach will only succeed where the teacher-student relationship is open and dynamic. Clearly an open, dynamic and supportive teacher-student relationship, in which teachers act as facilitators and guides, needs to be encouraged for this style of learning to occur and for the areas of interaction to contribute to the success of such a learning programme. Overall, it is difficult to envisage how the aims of the MYP can be realised without such an egalitarian, open and dynamic teacher-student relationship.

The importance of relationships between learners, and between young people and adults, is evident within the MYP literature, which points out, for instance, that 'as they learn to construct meaning by exploring other ways of being and different points of view, students become more informed about and sensitive to, the experiences of others, locally, nationally and internationally' (IB, 2002a: 5-6). Furthermore, the development and importance of relationships is promoted by encouraging students to consider multiple perspectives; intercultural awareness not only fosters respect, but also aims to develop empathy and understanding. An awareness of our interconnectedness brings with it our caring for others. Indeed, 'to be holistically authentic is to care; for if we see the connectedness to others then inevitably we care for them as well' (Miller, 2001: 179).

This theme of caring is evident in the IB statements above, and it emerges from the views, opinions, cultures and beliefs of others through the themes of intercultural awareness, the environment, communication and the approaches to learning within the MYP. It is evident that the MYP promotes genuine understanding at many levels that give voice to this important area of the holistic approach to education.

Life Experience

The scope of holistic education is broad and is

> ... concerned with life experience, not with narrowly defined 'basic skills'. Education is growth, discovery, and a widening of horizons; it is an engagement with the world, a quest for understanding and meaning. This quest goes far beyond the limited horizons of conventional curricula, textbooks, and standardised exams. (Miller, 1991: 3)

The IB literature indicates that students are positioned to acquire a wide range of intellectual, problem solving and social skills, many of which move beyond 'basic skills'. Within the MYP students are 'encouraged to make connections between their intellectual and social development and the benefits that they can contribute to the community ... students can discover the social reality of self, others and community' (IB, 2008).

The areas of interaction lead students to seek understanding and meaning beyond the immediate confines of textbooks and a conventional curriculum. Opportunities provided through the areas of interaction, particularly community and service, and environment, are well placed to contribute to this broadening of experience.

Reference to growth and discovery implies that students develop as lifelong learners, gaining and benefiting from experiences throughout their lifetimes. This aligns with the IB mission statement, which claims that 'the programmes encourage students across the world to become active, compassionate and lifelong learners' (IB, 2011b). It is further confirmed through the perception of the underlying concept of education as a lifelong process, of which the formal years of schooling are only a part.

These statements confirm that, within the MYP, the student is moved from a narrow knowledge-based curriculum to broader educational horizons. An educational vista beyond the school years is encouraged that leads to lifelong learning in the many situations that the student experiences. Consequently, the adolescent student emerges from the MYP as a learner who takes continuous advantage of the many learning opportunities with which they are presented through the MYP and beyond.

Cultural Development

Miller makes explicit the role of cultural development, stating that 'holistic education enables learners to critically approach the cultural, moral and political contexts of their lives. It recognises that cultures are created by people and can be changed by people if they fail to serve important human needs' (Miller, 1991: 3).

This characteristic demands that students are reflective and that they look critically at themselves and the position of their beliefs and values alongside those of others who are perhaps from very different backgrounds. The characteristic is addressed principally through the concept of intercultural awareness (IB, 2008), which asks the student to examine closely his or her own culture in the light of other cultures and beliefs. The output of these interventions is emotional and social growth through the development of empathy and respect (IB, 2008). Moreover, aligning with Miller's characteristics, the MYP calls on students to examine critically their beliefs through reflective thinking about ideas and behaviours including problem solving and analysis, clarification and discussion.

It would be naïve to believe that cultural awareness and understanding only develop in structured situations where such interactions are possible. Within the context of a school with a myriad of different cultures, it is unlikely that students will only mix with other students of their own nationality. They are much more likely to experience a large number of situations, both in and out of school, in which they will mix with other students and friends with differing beliefs, values and cultural norms. Such interactions can only add to the richness of their experiences in the MYP.

In summary, the MYP possesses a number of features that exemplify holistic education. The development of the whole person is well represented in IB literature, there is an emphasis on the development of relationships and, through the areas of interaction, MYP students are encouraged to be reflective in their cultural beliefs and moral standards. Students are also provided with opportunities to experience and understand the communities in which they reside and with which they interact, and to grow as individuals through the experiences that such interactions bring.

The development of skills, abilities and attitudes beyond those that could be described as 'basic skills' is well represented in IB literature. Furthermore there are descriptions that show that education for growth and discovery, leading to understanding and meaning beyond the subject disciplines, are elements of the MYP.

Interpreting what holistic education represents in an MYP student

Whilst there is good evidence that the MYP reflects the characteristics of a holistic approach to education, for the educator, student and parent/guardian the essential questions remain, namely:

• What will be the outputs of this approach?

• What skills and attributes will be developed in the student?

The absence of a working definition of holistic education need not be problematic, as long as the outcomes of holistic education can be identified in terms of student skills, behaviours and attributes. To this end, recurring themes within holistic education have been identified from various sources (Clarke,

1991a: 32; Clarke, 1991b: 40; Clarke 1991c: 61; Martin, 1997: 13; Miller, 1991: 3; Miller, 2001: 3). The themes have been described elsewhere (Hare, 2006a; Hare 2006b: 304-6) and can be summarised as follows:

- Our interconnectedness with all that is around us

- The development of relationships

- A sense of shared community

- A genuine sense of caring

- The management of personal development and growth of the whole person

- Developing personal goals

- The environment

The values and behaviours that arise from these common themes have been described previously (Hare, 2006a: 307-312; Hare, 2010) and lead to the identification of the skills, abilities and competencies that the student will develop within a programme of holistic education. These skills, abilities and competencies can be summarised in what has been described as a person profile.

The Holistically Educated Student: The Person Profile

The person profile (Appendix 1), developed as part of my earlier work (see, for example Hare 2006b), outlines important attributes that the student should be able to demonstrate or is in the process of developing and refining, which are presented as key indicators. These ten key indicators represent the major attributes that the student will be developing to the end of their middle years of education and beyond. A descriptor for each of the indicators provides additional information and clarification. A number of key indicators lend themselves to self- and peer-assessment rather than teacher-led assessment. For example, aspects of the following indicators:

- acts with social and academic maturity and integrity;

- through interpersonal skills develops and maintains relationships;

- demonstrates a reflective approach and an attitude of continuous improvement;

- seeks to bring clarity to decision making;

- demonstrates good meeting management and involvement behaviours;

can be assessed by the students themselves, supplemented by feedback from peer groups, as long as a culture of open and non-judgemental feedback is encouraged.

The key indicators are not prescriptive outcomes and it is not intended that the programme should deliver an 'ideal' holistically educated student. This would be far too ambitious a goal for a 16 year-old student for reasons outlined previously. Furthermore it is not intended that the student who demonstrates more of the key indicators than another student is necessarily more holistically educated than is their fellow student. Education is a dynamic process that elicits strengths and identifies development areas in all students; these will change as students progress through the MYP. Indeed, education is a lifelong dynamic process.

The person profile should be treated with caution. The student at this stage of education is not the 'finished article'. Holistic education prepares a student for lifelong learning and the middle years of education should be putting in place many of the values, attitudes and skills that will serve the individual well in later years.

All students react to, and benefit from, education in different ways and the proposed profile merely defines what the intended goals of the educational process may be. No weighting or value is given to any aspects of the values or behaviours and this is by design. The character of a student and the contribution that he/she brings to the community are a blend of strengths and development areas that they possess and are in the process of developing; it is what marks them out as individuals and makes their individual contributions unique and valued.

A comparison of the person profile with the IB learner profile

The IB learner profile describes the common attributes and aspirations of internationally-minded students engaged in the IB programmes. The origin of the profile is to be found in the IB Primary Years Programme (PYP) and much of the wording is found in PYP sources (IB, 2007), though the wording is equally appropriate for all the IB programmes. The learner profile (IB, 2006) can be found in Chapter 1 of this book. In the learner profile, the ten single-worded student attributes are described in terms of actions or activities that clarify each of these attributes. Similarly, the key indicators within the person profile (Appendix 1) are clarified through descriptors.

Both profiles identify outcomes of the educational process at the academic, personal and interpersonal levels. Despite their different origins, a comparison of the person profile and the IB learner profile reveals striking similarities in content. The learner profile applies to all three IB programmes and covers the entire school life of a student. The person profile has been developed only for the age range 11-16 years. There is little in the person profile to suggest that it could not be refined for the school age range of 5-18. Whilst the focus for development of the person profile was students within the middle years of education, the characteristics are common to holistic education regardless of the age-range of the educational programme. Consequently, the person profile can be applied to students throughout the school years, although the language of the descriptors would change to reflect the different age ranges of the students.

A comparison of the person profile with the learner profile reveals interesting similarities (see Appendix 2). Key indicators in the person profile have been compared with the attributes of the learner profile and comparisons made between the statements. Each of the key indicators and descriptors from the person profile compares well with an attribute and its descriptor in the learner profile. Whilst the wording may differ, the underlying themes within both documents show a high degree of similarity. For example, the person profile key indicators:

- acts with social and academic maturity; and

- demonstrates good meeting management and involvement behaviours,

have common features with 'communicators' in the learner profile. Similarly, the learner profile attribute 'knowledgeable' is comparable in content and purpose to the key indicators:

- seeks to bring clarity to decision making;

- through an understanding of their subject areas, their interdependencies and the areas of interaction can appreciate and debate global issues and their impact of the environment; and

- uses effectively information resources made available to them that assist in the acquisition of knowledge and its application.

These and the remaining comparisons included in Appendix 2 to this chapter highlight the notable similarities between the profiles.

A further point emerges from these comparisons. The person profile represents the attributes and qualities that students should possess as they emerge from a middle years programme of holistic education. The close similarities between the person profile and the learner profile suggest that students emerging from the MYP are also emerging from a programme of holistic education. This complements the evidence presented elsewhere (Hare, 2006a; Hare, 2007: 60-67) that the MYP represents a programme of holistic education.

Summary

The evidence above is persuasive; the MYP represents a holistic approach to education. The MYP reflects the characteristics of holistic education and the IB learner profile aligns well with the person profile of a student pursuing a programme of holistic education.

It could be argued that the holistic perspective is the aim of all education systems, and there are undoubtedly a number of schools that pursue such an approach, which has also been proposed elsewhere (UNESCO, 1996: 94). Nevertheless, a knowledge-based approach to education remains common (Peterson, 1987: 38-39) and fails to manage actively the broader education and development of the student.

The lack of a widely shared definition for holistic education is not problematic. This educational approach can be accessed through its outputs, which can be approached through well-designed teaching and support programmes. This moves the education process to the broad growth of the individual that is facilitated and guided by all around them, whether educators, parents or peers. Educating the individual is thus moved beyond the confines of the classroom; it is indeed a radical endeavour that can only benefit students and all who become part of their learning experience.

References

Clarke, E T (1991a): Holistic Education: A Search for Wholeness, in Miller, R (ed), *New Directions in Education*, pp53-62. Brandon, VT: Holistic Education Press.

Clarke, E T (1991b): Environmental Education as an Integrative study, in Miller, R (ed), *New Directions in Education*, pp38-52. Brandon, VT: Holistic Education Press.

Clarke, E T (1991c): The Search for a new international paradigm: The Implications of new assumptions about thinking and learning, in Miller, R (ed), *New Directions in Education*, pp16-37. Brandon, VT: Holistic Education Press.

Forbes, S H (2003): *Holistic Education: An Analysis of its Ideas and Nature.* Brandon VT: Foundation for Educational Renewal.

Hare, J R (2006a): *An Evaluation of the Holistic Credentials of the IB MYP.* Paper presented at the Alliance for International Education Conference, Shanghai, PR China. 27-29 October 2006.

Hare, J R (2006b): Towards an understanding of holistic education in the middle years of education, in *Journal of Research in International Education*, 5, 3: pp301-322.

Hare, J R (2007): *Holistic Education and the IB Middle Years Programme: towards a clearer understanding of the Relationship.* University of Bath: unpublished MPhil thesis.

Hare, J R (2010): *Holistic Education: An Interpretation for teachers in the IB programmes.* IB position paper. Available at:
http://occ.ibo.org/ibis/documents/general/g_0_iboxx_amo_1007_2_e.pdf

IB (2002a): *A Basis for Practice: The Middle Years Programme.* Geneva: International Baccalaureate.

IB (2002b): *Schools' Guide to the Middle Years Programme.* Geneva: International Baccalaureate.

IB (2002c): *International Baccalaureate Organisation Middle Years Programme: Areas of Interaction.* Geneva: International Baccalaureate.

IB (2002d): *A Continuum of international Education: The Primary Years Programme, The Middle Years Programme, The Diploma Programme.* Geneva: International Baccalaureate.

IB (2006): *IB Learner Profile.* Geneva: International Baccalaureate.

IB (2007): *The IB Primary Years Programme*, Available at: www.ibo.org/communications/publications/documents/PYPflyerEng.pdf [Accessed 17 January 2011]

IB (2008): *MYP: From Principles into Practice*, Cardiff: International Baccalaureate.

IB (2011a): *IB MYP Areas of Interaction-community service*, Available at: www.ibo.org/myp/curriculum/interaction/community/ [Accessed 17 January 2011]

IB (2011b): *IB Mission Statement*, Available at: www.ibo.org/mission/ [Accessed 17 January 2011]

Martin, C (1997): *The Holistic Educators: Education for the 21st Century.* Nottingham: The Educational Heretics Press.

Miller, J P (2001): *The Holistic Curriculum.* (Revised 2nd edn) Toronto: OISE Press.

Miller, R (1991): Introduction, in Miller, R (ed), *New Directions in Education*, pp1-3. Brandon, VT: Holistic Education Press.

Peterson, A D C (1987): *Schools Across Frontiers.* Chicago Ill.: Open Court.

UNESCO (1996): *Learning: The Treasure Within.* Report to UNESCO of the International Commission on Education for the Twenty First Century, chaired by Jacques Delors. Paris: UNESCO.

Appendix 1: Person profile of a student emerging from a programme of holistic education in the middle years of education

Key Indicators	Descriptor
Acts with social and academic maturity and integrity	The student would display social and academic maturity that would put them at ease within a group of people that they were previously unfamiliar with. They would also be confident in their approach to people that they had not previously encountered and exhibit respect for the culture, opinions and values of these individuals or group. They are ready to challenge accepted wisdom in a mature manner in order to clarify their own understanding and gain experience. In circumstances that an error is made, has the maturity to learn from the error and how it occurred. Takes responsibility and maintains integrity through not misrepresenting themselves for personal gain. Presents work that reflects their own efforts, acknowledges inputs from others and avoids plagiarism.
Takes ownership of their own development and learning and through planning, prioritisation and their own determination delivers tasks in a timely manner.	The student would take ownership of their own development and progress and take responsibility for the outcomes. To support this they would set themselves clear guidelines and targets and a realistic timetable for the achievement of these regardless of whether these are long or short term assignments. Can plan and prioritise task effectively so that tasks receive the appropriate time and effort to achieve the required outcome. In the face of adversity, they would persist with the task to achieve a quality outcome.
Demonstrates flexibility and a creative approach to problem solving.	They are able to think creatively and flexibly in addressing issues and problems that require approaches that are not readily apparent and result in drawing on approaches from a range of disciplines and experiences. In coming to conclusions and taking action, they are confident and feel empowered to take risks.
Through interpersonal skills develops and maintains relationships.	In their interactions with others from a range of different backgrounds and cultures, they will act with care, empathy, compassion and consideration especially in circumstances in which the views of others are at variance with their own. Through active listening and maintaining an open mind, the student actively reflects on their behaviours and values and modifies these accordingly.

Demonstrates a reflective approach and an attitude of continuous improvement.	Can review and evaluate the quality of their work objectively and identify areas of success and development. From these is able to modify their approaches and behaviours and continuously learn from and improve the work that they complete.
Demonstrates effective written and oral communication skills	Can demonstrate effective written and oral communication skills that facilitate the successful delivery of information in a variety of contexts and situations. This will be demonstrated through essay writing, oral presentations, analytical and creative writing and the effective use of IT skills.
Demonstrates good meeting management and involvement behaviours.	The student would actively and collaboratively contribute willingly and well to group discussions and meetings. They would actively listen to the opinions and values of others and support the team. They would challenge others with respect and consideration to move matters forward to achieve a decision and instigate constructive changes. In circumstances in which their decisions have been listened to, they would show maturity in accepting the group decision and actively support the majority view.
Seeks to bring clarity to decision making.	The student has consistently sought to bring clarity and simplicity to what they do to achieve a target or an outcome so that their efforts are directed effectively and in a timely way. In these efforts they would consistently seek to exceed standards and raise their own expectations.
Through an understanding of their subject areas, their interdependencies and interrelationships can take a global view of issues and appreciate and debate global issues and the impact of human activity on the environment.	Shows a knowledge and understanding of the subjects they study and can identify the features that draw the subjects and information together as a coherent whole. From their interaction with others, their experiences and learning, they take a considered global perspective on international concerns and bring a firm appreciation of the issues relevant to these concerns.
Uses effectively the information resources made available to them that assist in the acquisition of knowledge and its application.	Can use effectively data and information management methods, including electronic data and library resources.

Appendix 2: A Comparison of the Person Profile and the IB Learner Profile

The key indicators and supporting descriptors of the person profile (see Appendix 1) have been compared with the attributes and their corresponding descriptors of the IB learner profile (bold type in this appendix). Each key indicator and its descriptor from the person profile has been compared with the content of the learner profile. The comparable attributes and supporting descriptors in the learner profile have been identified. The results of this comparison are presented below.

Person Profile	IB Learner Profile (comparable attributes)
Acts with social and academic maturity... that would put them at ease within a group of people that they were previously unfamiliar with. **Demonstrates good meeting management and involvement behaviours** ... The student would actively and collaboratively contribute willingly and well to group discussions and meetings. They would actively listen to the opinions and values of others and support the team. They would challenge others with respect and consideration to move matters forward to achieve a decision and instigate constructive changes. In circumstances in which their decisions have been listened to, they would show maturity in accepting the group decision and actively support the majority view.	**Communicators** ... They work effectively and willingly in collaboration with others.
Takes ownership of their own development and learning and through planning, prioritisation and their own determination delivers tasks in a timely manner ... The student would take ownership of their own development and progress and take responsibility for the outcomes. Can plan and prioritise task effectively so that tasks receive the appropriate time and effort to achieve the required outcome.	**Inquirers** ... They acquire the skills necessary to conduct inquiry and research and show independence in learning. **Reflective** ... They give thoughtful consideration to their own learning and experience. They are able to assess and understand their strengths and limitations in order to support their learning and personal development.

Seeks to bring clarity to decision making ... The student has consistently sought to bring clarity and simplicity to what they do to achieve a target or an outcome so that their efforts are directed effectively and in a timely way. In these efforts they would consistently seek to exceed standards and raise their own expectations.	**Knowledgeable** ... they acquire in-depth knowledge and develop understanding across a broad and balanced range of disciplines.
Through an understanding of their subject areas, their interdependencies and interrelationships can take a global view of issues and appreciate and debate global issues and the impact of human activity on the environment ... Shows a knowledge and understanding of the subjects they study and can identify the features that draw the subjects and information together as a coherent whole.	
From their interaction with others, their experiences and learning, they take a considered global perspective on international concerns and bring a firm appreciation of the issues relevant to these concerns.	
Uses effectively information resources made available to them that assist in the acquisition of knowledge and its application ... Can use effectively data and information management methods, including electronic data and library resources.	
Through interpersonal skills develops and maintains relationships ... In their interactions with others from a range of different backgrounds and cultures, they will act with care, empathy, compassion and consideration especially in circumstances in which the views of others are at variance with their own.	**Open minded** ... They understand and appreciate their own cultures and personal histories, and are open to the perspectives, values and traditions of other individuals and communities. They are accustomed to seeking and evaluating a range of points of view, and are willing to grow from the experience.
Through active listening and maintaining an open mind, the student actively reflects on their behaviours and values and modifies these accordingly.	
Acts with social and academic maturity and integrity ... exhibit respect for the culture, opinions and values of these individuals or group.	**Caring** ... They show empathy, compassion and respect towards the needs and feelings of others.
Demonstrates a reflective approach and an attitude of continuous improvement ... able to modify their approaches and behaviours and continuously learn from and improve the work that they complete.	

Demonstrates effective written and oral communication skills ... Can demonstrate effective written and oral communication skills that facilitate the successful delivery of information in a variety of contexts and situations. This will be demonstrated through essay writing, oral presentations, analytical and creative writing and the effective use of IT skills.	**Communicators** ... They understand and express ideas and information confidently and creatively in more than one language and in a variety of modes of communication.
Demonstrates a reflective approach and an attitude of continuous improvement ... Can review and evaluate the quality of their work objectively and identify areas of success and development. From these is able to modify their approaches and behaviours and continuously learn from and improve the work that they complete. **Takes ownership of their own development and learning and through planning, prioritisation and their own determination delivers tasks in a timely manner** ... The student would take ownership of their own development and progress and take responsibility for the outcomes. To support this they would set themselves clear guidelines and targets and a realistic timetable for the achievement of these regardless of whether these are long or short term assignments. Can plan and prioritise task effectively so that tasks receive the appropriate time and effort to achieve the required outcome.	**Reflective** ... They give thoughtful consideration to their own learning and experience. They are able to assess and understand their strengths and limitations in order to support their learning and personal development.
Demonstrates flexibility and a creative approach to problem solving ... They are able to think creatively and flexibly in addressing issues and problems that require approaches that are not readily apparent and result in drawing on approaches from a range of disciplines and experiences. In coming to conclusions and taking action, they are confident and feel empowered to take risks.	**Thinkers** ... They exercise initiative in applying thinking skills critically and creatively to recognize and approach complex problems, and make reasoned, ethical decisions.

Chapter 5

Subject-based, interdisciplinary and transdisciplinary approaches to the MYP

Janet Field

When our school introduced the IB Middle Years Programme (MYP) in 1998, my colleagues and I seized the chance to design a curriculum for our own students, based upon what we considered good teaching. Characterized by experimentation and unhampered by the constraints of external curricula, our efforts were eclectic – if not to say haphazard! Only after several years wondering about the implications of the programme's principles and values did we start to ask ourselves how they could *best* be fulfilled. The 'what' of the programme had become fairly clear to us, but the 'how' has been taking much longer to figure out.

Recent MYP developments have shifted more towards the 'how' after a decade of consensus building about what the programme could, and should, be. *MYP: From principles into practice* (IB, 2008b) and the *Programme standards and practices* (IB, 2005; 2010d) have provided policy and guidance for implementing the programme. The *MYP Guide to interdisciplinary teaching and learning* (Boix-Mansilla, 2010) is intended to develop practice in schools by offering a research-based explanation of this approach.

In each case, matters concerning MYP subjects or disciplines arise. Guidance is provided regarding their organization, structures, status and the connections between them, as well as how they constitute the written, taught and assessed curriculum (IB, 2008b). Based mainly on the documents mentioned above, this chapter will first map out some of the conceptual terrain that faces MYP teachers when they consider the IB's guidance about the relationships between subjects. It will then discuss some of the associated challenges and tensions. I will suggest that the contrast between transdisciplinary and subject-based approaches will be less critical in future than the way in which we deal with the challenge of effectively implementing the MYP's approach to interdisciplinarity.

As this discussion does not require fine distinctions between 'subjects' and 'disciplines', both terms will be used to describe what Jacobs (1989) calls 'discipline fields': domains that represent a 'specific body of teachable knowledge with its own background of education, training, procedures, methods, and content areas'. In IB documents, the two terms tend to be used interchangeably (for example, in Boix-Mansilla, 2010: 5), which is how they will also be used in this chapter.

It is also important to observe from the outset that 'transdisciplinary' and 'interdisciplinary', and the associated terms, have not always been consistently used or understood in either practice or in the wider educational literature. They have sometimes been taken to mean more or less the same thing: a cross-curricular approach where the conventional boundaries between subjects are temporarily set aside. Another source of ambiguity has been the borrowing of terminology from one established context – such as the way transdisciplinarity is understood in the IB Primary Years Programme (PYP) – and its recontextualization elsewhere. The title of this chapter might seem to be misleading in that the three terms mentioned do not yet appear to represent completely distinct and stable conceptual approaches to curriculum. The chapter, however, uses them in the way, and with the meaning, that they are used in the particular IB documentation under discussion.

Approaches to the curriculum

MYP guidelines mention several approaches to the curriculum. A student's educational experience should be holistic, with interdisciplinary learning when appropriate. The curriculum is organized by subjects; these are studied concurrently, giving a sense of a balanced 'whole'. Before considering curriculum-related questions about 'taking the MYP forward', it is helpful to consider how these approaches are currently laid out.

Holistic learning

Holistic learning has been a fundamental concept of the MYP from its origins (IB, 2010a). It represents 'the notion that all knowledge is interrelated and that the curriculum should cater to the development of the whole person' (IB, 2008b: 10).

Two ideas are conveyed here – the whole experience and development of the learner, and the holistic conceptualization of what is learned. According to Hare, holistic education is also closely linked to the learning culture of the school:

> Through an understanding of their subject areas, their interdependencies and interrelationships, [students] can appreciate the interconnections in human knowledge; they can appreciate and debate global issues and the impact of human activity on the environment. They develop a sound knowledge and understanding of the subjects that they study and can identify the features that draw the subjects and information together as a coherent whole. They are able to transfer skills between disciplines. (Hare, 2010: 5)

Seemingly, it is the principle of holistic learning that gives us the mandate to take an interdisciplinary approach to teaching within a subject-based curriculum framework. The MYP model also includes a transdisciplinary core, formed by areas of interaction and the contexts for learning that they frame.

Consequently, three different disciplinary approaches must be balanced in the MYP curriculum as implemented by schools.

A transdisciplinary orientation

Whereas holistic learning is explicitly fundamental only to the MYP, transdisciplinarity features to some extent in each of the three IB programmes (Primary Years Programme, Middle Years Programme and Diploma Programme). Across the IB continuum, the programmes' structural dimension reveals different approaches to the relationships between subjects. Another dimension reflects the transdisciplinary process of learning to learn, which bridges all three (IB, 2008c: 5). (See Table 1)

Structure		
Primary Years Programme (PYP)	Middle Years Programme (MYP)	Diploma Programme (DP)
Transdisciplinary units of inquiry	Organized around disciplines with interdisciplinary areas of interaction	Organized around disciplines with theory of knowledge connecting the disciplines
Learning to learn		
PYP	MYP	DP
Transdisciplinary concepts and skills	Approaches to Learning	Theory of Knowledge

Table 1: from The IB continuum of international education *(IB, 2008c: 5)*

Transdisciplinarity has been defined as learning that is 'beyond the scope of the disciplines; that is, to start with a problem and bring to bear knowledge from the disciplines' (Jacobs, 1989). However, IB programmes differ in the extent of their transdisciplinary orientation. Such an orientation prevails in the PYP where younger students hardly need to compartmentalize their learning even though their teachers are already laying the foundations of disciplinary understanding (IB, 2007). As with the PYP, the MYP and the DP both have student-centred 'cores' in their curriculum models, of which the IB learner, represented as a profile of attributes, is the conceptual centrepiece. The learner is in the position of actor in relation to the discipline fields that surround him or her; the relationships between student and subjects are mediated to some extent through generic, over-arching or interactive elements. In the DP, the core comprises the theory of knowledge and extended essay, along with creativity, action, service (CAS). Teachers and students can 'make links between experiences in the core and the academic subjects that are being studied, ...based on the belief that the total educational experience is more than the sum of its parts' (IB, 2009: 6). Similarly, the MYP areas of interaction prompt students to contextualize their subject-based learning, the 'problems' mentioned above being those to which students can relate in real terms as they apply their subject-based learning. Also, approaches to learning are identified when teachers analyse the processes, skills and attitudes that students will need. This provides a transdisciplinary 'metacurriculum' (Ackerman and Perkins, 1989), 'comprised of learning skills and strategies selected on the basis of their value in helping students (1) acquire the curriculum content being taught and (2) develop the capacity to think and learn independently.' The metacurriculum is integrated across subjects.

There is also a transdisciplinary or interdisciplinary thread running through the PYP exhibition, the MYP personal project and the DP extended essay, the last of which now has an interdisciplinary 'World Studies' option that requires students to 'pursue independent research on a focused topic, *using concepts, perspectives, findings, or examples from at least two different subjects/disciplines*' (IB, 2010e: my emphasis). In each case, students start with a problem or question and then select disciplinary fields from which to draw. The personal project meets the criteria for quality interdisciplinary learning by addressing multifaceted topics in a purposeful way and integrating several disciplinary perspectives (Boix-Mansilla, 2010). Students discover this when they realize that they must venture beyond subject boundaries, locating and bringing together knowledge and skills from different areas so that they can achieve their project's goal.

Interdisciplinary teaching and learning

Like holistic learning, interdisciplinarity has been present from the MYP's start (IB, 2010a), but over the past decade it has been difficult to feel secure about this approach. Grossman *et al* wrote of 'the lack of common definitions about what constitutes interdisciplinarity', suggesting that 'the lack of agreement over the terms of the debate simply reflects the disorderly state of the art' (2000: 10). Ideological support for cross-curricular teaching co-existed with pragmatic interests that sought to increase the amount of time available for 'pressure-point' issues such as literacy, numeracy and content expansion. Criticism has focused on both its lack of demonstrable impact on student learning (Stevens *et al*, 2005) and on the proliferation of 'overloaded, over-framed curriculum units' (Hameyer, 2007: 423; see also Boyle and Bragg, 2008). The 'fuzziness' of the whole approach was one of the factors that affected the MYP's early reputation, as acknowledged in a recent account of the MYP's development:

> In the very beginning of its existence the MYP had been criticised in some quarters for the interdisciplinary nature of the programme and the perceived subsequent lack of disciplinary rigour in comparison to the IGCSE... In 2006, the MYP team started collaborating with Harvard Project Zero in order to address misconceptions and to provide clear research-based guidance. Veronica

Boix-Mansilla authored *MYP: A guide to interdisciplinary teaching and learning in the MYP*. She had access to outstanding work in MYP schools and used case study examples as part of the guide published in May 2010. (IB, 2010a: 34)

This new guide supports learning that 'bring(s) together concepts, methods or forms of communication from two or more disciplines or established areas of expertise to explain a phenomenon, solve a problem, create a product or raise a new question in ways that would have been unlikely through single disciplinary means' (Boix-Mansilla, 2010: 13). It advocates teaching that is grounded in the disciplines, provides problem-spaces in which integration can occur, and crafts sequences of understanding performances that guide students to develop their thinking as they pursue authentic lines of inquiry in a purposeful way.

The interdisciplinary approach is introduced from the start: 'MYP schools have a responsibility to ensure that there is a smooth transition from the transdisciplinary model [of the PYP] into a model where disciplinary concepts are taught' (IB, 2008b: 3). Also bordering the MYP is the subject-based DP, which has little space for interdisciplinarity even though the IB 'will continue to explore ways of offering DP students more opportunities to study in an interdisciplinary way in order to allow them to explore multidisciplinary global issues and to enhance their learning in general' (IB, 2008c: 11). Questions raised by this statement illustrate the need for clearer definitions of such concepts, and for building consensus within and across the programme communities about how various curriculum approaches might appear in practice.

Central to the process of ensuring appropriate implementation of the IB programmes is a set of standards and practices, some of which are common and some which are particular to each programme. The classification of the practices and the way in which they align provide clues about the intentions behind various aspects of the programmes (IB, 2010d). Three of the four common standards set expectations regarding the relationship between disciplines within the curriculum. In these, we can compare the references to transdisciplinary, interdisciplinary and subject-based approaches across the three programmes.

Standard A: Philosophy

Transdisciplinarity is considered essential to the philosophy of the PYP but there are no such claims for interdisciplinarity in the MYP. However, as explained above, the latter is associated with holistic learning and, as a fundamental concept of the MYP, this is identified as essential. Even though there are several transdisciplinary or interdisciplinary elements within the DP, this does not signal a shift away from a philosophy that is firmly subject-based.

Standard B2: Resources and Support

The relevant practices here refer to scheduling and time resources for subjects; parallel MYP and DP practices relate to minimum time requirements and the 'concurrency of learning'. This is a 'principle promoted in the Middle Years Programme and the Diploma Programme. Students deal with a balanced curriculum each year in which the required subjects are studied simultaneously' (IB, 2010d: 25). Concurrent learning across all eight MYP subject groups supposedly increases the likelihood of students perceiving the curriculum as a balanced whole and making their own connections across subject boundaries.

Standard C: Curriculum

Here, the relevant practices are not directly associated with the written, taught or assessed curriculum. Instead, collaborative planning is emphasized. Whereas in the PYP this is expected to lead towards a transdisciplinary curriculum, the requirement in the MYP is that 'collaborative planning and reflection facilitates interdisciplinary learning to strengthen cross-curricular skills and the deepening of disciplinary understanding' (IB, 2010d: 15). The DP practices refer to the transdisciplinary aspect of theory of knowledge. Significantly, DP practice 1b, 'Collaborative planning and reflection explores connections and relations between subjects and reinforces knowledge, understanding and skills shared by the different disciplines' (IB, 2010d: 22), indicates a shift towards awareness of the relationships between subjects.

The status of transdisciplinarity in the DP is less secure than in the other programmes, given the newness of the innovations there. Unlike the PYP and the MYP, which are frameworks, the DP has a prescribed curriculum (IB, 2008c: 5) and therefore its subject-based structure is largely beyond the control of schools. Any further shifts in the DP towards transdisciplinarity or interdisciplinarity are likely to be supported more readily by teachers who also teach in the MYP and who value the rigour and method that underlies the approach there; similarly, the regard for interdisciplinarity in the MYP is likely to increase if its wider acceptance should develop in the DP.

These standards and practices amount to policy and form the basis for evaluating schools' implementation of the MYP. Consequently, this is where the expectation is mandated that MYP teachers will collaborate to bring about interdisciplinary teaching and learning.

The subject-based approach

Having outlined the transdisciplinary and interdisciplinary curriculum approaches, I will mention the subject-based approach briefly before looking at some reasons why these approaches should not be viewed as opposing one another.

The MYP is organized around eight subject groups or disciplinary fields. These involve more than just the acquisition of knowledge and skills; they comprise various dimensions which require understanding. Boix-Mansilla points out that

Quality understanding in a discipline or an established area of expertise involves not only having adequate information about the core concepts, theories, and findings in the domain, but also calls upon students to learn about the methods by which disciplinary knowledge is produced...; the purposes and applications for which knowledge is pursued...; and the typical ways in which information is communicated in the discipline. (2010: 10)

The objectives of each subject group are expressed as sets of knowledge, concepts, skills and attitudes. Clear boundaries between the groups, and the subjects within them, assist us to plan the curriculum and organize schools. This can amount to a type of insularity where curriculum territory is protected and there are only limited possibilities for crossing disciplinary boundaries, incorporating everyday knowledge into the curriculum and involving non-specialists in curriculum decisions (Young, 2006).

Beane (1995) argues that such subject-based approaches can result not just in the fragmentation of learning, and in territory and status distinctions across the curriculum, but also in schools that are organized around countless boundaries and roles: 'When we come up with a new area that has to be taken care of, we add a new "compartment" to the curriculum ... making new timeslots and defining teachers and groups of students accordingly.' Ironically, one way of organizing interdisciplinary learning is to create 'new areas' in which to contain it: special timetable days or weeks, supplementary units or classes organized around themes, topics or events, or hybridized subjects that gain their own place in the curriculum. Providing interdisciplinary learning opportunities within an insular subject-based framework does not necessarily provide for integration and a more open approach to subject boundaries, since new hybrid subjects can become curriculum entities that are almost as insular as those that already exist. We have noticed this in our school where a science-humanities investigation that has been running for several years is widely referred to as 'the interdisciplinary unit'. The students' values are not focused so much on the unit's purpose or approach, but on the characteristics of the entity and the basis of its place in the curriculum; their questions normally cluster around assessment and 'grades'.

Young has explained the dynamics of subject-based insularity and hybridization as a reflection of globalizing political and economic factors, expressed through the structures, compartmentalization and control of knowledge. His assumption is that the future will 'be one of increasing homogeneity in which the acquisition and production of knowledge are not distinct phenomena – just two among many diverse social practices' (Young, 2006: 739). He also argues that knowledge is not independent from the contexts in which it is developed, is socially produced and is constantly emerging. It is interesting to look at some of the characteristics of what Young refers to as 'the curriculum of the future' and to see how well they complement the approach to interdisciplinary learning that is being advocated for the MYP. (See Table 2)

Young's 'curriculum of the future' raises questions about where the student is positioned in a supposedly student-centred MYP curriculum, and whether

Curriculum of the past	Curriculum of the future
Academic disciplines/subjects in the curriculum are kept separate.	Academic disciplines/subjects in the curriculum are connected.
Students acquire knowledge first and then apply it later.	Acquiring knowledge and applying knowledge are integrated.
Knowledge falls into a coherent 'whole' which can be gained in a systematic way.	Knowledge can be broken up into separate elements and put together by learners or teachers in any numbers of combinations.

Table 2 (Young, 2006: 740)

this will change as the curriculum evolves. We do not know enough about students' experiences of learning in the MYP and how the elements of its curriculum model affect them, other than from observation and anecdote. Stevens *et al* have suggested that if we were to focus on the 'temporal, material, emotional, and social organizational conditions of the school day, [we may notice] a perceived imbalance between how little we know about the whole (*ie*, students' experience of the whole school day) and how much we know about its parts (*ie*, subject-specific studies)' (2005: 146). Greene also considers that the student's consciousness should play a more active role in the curriculum. She refers to the curriculum as a map or a network, where the structural relationships between subjects are less significant than the meaning-making that students do when they negotiate their way through them. 'Curriculum can offer the possibility for students to be the makers for such networks. The problem for their teachers is to stimulate an awareness of the questionable, to aid in the identification of the thematically relevant, to beckon beyond the everyday.' (Greene, 1997: 148) One reason to move away from a completely subject-based curriculum design is the possibility of finding opportunities to make it more student-centred, enabling students to have a greater influence over the selection and combination of knowledge.

Understanding the MYP approach to interdisciplinarity

Despite Young's categorization of past and future curriculum, and the supporting theory that considers the structural relations of subject boundaries as a matter of strong or weak framing (Bernstein, 1975), I suggest that we use a continuum to make sense of the differences between the three approaches that are being discussed here. At one end of the continuum, self-contained subjects can seem to be almost impenetrable in their specialized qualities. At the other end sit transdisciplinary engagements that lend themselves so well to synthesis that any delineation between the disciplines is hard to detect. In between is the MYP approach to interdisciplinary teaching and learning where the integrity of the disciplines is still apparent and there is both 'rigorous learning in the disciplines and interdisciplinary synergy' (Boix-Mansilla, 2010: 121). This illuminates the balance that should be our aim: not so much a compromise between approaches as an incorporation of various elements that are supported by the MYP's philosophy, if not by the almost hegemonic reality of the way schools organize themselves around subjects.

From my own perspective as an MYP teacher, the immediate challenge is better to understand the nature of this balance and how to negotiate it in different situations and with different purposes. Still in an 'investigation/exploration' stage of learning, I am glad when I see students grappling with the same issues of integration, balance and the urge to cling too tightly to subject boundaries. The following example comes from a drama/design technology (DT) unit. Students were working towards a performance that they had scripted themselves, using puppets they had created. The unit was integrated around a common context and had a single unit question. One afternoon, an email arrived from a student who was doing her drama homework and evidently struggling with the question's ambiguous subject framing:

> I was wondering about the unit question: 'How can we create puppets that seem to be real enough?' Is the question not more linked to the DT part? Would it not be better to ask how the technical components act in suspending disbelief? And the end: 'seem to be real enough' – are you saying, is the puppet created well enough to suspend disbelief or are you asking something different?

For interdisciplinary learning to be effective it needs 'carefully conceived design features' including selection, sequence, a cognitive taxonomy, indicators of attitudinal change and evaluation (Jacobs, 1989), along with indications of the integrative understandings that are sought, opportunities for students to show their developing understanding and an inclination to reflect on the quality of the learning (Boix-Mansilla, 2010):

> Interdisciplinary instruction does not replace disciplinary teaching; rather it builds on it, selecting and reorganizing disciplinary learning goals and objectives in meaningful and connected ways in the areas of interaction. Students exhibit quality interdisciplinary understandings when they:
>
> • know, understand and apply knowledge, concepts, findings, tools, methods of inquiry, or forms of communication in the selected disciplines – that is, as framed in subject group objectives;
>
> • employ such concepts and modes of thinking in ways that echo that of experts working in the discipline – avoiding misconceptions or oversimplifications. (Boix-Mansilla, 2010: 15)

'Misconceptions or oversimplifications' here refers to naïve or intuitive ideas or misdirected reasoning that students might bring into an interdisciplinary setting. In the example above, the student thought that 'creating' in this context meant constructing puppets, rather than achieving a performance that would bring the puppets 'to life'. Her limited understanding of 'realization' was misleading her and making it difficult to grasp a new concept – 'suspension of disbelief'. This misconception was only exposed because drama and technology came together at a particular point and the limits of her conceptual understanding became obvious to her as she reflected upon her work.

Teachers can also have misconceptions, and some will need to challenge beliefs or sharpen skills as they develop their approach to interdisciplinary planning and teaching. For example, teachers may think that the main challenge of interdisciplinary teaching is just scheduling it. Boix-Mansilla (2010: 62) likens this to having a black box into which elements are placed without any sense of control over how they will interact. Another problem area is the difference between thematic and interdisciplinary teaching. Themes provide novel contextual or content links; disciplinary grounding is missing, as are integration and a purpose for bringing the subjects together in the first place. Similarities between the formats of thematic and interdisciplinary teaching, viewed from outside, may explain why some people assume that interdisciplinary units are more suitable for younger students. However, Boix-Mansilla (2010: 58) mentions a different question that some teachers have: whether students should 'master' the separate disciplines before being asked to integrate them.

Foremost amongst the technical challenges will be the unit planning process that was recently introduced into the MYP (IB, 2008b). Integration, and exactly where and how it is denoted in a plan, is the issue that will be of the most practical interest to teachers. In the first stage of the process, the intended enduring conceptual understandings, meaningful contexts and the question directing student inquiry are all laid out. Ideally, integration should occur at some or all of these 'axis points', where elements from different disciplinary perspectives may come together and, through their interaction, generate new understanding. A rubric provided for guidance states, for example, that the significant concept 'is evidently grounded in the subject without identifying subject-specific knowledge, skills or attitudes' (IB, 2010c), thus enabling concepts to transcend the boundaries of individual disciplines. However, finding pivotal ways to stimulate new understanding is more difficult than just arranging common contexts or related content. If successful implementation of the interdisciplinary approach is going to depend upon effective use of the unit planning process, without elements from different subjects being forced together in implausible ways, then it is essential that teachers can use that process confidently in the first place, with a clear understanding of all of its elements and relationships.

A continuum of disciplinary approaches is helpful when considering assessment because, in this regard, the MYP is still entirely subject-based for reasons of both practicality and validity. Even the personal project is classified as a subject where assessment is concerned. Each subject has its own objectives and assessment criteria; these are applied to separate aspects of an interdisciplinary assessment task for the sake of rigour and clarity, even if the task itself calls for integration or synthesis:

> Although interdisciplinary work is encouraged in the MYP, teachers must ensure that they have used the assessment criteria from different subject groups to assess different aspects of a task. ... If teachers from both subject groups wish to submit it for moderation, it must be made clear how teachers have ensured that the assessment criteria used have assessed different aspects of the task. (IB, 2010b: 52, 63)

The predicament here is not just that assessment is positioned differently from other aspects of interdisciplinarity, but that there is an additional need for collaborative assessment of the quality of learning, 'to move from a multidisciplinary assessment in which teachers only consider the perspective of their subject to an interdisciplinary one' (Boix-Mansilla, 2010: 98). A protocol is provided in the guide that is sure to evoke valuable evidence-based reflection, but it is unconnected to the MYP assessment procedures that relate to subject objectives. In effect, an extra layer is added and it is not immediately clear how well subject-based assessment, collaborative evaluation of the interdisciplinary qualities of the student work and, in some cases, external moderation will cohere. If short cuts are taken, the reflective component is almost sure to be omitted due to its lesser impact on students or their grades, even though it is likely to be most valuable when it comes to professional growth.

Structure or process

One useful distinction is that between structure and process: the process being teaching and learning. As mentioned above, both subject-based and transdisciplinary approaches are inherent in the structure of the IB curriculum models. However, interdisciplinarity – in the MYP sense – should be thought of in pedagogical terms as it relies on cognitive strategies such as integration, 'crossover tooling' and transfer. To the extent that it requires structures, we can see that creating an interdisciplinary unit reflects an 'effort to prepare a space that is conducive to students constructing a series of synthetical moments' (Slattery, 1995: xii). As Boix-Mansilla points out:

> In the MYP interdisciplinary learning is generally defined as the process by which students come to understand bodies of knowledge and modes of thinking from two or more disciplines or subjects and integrate them to create a new understanding. (2010: 13)

Despite this, the temptation to regard interdisciplinarity as a function of the way in which schools are structured is strong. Subject organization generally determines time and group arrangements; the curriculum is understood in terms of courses and units. In the past, some MYP schools have even set quotas for the number of interdisciplinary units that a class should undertake or that a subject should deliver during the year. A small clue about the pull of the structural approach is the creeping acceptance of the term 'IDU' (interdisciplinary unit) amongst some MYP teachers who are signifying this as an entity within a content-delivery paradigm, seemingly unaware of the tension between this approach and a pedagogical, process-orientation. 'There are teachers who accept, or even embrace, the category of interdisciplinary teaching,' says Siskin, 'and then search for the appropriate content to place within it.' (2000: 174)

Regardless of our personal enthusiasm for an interdisciplinary approach, there will always be structural challenges that come with the subject territory. These include timetabling, scheduling, a written curriculum that has to be organized into recognisable categories and the demarcations of teachers' professional expertise and identities. We are compelled constantly to define our 'school reality' in terms of the knowledge domains and structures in which we are working, locating ourselves strategically according to structural arrangements, even if the link to the process of learning – not to mention the students' needs, purposes and interests – is not always clear.

However, we are also reminded that teachers mediate the curriculum – interpreting it according to what makes them feel most comfortable, what excites them and what seems appropriate (Catling, 2001). Their social behaviour and the way in which they communicate are critical to the effectiveness of collaborative planning. The coordinator's handbook spells out the expectation, in stating that:

> The MYP, by its very nature and driving principles, requires whole-school discussions of basic pedagogical issues and concerted efforts in the development of interdisciplinary activities and projects within and across traditional departments (horizontal articulation) and grade levels/years (vertical articulation). (IB, 2010b: 9)

As with other aspects of MYP curriculum policy, this instruction seems more straightforward in principle than it does at the school level. Investigating how effectively to implement a similar approach, Siskin (2000) has referred to a study of small high schools, in which several of the findings were that:

- Teachers kept their own subject identities intact, protecting their own disciplinary values while they collaborated with other disciplines.

- It was more difficult to define meaningful disciplinary work and to collaborate than the teachers expected.

- Some subjects seemed more accessible to interdisciplinary collaboration than others.

- When there were problems, they were likely to be interpreted as being due to personal or local reasons, rather than being due to the structural difference between the subjects.

It would certainly be interesting to explore whether implementation of interdisciplinary teaching in the MYP follows a similar pattern.

Moving forward: from 'what' to 'how'

Professional development and research both have roles in advancing understanding of the dynamics of the MYP curriculum, at the programme and school levels. The IB can assist by ensuring that the release of curriculum policy is supported by appropriate guidance, support, and professional development opportunities. Teachers should find these easy to access and consistent, so that the gradual process of consensus-building across the MYP professional community does not amount to different 'versions' of understanding that rest upon misconceptions. In addition, the IB's research agenda should include follow-up investigation after the release of curriculum policy documents such as the interdisciplinary guide so that there can be a proper evaluation of the impact and effectiveness of its implementation (IB, 2008a: 23; see also IB, 2010a: 39). It would also be useful to know how the different approaches to the curriculum impact upon student learning (Stevens *et al*, 2005).

In summary, these are some of the questions which emerge from the previous discussion:

- What do we mean by subject-based, interdisciplinary and transdisciplinary approaches to the curriculum in the three IB programmes, how do the approaches differ, and how does each approach meet the needs of students?

- What kind of balance of approaches is optimum for our situation?

- Where do we see the characteristics of quality interdisciplinary teaching and learning in practice, especially in our own school?

- How can we broaden our approach to assessment so that we can evaluate the quality of interdisciplinary learning in a way that is more coherent with the need for subject-based rigour and clarity?

- How can we balance the tensions between structure and pedagogy, bearing in mind the student-centred philosophy of the programme?

- How can we transform our perspective of interdisciplinarity so that it comes to be regarded as an essential MYP learning strategy along with reflection, collaboration and inquiry?

- What support, in terms of policy, guidance, professional development and research, would help teachers and schools to implement interdisciplinary teaching and learning effectively? How can we support the process of school transformation that will inevitably occur as we move towards a 'curriculum of the future'?

For most schools that are implementing the guide to interdisciplinary teaching and learning, some transformation will be required during their journey from 'what' to 'how'. The guide signals a paradigm shift from one view of effective interdisciplinary teaching to another. However, there is still much to be done before the approach that is described is widely understood and supported. Even though the research upon which the guide is based was carried out inductively, this does not necessarily mean that there is an abundance of quality interdisciplinary teaching and learning occurring in MYP schools. There is likely to be a gap between the policy and guidance and what schools consider as the best practical balance between subject-based and other disciplinary approaches, whether their curriculum is entirely MYP or combined with other curriculum requirements. Within schools, it will be the 'creative teacher professionalism' of teachers – that open-mindedness, intellectual risk-taking and ongoing professional inquiry that MYP teachers bring to their teaching – that will have a major impact upon whether or not meaningful learning can be facilitated in the way that the guidance suggests (Stobie, in IB 2010a: 24).

In this regard, Hameyer (2007: 418) outlines the process of transforming a knowledge domain into school practice. He suggests that a number of factors come into play: quality standards, working patterns, control systems, commitment profiles, time limits, teacher identities, gratification/reward schemes, programme establishment, school policies and shared aims. These provide a systemic framework for transformation when it comes to subjects in the curriculum. Perhaps it might also be useful when we are thinking about transforming disciplinary approaches into school-level curriculum. Some elements will be in place due to IB policies, requirements and procedures; other elements will need to be institutionalized by schools in order to facilitate and embed interdisciplinary teaching and learning within the curriculum. The process of doing this, and exploring with teachers the 'how' as much as the 'what', should occur in the context of wider discussion and continued consensus building within the MYP community about how we understand the balance between various curriculum approaches and how we see this evolving. I suggest that the contrast between transdisciplinary and subject-based approaches is likely to be less critical in future than the way we deal with the challenge of effectively implementing the MYP's approach to interdisciplinarity, as it sits most closely to the point of balance between the others. Furthermore, because of its pedagogical orientation towards process rather than structure, this approach is better placed to illuminate some of the 'how' in relation to the 'what' that we have in mind – a more meaningful, intellectually challenging and holistic education for students.

References

Ackerman, D and Perkins, D (1989): 'Integrating thinking and learning skills across the curriculum' in *Interdisciplinary curriculum: design and implementation*. From: www.ascd.org/publications/books/61189156.aspx [Accessed 23 November 2010]

Beane, J (1995): 'What is a coherent curriculum?' in *Toward a coherent curriculum*. ASCD Yearbook 1995.

Bernstein, B (1975): *Class, Codes and Control - Towards a Theory of Educational Transmissions*. London: Routledge and Kegan Paul.

Boix-Mansilla, V (2010): *MYP guide to interdisciplinary teaching and learning*. Cardiff: International Baccalaureate

Boyle, B and Bragg, J (2008): 'Making primary connections: the cross-curriculum story', in *Curriculum Journal*, 19 (1) pp5-21.

Catling, S (2001): 'Developing the curriculum in international schools' in *Managing International Schools*. Blandford, S and Shaw, M (eds). London: RoutledgeFalmer.

Greene, M (1997): 'Curriculum and consciousness' in *The Curriculum Studies Reader*. Flinders, D and Thornton, S (eds). New York: Routledge. First published 1971.

Grossman, P Wineburg, S and Beers, S (2000): 'When theory meets practice in the world of school' in *Interdisciplinary curriculum: challenges to implementation*. Wineburg, S and Grossman, P (eds). New York: Teachers' College Press.

Hameyer, U (2007): 'Transforming domain knowledge: a systemic view at the school curriculum', in *Curriculum Journal*, 18 (4) pp411-427.

Hare, J (2010): *Holistic education: An interpretation for teachers in the IB programmes*. IB Position Paper. From: http://occ.ibo.org/ibis/occ/ [Accessed 19 November 2010]

IB (2005): *Programme Standards and Practices*. Cardiff: International Baccalaureate.

IB (2007): *Making the PYP happen: A curriculum framework for international primary education*. Cardiff: International Baccalaureate.

IB (2008a): *A review of research relating to the IB Diploma Programme*. Cardiff: International Baccalaureate.

IB (2008b): *The Middle Years Programme: From principles into practice*. Cardiff: International Baccalaureate.

IB (2008c): *Towards a continuum of international education*. Cardiff: International Baccalaureate.

IB (2009): *The Diploma Programme: From principles into practice*. Cardiff: International Baccalaureate.

IB (2010a): *History of the Middle Years Programme*. Cardiff: International Baccalaureate.

IB (2010b): *MYP coordinators' handbook 2010-11*. Cardiff: International Baccalaureate.

IB (2010c): *MYP coordinators' teacher support material.* From: http://occ.ibo.org/ibis/occ/ [Accessed 17 November 2010]

IB (2010d): *Programme standards and practices.* Cardiff: International Baccalaureate.

IB (2010e): *IB Diploma Programme Extended Essay guidelines: World Studies.* From: http://occ.ibo.org/ibis/occ/ [Accessed 13 November 2010]

Jacobs, H (1989): 'The growing need for interdisciplinary curriculum content' in *Interdisciplinary curriculum: design and implementation.* From: www.ascd.org/publications/books/61189156.aspx [Accessed 23 November 2010]

Siskin, L (2000): 'Restructuring knowledge: mapping (inter)disciplinary change' in *Interdisciplinary curriculum: challenges to implementation.* Wineburg, S and Grossman, P (eds). New York: Teachers' College Press.

Slattery, P (1995): *Curriculum Development in the Postmodern Era.* New York: Garland.

Stevens, R, Wineburg, S, Herrenkohl, L and Bell, P (2005): 'Comparative understanding of school subjects, past, present and future', in *Review of Educational Research,* 75 (2) pp125-157.

Young, M (2006): 'Curriculum Studies and the Problem of Knowledge; Updating the Enlightenment?' in *Education, Globalization and Social Change.* Lauder, H, Brown, P, Dillabough, J and Halsey, A (eds). Oxford: Oxford University Press.

Chapter 6

Creativity and the MYP

Éanna O'Boyle

Introduction

It is easy to see why many involved with education might be impressed with the IB Middle Years Programme (MYP). Any approach that claims to help adolescents 'find a sense of belonging in the ever-changing and increasingly interrelated world around them and to foster a positive attitude to learning' (IB, 2007: 2) will receive instant support amongst those who, sadly, see how schools carry on isolating people from the dynamism, richness, challenges and fun of a good life. It is gratifying to learn how the programme develops self-identity through teaching for metacognition, community, values and communication, all in the context of meaningful student-initiated inquiry and action. A successful action-driven inquiry of formulating a question and trying to answer it through 'research, experimentation, observation and analysis' (IB 2008a: 62) seems to require some degree of creative thought, the promotion of which in schools, at least in the 21st century, is generally seen as a good thing. This chapter thus aims to explore how the MYP views and fosters creativity.

Why creativity in school?

For various reasons, particularly in the past ten years, there have been numerous calls and initiatives worldwide to foster the creativity of young people in schools (Craft, 2006; Robinson, 2001). These reasons reflect a view of what creativity is and why it is important. Educational policies and national enquiries related to creativity have recently been developed, for instance, in Australia, Canada, Finland, France, Hong Kong, Iceland, India, Japan, Netherlands, Serbia, Singapore, Slovenia, South Korea, Switzerland, UK, and US (Craft, 2006, Kaufman and Sternberg, 2007; OECD, 1998; Tan and Gopinathan, 2000). Perhaps the most audible calls embed creativity in an economic and market-driven context. The political argument for more creativity in schools starts with the premise that we live in a knowledge economy in which the production and distribution of information and ideas, rather than of things, is central for successful economies (OECD, 2008). It is claimed that an increasing focus on creativity in education will help young people to learn skills required by employers and so better support and drive the globalised capitalist marketplace (Craft, 2006; Tan and Gopinathan, 2000). Along similar lines, many have pointed out that future workers need to be creative learners since they will likely pursue multiple career paths (Cropley, 2001; Hargreaves, 2004).

In effect, the message is that young people should develop their creativity because the workforce needs these skills. Interestingly, Brown *et al* question the assumption that the workplace increasingly needs people with creative skills. By interviewing 180 senior managers and executives in 20 leading transnational companies in financial services, telecoms, electronics and the automotive sector, they report that it is only the elite few who have 'permission to think' and that most workers, at least in Europe, have limited opportunities to be creative (2008). However, this does not imply that schools should not teach for creativity; rather that teaching for creativity may serve other purposes.

A link is sometimes made, in a market-driven justification for fostering creativity in schools, with improved self-esteem and mental health (Cropley, 2001; Learning and Teaching Scotland, 2007). In the latter publication it is argued that promoting creativity helps young people to have greater self-esteem so that they are better prepared for the life of work after school; they achieve more, tend to discover ideas and things, are better able to solve problems, are comfortable with uncertainty and new ideas, and get on better with others. There is a hint however that the authors consider them better prepared not because of self-worth, but because of the worth likely to be bestowed on them by the various employers they will have in their lifetime. In other words, the fostering of creativity is embedded in an individualistic competitive framework in which high self-esteem and happiness arise from a successful career (2007).

Some have seen the need to foster creativity primarily as an issue of personal wellbeing. This approach was evident in the 1960s through, for example, the Plowden report in the UK in which teaching for creativity with a discovery-based pedagogical approach aimed to ensure that the child's needs were primarily met before those of the state (Craft, 2001). This view is supported by Dabrowski (in Terry and Bohnenberger, 2003) who observed that the most creative individuals tended to show admirable qualities such as high levels of empathy, sensitivity, moral responsibility, self-reflection, and autonomy of thought. Through empirical research, Csikszentmihalyi (1997) and Ardelt (1997) each see the value of creative process in the happiness that it brings to the creator. Creative people can devote many hours to their passions without any obvious rewards, although the feelings involved in the activity (such as pain, risk, challenge, novelty and discovery) cause an optimal experience which Csikszentmihalyi calls 'flow' (1997). Considering the relationship between happiness and creativity from the opposite direction, Minkel reports on findings that suggest happiness induces creativity because happy people are more easily distracted and as a result more receptive to information of all kinds (2006). Although rarely making links with creativity, Noddings has urged policy makers in education to consider the development of personal happiness as a major goal of education (2003). She considers it a disservice to define happiness in terms of financial success, and she stresses the need for schools to help young people to think imaginatively in the context of their families, their homes, and their communities (2003). In addition, she would like to see young people being challenged more, and at a deeper level, to think about the moral dimensions of their own and others' actions (2003, 2006).

One way to begin a discussion on the extent to which creativity is fostered in the MYP is to examine why the IB would want to do this in the first place. The answer is not readily available from IB documentation. In the main reference guide to the MYP, *From Principles into Practice,* (IB, 2008a) a word search shows that although words such as *creative* (seven times), *creatively* (four) and *creativity* (two) appear throughout, there is no section devoted to the topic. In more general terms, IB literature clearly emphasizes a more humanistic, collective goal for education than one which is political and individualistic. This is evident in the IB's mission statement, in which there is a commitment to enabling today's youth to create a better world:

> The International Baccalaureate aims to develop inquiring, knowledgeable and caring young people who help to create a better and more peaceful world through intercultural understanding and respect. (IB, 2008b: 3)

Developing in students the capacity to create a better and more peaceful world contrasts with the ideals espoused by political, market-driven initiatives. Furthermore, the type of person who can make such a difference in the world is described by the attributes of the IB learner profile, which serve as an 'educational compass' in teaching and curriculum development (Boix-Mansilla, 2010: 3). In the IB's explanation of these attributes, the goal of developing creativity becomes more explicit. *Thinkers,* for instance, 'exercise initiative in applying thinking skills critically and creatively to recognize and approach complex problems, and make reasoned, ethical decisions', while *communicators* 'understand and express ideas and information confidently and creatively in more than one language and in a variety of modes of communication', and *risk-takers* 'approach unfamiliar situations and uncertainty with courage and forethought, and have the independence of spirit to explore new roles, ideas and strategies' (IB, 2008a: 8).

In relation specifically to the MYP, the IB also emphasizes an approach focusing on 'the development of the whole person – affective, cognitive, creative and physical – and its effective implementation depends on the school's concern for the whole educational experience, including what students learn outside the classroom' (2008a: 16). Perhaps the most explicit declaration of the important role of creativity in the MYP is found in a more recent publication whereby the programme is seen to 'nurture students' capacity to engage in and employ multiple sources of expertise to solve problems, create products, produce explanations and raise new questions about the world in which they live' (Boix-Mansilla, 2010: 3).

This preliminary exploration of creativity in the MYP indicates that it seems to be encouraged within a humanistic framework. Before delving more deeply, it will be helpful to discuss in more detail what is meant by creativity.

What is creativity?

Although creativity was initially associated with artistic domains, it is now seen in more general terms as encompassing many disciplines such as mathematics, science, architecture, engineering, business, management, leadership, government and writing (Cropley, 2001; Robinson, 2001). Many definitions of creativity focus on two elements: *novelty* and *effectiveness*. For example, Robinson describes creativity as 'imaginative processes with outcomes that are original and of value' (2001: 118). Similarly, Sternberg, a pioneer in this area of research, has defined creativity as the 'ability to produce work that is novel (that is, original, unexpected), high in quality, and appropriate (that is, useful, meets task constraints)' (2003: 89).

It is clear that a novel idea is not necessarily creative if it simply involves uninhibited self-indulgent activity that does not conform to societal norms; this can be described as 'pseudocreativity' (Cropley, 2001). Writing an outrageous poem or playing random chords on a guitar will be pseudocreative if society deems it useless. Nor is it considered creative if the novel idea has few connections with the real world; this can be called 'quasicreativity', and 'creative' daydreams would be an example (Cropley, 2001).

In highlighting the usefulness or appropriateness of creativity, many have argued for the necessity of emphasizing the societal context in which an idea is seen to be creative (Craft, 2008). Felhusen and Westby (2003: 95) capture the essence of this shift by defining creativity as:

> ... the production of ideas, problem solutions, plans, works of art, musical compositions, sculptures, dance routines, poems, novels, essays, designs, theories, or devices that are at the lowest level new and of value to the creator and at the highest level are recognized, embraced, honored, or valued by all or large segments of society.

However, this may seem limiting. Is it possible to be creative in the absence of social recognition? Perhaps, but this only becomes evident when, in retrospect, society recognizes creative exploits. Unfortunately, many creative people are recognized as such only after their deaths (for example, Vincent Van Gogh, Gregor Mendel and Lev Vygotsky). Thus, it can be said that society sometimes does not recognize the potential that creative acts can have. Although apparently limiting, it is society (whether in a global, cultural, or discipline-specific sense) that judges what is creative and what is not.

Felhusen and Westby's definition, like any attempt succinctly to define creativity, may also appear limiting because views of creativity vary between cultures (Boden, 1994; Lubart and Sternberg, 1995, Sternberg, 2008; Lopez, 2003). It has often been noted that there are differences between the western individualist and eastern collectivist views of creativity, the latter nurturing values such as interdependence, consensus, social order and conformity with tightly structured social norms, while the former emphasizes independence, personal opinions, open exchange of ideas, and differentiated interpretation of social norms (Craft, 2008). Yet it is the western view that dominates discourse around creativity (Craft, 2006; Lopez, 2003). High value is placed on individuality, generating ideas outside of social norms, and on engaging innovatively with the economy as both producer and consumer (Craft, 2006). Zhou Nanzhao, a former member of the IB's Council of Foundation (its then governing body), notes that eastern cultures stress the moral cultivation of personality rather than the materialistic cultivation of self (1996). Certainly, what teachers recognize as creative can be greatly influenced by their cultural histories, which in turn affect their success in fostering creativity (Craft, 2008). In which case, perhaps it is the wise teacher who can differentiate effectively between, and celebrate, diverse cultural views of creativity – while not ignoring the more critical theory perspective that all students, particularly the marginalized, ought to have access to the predominant social and economic culture of the society in which they will likely grow up (Freire, 1968).

Another dimension lacking in many definitions of creativity is a moral one. An implication of this is that when a person uses creativity, he/she may seek outcomes that are good for him/herself but bad for others (Sternberg *et al*, 2007). Rowson (2008) describes creativity as integrating motivation that is intrinsic, extrinsic, egocentric (seeing all relationships to people and objects in reference to 'me') and allocentric (seeing all relationships in an objective way), but without necessarily doing so in an ethically progressive way. It does not seem appropriate to describe as creative a burglar who uses his three-year-old son to slip through the metal bars of the house of a rich neighbour. Such an act may clearly not qualify as creative, but other common examples throw light on the rather loose connections between creative and morally acceptable actions. Creativity in disciplines such as the business sector may be judged less on moral or ethical grounds and more on the basis of its entrepreneurship. For example, we may describe as creative, but morally questionable, a clever advertisement campaign to sell cigarettes to teenagers, or the development of a new brand of coffee that is more addictive. Creativity without this moral dimension has been critically questioned by Craft (2006) and Cropley (2001). Indeed, Cropley (2001) adds *ethicality* as a third element of creativity (in addition to novelty and effectiveness).

In relation to its appropriateness and ethicality, Craft points out that the products of creativity may be encouraged without regard to society's genuine needs (2008). For example, Craft questions the current culture in westernized societies whereby we create new things rather than using and creatively adapting what we have already so as to conserve resources more carefully (2008). As Claxton *et al* note, 'the focus of concern, if creativity is to become wise, has to be people, not gadgets', adding that 'educational practice has to concern itself as much with the functionality and appropriateness of the solution as with its mere originality' (2008: 174). Teaching for an ethical and environmentally sustainable dimension to creativity challenges learners to look more carefully at the wider societal implications of their own and others' creative actions.

Creativity and the MYP

Perhaps a more pragmatic pursuit than exploring how the MYP defines and speaks about creativity is to address the pedagogical practices that encourage creativity, and consider how the MYP framework might support such practices. There appear to be several elements of the MYP that indicate a commitment to fostering creativity, which I have summarized in Table 1. Inevitably, these six elements overlap in terms of how they foster creativity.

Element of MYP	To foster creativity, students are encouraged to
Constructivist approach to learning	• learn in meaningful contexts • manage uncertainty • inquire into their interests
Areas of interaction, significant concepts and unit questions	• take an interdisciplinary approach to inquiry • inquire into open-ended questions for an extended time • see teachers role-model creativity in their planning
Thinking 'skills'	• see connections between subjects • develop dispositions, not only skills, for effective inquiry • generate and develop questions, identify problems and create novel solutions
Assessment	• be creative in assessment tasks • analyze and critique their own ideas so that problems can be reformulated and creative solutions developed • collaborate and not compete • self-assess and reflect frequently
Socializing creativity	• learn in groups • communicate with others what they are learning
Specialized knowledge	• understand that each subject uses specific methods and skills to find out knowledge • develop expertise and creativity in several fields of knowledge

Table 1: Elements of the MYP that encourage student creativity

Constructivist Approach to Learning

The MYP requires a constructivist approach to teaching, which recognises that a learner's existing knowledge is used to build new knowledge (Brooks and Brooks, 1993) and a learner's basis of meaning is found in personal and social experiences. The following is probably the clearest indication of how the IB believes we should teach in the MYP (bold in original):

> As outlined in the programme model, the curriculum framework recognizes and values students' efforts to construct meaning when exploring the world around them. To support this, the MYP requires teachers to provide learning experiences that draw on students' prior knowledge and provide the time and opportunity for reflection and consolidation. This **constructivist** approach respects students' ongoing development of ideas and their understanding of the wider world. It implies a pedagogy that includes student inquiry into significant content in real-world contexts. This pedagogy leads to the most substantial and enduring learning. (IB, 2008a: 62)

The connection between this constructivist approach and creativity is made in the next paragraph:

> The construction of meaning and the development of conceptual understanding are supported in the MYP by the acquisition of knowledge and the development of skills and attitudes that have a context. This is the way in which students learn best – they should be invited to investigate significant issues by formulating their own questions, designing their own inquiries, assessing the various means available to support their inquiries, and proceeding with research, experimentation, observation and analysis that will help them find their own responses to the issues. The starting point is students' current understanding, and the goal is the active construction of meaning by building connections between that understanding and new information and experience, derived from the inquiry into new content. (IB, 2008a: 62)

Furthermore, this constructivist platform of teaching for creativity encourages learners to approach uncertainty, ambiguity, diversity and the tentative nature of knowledge with confidence and optimism. Such approaches are central components of creativity (Haste, 2008).

A constructivist approach to teaching also helps children to learn more about what they love to do, which can lead to creative thought and action (Cropley, 2001; Sternberg, 2003). The MYP encourages open-ended tasks in which students can integrate their own interests in responding to unit questions, and the personal project particularly encourages students to unleash their creativity in an area about which they are passionate.

Areas of interaction, significant concepts and unit questions

A multidisciplinary approach to curriculum encourages the cross-fertilization of ideas (Sternberg, 2003) and creativity (Cropley, 2001; Houtz, 2003). Holistic learning comprises one of the three fundamental concepts of the programme, which is described as stressing 'the interrelatedness of various disciplines and issues, and the education of the whole person' (IB, 2008a: 104). A unique aspect of the MYP, evident from its early development, was the inclusion of areas of interaction (AOI) as a tool for students to see connections between themselves and the real world, to make interdisciplinary connections, and ultimately to enable inquiry (IB, 2008a). The AOI aim to decontextualize important concepts and 'big' questions away from a single disciplinary angle, so that students appreciate the richness of knowledge, perspectives and creative potential of an interdisciplinary approach. In other words, the contexts for learning are provided by the AOI (IB, 2010a). Creativity is perhaps brought out most explicitly in the human ingenuity AOI, which is described as being 'concerned with the evolution, processes and products of human *creativity*, and their impact on society and on the mind' (IB, 2008a: 104, italics added). In community and service, students are expected to reflect critically on the ethical aspects of their activity or non-activity within the community. Haste reports that when students want to help others by participating in community service projects, they show increased awareness of the social and political conditions that create disadvantage and deprivation, and this leads to a sense of personal responsibility for challenging injustice (2008). Thus, fostering creativity in the MYP appears to be promoted with sensitivity to its ethical, cultural and global dimensions.

The MYP unit planner, at first glance, cements this commitment to creativity by offering teachers a template to describe explicitly the so-called 'units of work'. Developing unit planners begins with stating 'significant' concepts, AOI links and the 'big' or unit question. As a result, the unit planner links the contexts and concepts with the factual content. Or put another way, the content is made relevant and meaningful through the contexts provided by the AOI and by the significant concepts. The unit question provides students with opportunities to inquire creatively about a question for a long time, finding the problems inherent in the question, and gradually seeing it more clearly (Claxton *et al*, 2006).

Nevertheless, recent guidelines for developing these unit planners raise some questions. When the unit planner was first published, it was *recommended* to have one AOI focus (rarely 'approaches to learning', which already had its own section in the template) and one or few significant concept(s) (IB, 2008a). Newer guidelines (IB, 2010a) make it clear that there *should* only be one AOI so that a theme can be explored in sufficient depth. This seems to my mind to restrict students' thinking about content, to limit contextualized and meaningful understanding of concepts, and to offer less possibility for creative responses to the big question. A deep understanding of how one AOI contextualizes concepts would seem to be actually enriched by careful consideration of other AOI. After all, the AOI do not have strict boundaries but overlap and merge to form a context for learning (Boix-Mansilla, 2010). It is interesting to note that the joint IB/Harvard Project Zero publication, *The Middle Years Programme: An Interdisciplinary View*, does not explicitly advise focusing on just one AOI when developing an interdisciplinary unit, and gives an example in which there is a focus on two AOI in a unit on ancient civilizations (Boix-Mansilla, 2010). This contrasts with the IB published example of an interdisciplinary unit planner in which the focus is on one AOI (IB, 2010b). Similarly, students are encouraged to focus on one AOI and on no more than two in the personal project.

Perhaps in a similar vein, the MYP encourages one or few significant concepts, as follows:

> When developing a unit, the teacher will start by considering all the concepts that will be taught. By listing these concepts, teachers will reflect upon the underlying (or overarching) concept they want their students to remember and apply in the long term. This will then become the significant concept or big idea for the unit and will be written as a statement. (IB, 2010c)

Again, to my mind this is limiting. One example of what is considered a 'good' significant concept published by the IB is 'The importance of plants for life on our planet'. As a scientific aside, it might be challenged that there was life on Earth before plants evolved, so a better phrasing might be 'The importance of plants for life, *as we know it,* on our planet'. This minor criticism notwithstanding, it is useful to look at what the IB considers an appropriate AOI focus and unit question corresponding to this concept. The AOI focus is the effect of the environment on the growth of plants and the effects of plants on the environment, with a unit question asking to what extent humans are dependent upon plants (IB, 2009).

It can easily be seen how this environments AOI focus helps clarify the context for the unit question. Yet it seems that other AOI could enrich engagement with this question. The following are just some possible examples:

• Health and social education: How do plants seem to affect our moods? How healthy are vegetarians?

• Human ingenuity: Why are plants, particularly flowers, such meaningful symbols in different cultures? To what extent is homeopathy a valid medical discipline?

• Community and service: How can we highlight to a community the dependency of humans upon plants? Should rare flowering plants be protected with the same vigour as rare mammals?

Note that many of these questions could fit in with another AOI. The point is that the exploration of all the AOI would seem to give learners a much richer and more meaningful contextual understanding of a concept. Even if environments is the AOI focus, other AOI deserve thoughtful consideration to help guide students' inquiries in tinkering with the unit question creatively. Admittedly, the IB states that only one AOI should be *documented* and there may be an implicit assumption that learning should happen in the context of more AOI. If so, there would be benefit in this being made clearer in MYP documentation.

These minor criticisms do not detract from the fact that the development of unit planners helps students to take an interdisciplinary and open-ended approach to inquiry. Developing unit planners also demands a creative approach by teachers. Although teaching creatively is not the same as teaching for creativity, role-modelling is a powerful way to develop creativity in children (Sternberg, 2003). Claxton (2007) reports how the disposition towards imitating others is one of the main ways in which cultural habits of thinking and learning transmit themselves from generation to generation.

Thinking 'skills'

The central role given to approaches to learning (ATL) in curriculum development and teaching is perhaps the most obvious element of the MYP to encourage creativity. An essential aspect of ATL is appreciating the uncertainty of knowledge that is a necessary pre-cursor to creativity. The MYP has identified seven groups of skills that encompass ATL, including 'thinking', which is described as the skills of generating ideas, inquiring, developing questions, identifying problems and creating novel solutions (IB, 2008a: 24). The MYP emphasizes the acquisition of ATL skills and yet a simple activity brings home the point that learning ATL skills is not enough. Ask a group of teachers to rate the ATL skills of a particular group of students, and I predict that you will find disagreement (the author has done this activity many times in different schools). As a typical example, one teacher might state that the students reference appropriately and another might state that they do not. Even taking into consideration that teachers might have varying expectations, it becomes clear that students will indeed reference appropriately in one class but will not do so in another class. Similarly, one teacher may be proud of how skilled the students are in collaborating but, if this is not the case in other classes, then doubts arise about the extent to which they are using the skill. In other words, students may learn ATL skills but that does not mean that they have learned to use the skill independently and without prompting. They may not have learned the *disposition* to reference appropriately or to collaborate. Creativity relies not just on knowing ATL skills but also on developing habits and dispositions of mind to be inclined to use them (Claxton *et al*, 2006). Moving from skills to dispositions also means refining and broadening the sense of when and where it is appropriate to use the skills, in other words being ready (Claxton, 2007). As Ritchhart (2002) points out, emphasizing dispositions addresses the gap often noticed between what we are able to do and our actions.

Assessment

For creativity to be fostered, it ought to be assessed (Sternberg, 2003). The holistic learning of the MYP is not only apparent in the making of connections between disciplines through the AOI; it is also evident through the holistic assessment rubrics, which 'offer general, qualitative value statements about student achievement' (IB, 2008a: 51). The highest descriptors in many subjects' assessment rubrics challenge students through open-ended tasks to tackle complex problems in unfamiliar situations and to see things through; this helps to foster creative thought (Houtz, 2003; Torrance, 1975 in Esquivel and Hodes, 2003). Providing extended time to complete these tasks allows thoughts to incubate, which is an important component of creativity (Sternberg, 2003). Perhaps the extended time allows learners to switch fluidly between concentrated and diffused awareness, and between sociable and solitary thinking – all of which seem to promote creativity (Claxton, 2007). The lack of creative thought assessed in multiple-choice tests means they are rarely appropriate except when testing basic understanding or simple application, a point made explicitly by the IB in relation to the MYP (2008a).

It is also worth noting that MYP assessment structures ensure that assessment is not overly competitive because grades are not norm-referenced. This point is relevant since those who believe they are continually competing with others on tasks tend to be less creative than those who believe they are not competing (Tighe *et al*, 2003). Because grading in the MYP is criteria-related, all students can achieve at the highest levels.

In order to develop creativity, there needs to be opportunities for students to self-assess and reflect (Houtz, 2003; Cropley, 2001). These opportunities are built explicitly into the assessment criteria of some subjects – mathematics, the arts, and technology. In MYP, reflection is an essential element of the inquiry cycle associated with each AOI (along with 'awareness and understanding' and 'action'). In allowing ideas to incubate and emerge, reflection enables students to analyze and critique their own ideas so that problems can be reformulated and creative solutions developed (Sternberg, 2003).

Socializing creativity

It has been suggested that schools ought to encourage creative collaboration (Cropley, 2001; Sternberg, 2003). In describing how the taught curriculum should emphasize the active construction of knowledge, the MYP 'encourages teachers to provide opportunities for students to build meaning and refine understanding through structured **inquiry**. As the learning process involves communication and collaboration, this inquiry may take many forms, with students sometimes working on their own or collaboratively with partners or larger groups' (IB, 2008a: 18, bold in original). Creativity is promoted when, in a safe environment, students have opportunities to communicate with others what they learn in tasks (Torrance, 1975 in Esquivel and Hodes, 2003). Communication is one of the underlying fundamental concepts of the programme, as well as being encouraged through the learner profile. Criteria that assess communication come under different titles in different subjects: communication (language B, mathematics, and science), organization (humanities, language A), application (arts) or social skills (physical education: PE).

Specialized knowledge

Expertise and creativity in a narrow field of knowledge often go hand-in-hand. The MYP does not lose sight of subject-specific knowledge and skills, as is evident in subject-specific assessment criteria and objectives. However, it is not just about factual recall and processing of information. It highlights other subject-specific skills such as experimentation and analysis of new data (science), collaboration (science, physical education, the arts), organization of thought (humanities) and planning and design (technology).

Pedagogy

It is clear that the MYP provides schools with a powerful framework for developing creativity, although there are opportunities to provide more pedagogical guidelines for teachers with respect to how they might do so. The MYP literature focuses on providing technical guidelines on developing and documenting curriculum, on what to teach, and on assessment procedures. Understandably, the IB may not wish to mandate explicit and specific MYP teaching strategies because of its emphasis on empowering schools to contextualize teaching and the curriculum within the uniqueness of the school setting. However, to my mind it would make sense to highlight teaching strategies that appear to enhance learning, including those that foster creativity.

Awareness of current understandings of creativity may already be helping many to teach for creativity more effectively. On the other hand, myths about creativity may be inhibiting this progress. For example, some creative behaviours such as questioning and challenging the *status quo* seem to be actually discouraged by teachers (Cropley, 2001). It is also worth referring to the research of Ellen Langer, which indicates that stressing the uncertain and conditional nature of current knowledge tends to make the content more interesting, and leads to more creative thought than if knowledge was presented as fixed (1997). Thus, teachers would be encouraged to use more often words such as 'may', 'could', 'often' and 'probably' when presenting information to students. Similarly, Dweck places emphasis on the directions we give to students and how these foster or inhibit creativity (2008). Dweck told one group of students (A) before a test that 'part I consists of a 30-minute video that will introduce a few basic concepts of physics; part II involves a short questionnaire in which you apply the concepts shown in the video'. The other group (B) was told the same thing, but in addition they were told 'please feel free to use any additional methods you want, to assist you in solving the problems'. Group B performed better and were more creative.

Byrge and Hansen report on other ways in which teachers' practices may influence creativity by describing how increasing arousal (or stimuli such as time pressure and rewards) beyond an ideal amount seems to make behaviours such as writing, speaking and thinking more stereotypical (2009). The arousal provoked, particularly in adolescents, by being watched by others, speaking on the spot, rushing a task, or giving an oral presentation is therefore likely to decrease creativity. In schools, the arousal often stems from uncertain relations with others. Byrge and Hansen suggest that this may be the reason why brainstorming and group activities often lead to less creative action than if participants were on their own, or at least made to feel that they were alone even while being with others (2009).

One final point needs mentioning – the role of dialogue in fostering creativity. In the context of promoting student voice and community learning, Lodge favours the notion of having dialogues with students rather than debates, the latter of which she associates with being confrontational and win-lose (2005). Dialogue, on the other hand, is about 'engagement with others through talk to arrive at a point one would not get to alone' (Lodge, 2005: 134) or, from a critical theory perspective, having 'the possibility that the oppressed will produce a "counter sentence" that can suggest a new historical narrative' (Alcoff, 1991/92 in Fielding, 2004: 23). Similarly, Bohm sees dialogue as an interpersonal practice for cultivating deep wisdom (1996). Dialogues between adults and young people involve people who are open to 'questioning their fundamental assumptions' (Bohm, 1996: 7). Understanding the nature of dialogue helps us to appreciate the challenge of genuinely enabling dialogues not only between teachers and students but also between students themselves. Creativity stoppers such as 'oh, that's been tried before', 'here's an even better idea', 'why are you being so awkward?' or 'what makes you think that you are an expert on this?' may occur more often than we wish to admit. In the MYP, the AOI are stated to 'provide opportunities for further discussion' (IB, 2008a: 31); perhaps this can be extended further to encourage more dialogue between teachers and students as well as between students themselves.

Conclusion

It would be difficult to argue with the view that the MYP encourages young people to think for themselves and to contribute creatively, in a morally acceptable fashion, to their own and other community/ies. The MYP maintains that young people need daily opportunities to inquire, assess and try out ideas in an environment in which they feel comfortable with their own and others' uncertainties. These ideas very often come to fruition through the expert guidance of teachers. It is also possible that unintentional misguidance by teachers stifles creativity or gives it an individualistic, environmentally unsustainable or morally questionable dimension.

It has become a cliché to say that we live in radically changing times and that we do not know what young people will need to know in ten years time, never mind in 30 years from now. Perhaps it is more useful to say that, although we are unsure what facts, techniques and theories will be of use to adolescents in the future, it is likely that they will be a lot wiser, as well as happier, if they develop dispositions to think and act creatively. Instead of assuming that creativity will simply happen, the MYP may need to guide more consciously the development of dispositions that enhance creativity through its documentation and the opportunities it offers for professional development.

References

Ardelt, M (1997): 'Wisdom and Life Satisfaction in Old Age', in *The Journals of Gerontology: Series B, Psychological Sciences and Social Sciences*, 52B (1) pp15-27.

Boden, M A (1994): 'Introduction' in Boden, M A (ed), *Dimensions of Creativity*, (pp1-11). Cambridge: Massachusetts Institute of Technology.

Bohm, D (1996): *On dialogue*. London: Routledge.

Boix-Mansilla V (2010): *MYP guide to interdisciplinary teaching and learning*. Cardiff: International Baccalaureate.

Brooks, J G and Brooks, M G (1993): *In Search for Understanding: The Case for Constructivist Classrooms*. Alexandria, VA: ASCD.

Brown P, Lauder, H and Ashton, D (2008): 'Education, globalisation and the future of the Knowledge Economy', in *European Educational Research Journal*, 7 (2) pp131-147.

Byrge, C and Hansen, S (2009): 'The creative platform: A new paradigm for teaching creativity', in *Problems of Education in the 21st Century*, 18: pp33-50.

Claxton, G, Edwards, E and Scale-Constantinou, V (2006): 'Cultivating creative mentalities: A framework for education', in *Thinking Skills and Creativity*, 1: pp57-61.

Claxton, G (2007): 'Expanding Young People's Capacity To Learn', in *British Journal of Educational Studies*, 55 (2) pp115-134.

Claxton, G, Craft, A and Gardner, H (2008): 'Concluding thoughts: good thinking – education for wise creativity' in Craft, A, Claxton, G and Gardner, H (eds) *Creativity, Wisdom and Trusteeship: Exploring the Role of Education*. Thousand Oaks, CA: Corwin Press.

Craft, A (2001): *An analysis of research and literature on creativity in education*. London: Qualifications and Curriculum Authority.

Craft, A (2006): 'Fostering creativity with wisdom', in *Cambridge Journal of Education*, 36(3): pp337-350.

Craft, A (2008): 'Tensions in creativity and education: Enter Wisdom and Trusteeship' in Craft, A, Claxton, G and Gardner, H (eds) *Creativity, Wisdom and Trusteeship: Exploring the Role of Education*. Thousand Oaks, CA: Corwin Press.

Cropley, A J (2001): *Creativity in Education and Learning: a guide for teachers and educators*. Abingdon: RoutledgeFalmer

Csikszentmihalyi, M (1997): 'Happiness and Creativity: Going with the Flow', in *The Futurist*, 31(5) pp8-12.

Dweck, C S (2008): 'Brainology: Transforming Students' Motivation To Learn', in *Independent School*, 67(2) pp110-119.

Esquivel, G B and Hodges, T G (2003): 'Creativity, development and personality' in Houtz, J (ed), *The Educational Psychology of Creativity* (pp135-166). New York: Hampton Press.

Felhusen, J F and Westby, E L (2003): 'Creative and affective behaviour: cognition, personality and motivation' in Houtz, J (ed), *The Educational Psychology of Creativity* (pp95-105). New York: Hampton Press.

Fielding, M (2004): 'Transformative approaches to student voice: theoretical underpinnings, recalcitrant realities', in *British Educational Research Journal* 30 (2) pp296-311.

Freire, P (1968): *Pedagogy for the Oppressed*. New York: Continuum.

Hargreaves, D H (2004): *Learning for Life: the Foundations for Lifelong Learning*. Bristol: Policy Press.

Haste, H (2008): 'Good thinking: the creative and competent mind' in Craft, A, Claxton, G and Gardner, H (eds), *Creativity, Wisdom and Trusteeship: Exploring the Role of Education*. Thousand Oaks, CA: Corwin Press.

Houtz, J (2003): 'Objective 3: fostering creativity' in Houtz, J (ed), *The Educational Psychology of Creativity* (pp135-166). New York: Hampton Press.

IB (2007): *The IB Middle Years Programme: 21st Century Education*. Geneva: International Baccalaureate.

IB (2008a): *MYP: From Principles into Practice*. Geneva: International Baccalaureate.

IB (2008b): *Towards a Continuum of International Education*. Cardiff: International Baccalaureate.

IB (2009): Unit Planner PowerPoint Presentation from: http://occ.ibo.org/ibis/occ/general/Unit_planner(e).ppt [Accessed 8 February 2010]

IB (2010a): Coordinator Support Material. From: http://xmltwo.ibo.org/publications/MYP/m_g_mypxx_mon_1008_1/html/production-app3.ibo.org/publication/242/part/5/chapter/2.html [Accessed 20 November 2010]

IB (2010b): Example of Unit Planner. From: http://xmltwo.ibo.org/publications/MYP/m_g_mypxx_mon_1008_1/html/xmltwo.ibo.org/publications/MYP/m_g_mypxx_mon_1008_1/PDF/Example of unit planner.pdf [Accessed 20 November 2010]

IB (2010c): MYP Coordinator Support Material, *Unit Planner Rubric, Rubric for Stage 1*. From: http://xmltwo.ibo.org/publications/MYP/m_g_mypxx_mon_1008_1/html/production-app3.ibo.org/publication/242/part/5/chapter/2.html [Accessed 7 November 2010]

Kaufman, J C and Sternberg, R J (2007): 'Creativity', in *Change*. July/August.

Langer, E J (1997): *The Power of Mindful Learning*. New York: Addison-Wesley Publishing Co Inc.

Learning and Teaching Scotland (2007): *Teaching for Effective Learning: Creativity and learning*. Glasgow: Learning and Teaching Scotland.

Lodge, C (2005): 'From hearing voices to engaging in dialogue: problematising student participation in school improvement', in *Journal of Educational Change*, 6: pp125-146.

Lopez, E C (2003): 'Creativity issues concerning linguistically and culturally diverse children', in Houtz, J (ed), *The Educational Psychology of Creativity* (pp107-127). New York: Hampton Press.

Lubart T I and Sternberg, R J (1995): 'An investment approach to creativity: Theory and data', in S M Smith, T B Ward, and R A Finke (eds), *The creative cognition approach* (pp269-302). Cambridge: Massachusetts Institute of Technology.

Minkel, J R (2006): 'Happiness: Good for Creativity, Bad for Single-Minded Focus', in *Scientific American*, December.

Noddings, N (2003): *Happiness and Education.* Cambridge: Cambridge University Press.

Noddings, N (2006): *Critical Lessons: What Our School Should Teach.* New York: Cambridge University Press.

OECD (Organisation for Economic Co-operation and Development) (1998): *Making the Curriculum Happen.* Paris: OECD Centre for Educational Research and Innovation.

OECD (2008): *Innovating to Learn, Learning to Innovate.* Paris: OECD Centre for Educational Research and Innovation.

Ritchhart, R (2002): *Intellectual Character: What it is, Why it Matters, and How to Get it.* San Francisco: Jossey-Bass.

Robinson, K (2001): *Out of our Minds: learning to be creative.* Bloomington, MN: Capstone Publishing Company.

Rowson, J (2008): 'How are we disposed to be creative' in Craft, A, Claxton, G and Gardner, H (eds), *Creativity, Wisdom and Trusteeship: Exploring the Role of Education.* Thousand Oaks, CA: Corwin Press.

Sternberg, R J (2003): *Wisdom, intelligence and creativity synthesized.* New York: Cambridge University Press.

Sternberg, R J (2008): 'Leadership as a basis for the education of our children' in Craft, A, Claxton, G and Gardner, H (eds), *Creativity, Wisdom and Trusteeship: Exploring the Role of Education.* Thousand Oaks, CA: Corwin Press.

Sternberg, R J, Reznitskaya, A and Jarvin, L (2007): 'Teaching for wisdom: what matters is not just what students know, but how they use it', in *London Review of Education*, 5 (2) pp143-158.

Tan, J and Gopinathan, S (2000): 'Education Reform in Singapore: Towards Greater Creativity and Innovation?' in *NIRA Review*, 7 (3) pp5-10.

Terry, A W and Bohnenberger, J E (2003): 'Service Learning: Fostering a Cycle of Caring in Our Gifted Youth', in *Journal of Secondary Gifted Education*, 15 (1) pp23-32.

Tighe, E, Picariello, M L and Amabile, T M (2003): 'Environmental Influences on Motivation and Creativity in the Classroom' in Houtz, J (ed), *The Educational Psychology of Creativity* (pp199-222). New York: Hampton Press.

Zhou Nanzhao (1996): 'Interactions of education and culture for economic and human development: an Asian perspective' in *Learning: the treasure within.* Paris: UNESCO Publishing.

Chapter 7

21st century learning: community and service in the MYP

Chris Charleson, Tracy Moxley and David Batten

Introduction

In this chapter, we hope to show that 21st century learning is much more than a collection of new skills that needs to be integrated into the curriculum, or a raft of new technologies that will drain a school budget. It is an approach that requires a fundamental shift to an internationally-minded and globally-connected learning environment, with a focus on developing competencies for this new world. Our contention is that MYP community and service (C&S) can provide the 'spine' of an innovative, experiential curriculum for young people, through which students can develop many of the key competencies necessary for the 21st century global society.

Many observers point out the disjuncture between school and 'real' life experiences for students. Heidi Hayes Jacobs conjures up a challenging scenario for us: 'I often wonder if many of our students feel like they are time travelling as they walk through the school door each morning. As they cross the threshold, do they feel as if they are entering a simulation of life in the 1980s? Then, at the end of the school day, do they feel that they have returned to the 21st century?' (Jacobs, 2010a) If schools are not entering into the 21st century world of global connectedness and multimedia richness, and are not facilitating the development of the competencies needed for that world, then we are doing a disservice to our students.

21st century skills

There has been much discussion about 21st century skills in recent years and suddenly the 21st century is upon us: the future is here and now. It really is time for schools to catch up with the 21st century and match the experience that students have of a technological and inter-connected society, outside school, with the one they experience in school. We need to overhaul and invigorate our curriculum and radically change how schools operate to meet the needs of students in the 21st century. 'Our responsibility is to prepare the learners in our care for their world and their future' says Jacobs (2010b). The world and future for which we are preparing our students is complex and uncertain. In the executive summary of its report, *College Learning for the New Global Century*, the National Leadership Council for Liberal Education

America's Promise (LEAP) states that: 'The world in which today's students will make choices and compose lives is one of disruption rather than certainty, and of interdependence rather than insularity.' (National Leadership Council for Liberal Education America's Promise, 2008: 2) The 21st century student can only deal with the complexity and diversity of our world by becoming more adaptable and innovative, and developing the ability to filter and respond flexibly to information overload and sometimes apparently contradictory stimuli.

Technology has provided the means for us to touch and experience the diverse 'global village' and offers students the opportunity to learn, understand and know their place in relation to other global villagers. 'The revolution in communications technology, particularly the ubiquity of the internet, has rendered access to the information about and contact with other countries virtually instantaneous' says Lewin (2009). The ability to make these exciting connections offers further opportunities for new curricula to provide the skills, knowledge and attitudes that students need for an ever-changing global landscape. These 21st century skills are the key to our future and a modern curriculum must address contemporary global issues and the questions that are important to humanity. We contend that these skills can only be fully developed through an education with a significant global citizenship element.

Hargreaves and Shirley suggest the key 21st century skills that will drive new knowledge economies are 'creativity, innovation, intellectual agility, teamwork, problem solving, flexibility and adaptability to change'. They further assert that 21st century schools 'must also embrace deeper virtues and values such as loyalty, perseverance, courage, service, and sacrifice' (Hargreaves and Shirley, 2009). It is clear that the modern global environment requires more than just thinking skills and content knowledge. The ability to navigate the complex, interconnected, competitive information world requires students to develop flexible life and career skills. It requires students to have a solid reference point, based on deeply embedded values and principles that are learned through intimate and direct experiences and interactions with a diverse range of people from across the globe.

We believe strongly that students require a learning environment that stimulates the imagination and enables them to construct meaning and bring coherence to disparate information. Learning should include the ability to think critically and solve problems, and to make informed judgements based on sound principles. Hersh states that students will require 'soft skills' such as 'valuing and embracing diverse ideas and people, working cooperatively with others, tolerating ambiguity, and possessing the resilience to bounce back after setbacks' (Hersh, 2009). Resilience and perseverance are also key components in the armoury of our students, who should be given the opportunity to develop those attributes by exposure to inevitable setbacks in their direct experience of an ever-changing and often inequitable world.

The 21st century skills movement has many advocates and manifests itself in a number of different frameworks. We will examine some of these and draw out the key common skills that could be developed through MYP C&S. Perhaps the most widely known and influential of these frameworks is that of the Partnership for 21st (P21) Century Skills (2009). The P21 framework describes the skills, knowledge and expertise needed to succeed in work and life; it is a blend of content knowledge, specific skills, expertise and literacies. The framework is divided into four skills sections including core subjects; learning and innovation; information, media and technology; life and career; plus a fifth section on 21st century interdisciplinary themes that would infuse all areas. In the context of skills that could be developed through C&S, the sections of interest in the P21 framework are creativity and innovation; critical thinking and problem solving; communication and collaboration; flexibility and adaptability; initiative, leadership, responsibility and self-direction; social and cross-cultural skills; financial, economic, business and entrepreneurial skills; global awareness; and civic, environmental and health literacy (Partnership for 21st Century Skills, 2009). Development of these skills will require an innovative approach from schools, and can only be developed through an active and experiential programme; indeed, we contend that they would be best learned through a programme of C&S.

One of P21's major proponents, Johnson, argues that to be successful in a globally competitive work environment, 'schools must align classroom environments and core subjects with 21st century skills. By combining both skills and content, educators can impart the expertise required for success in today's world' (Johnson, 2009). To some extent we concur with Dede (2010), in believing that the skills people need for work, citizenship and self-actualization in the 21st century are due to the emergence of very sophisticated information and communications technologies (ICT). It is essential that educators nurture those skills in our schools, not only locally and nationally but also internationally. However, our strong belief is that it is necessary to go beyond mastery of skills to a realisation that through sophisticated ICT, the world has indeed become, in the words of Friedman (2005), 'flatter' and more interdependent. The challenge for schools is how to enable students to become more aware of their place in this 'flat' world.

Salganik and Rychen, for OECD, have defined key competencies for a successful life and well-functioning 21st century society. They indicate that globalisation and modernisation are creating an increasingly diverse and interconnected world and in order to make sense of, and function well in, this world 'individuals need to master changing technologies and to make sense of large amounts of available information. They also face collective challenges as societies – such as balancing economic growth with environmental sustainability, and prosperity with social equity' (Salganik and Rychen, 2005).

Competency Category 1: Using Tools Interactively
A. Use language, symbols and texts interactively
B. Use knowledge and information interactively
C. Use technology interactively
Competency Category 2: Interacting in Heterogeneous Groups
A. Relate well to others.
B. Co-operate, work in teams
C. Manage and resolve conflicts
Competency Category 3: Acting Autonomously
A. Act within the big picture
B. Form and conduct life plans and personal projects
C. Defend and assert rights, interests, limits and needs

Table 1: OECD competencies: adapted and summarised from Salganik and Rychen (2005)

A summary of the competencies defined by OECD is shown in Table 1.

OECD suggest that the competencies required to succeed in our globalised society are more complex than simply mastering a set of narrowly defined skills, and that we will need to be able to integrate 'seemingly contradictory or incompatible goals as aspects of the same reality' (Salganik and Rychen, 2005). This reflects our belief that it is important for students to be not only technologically competent but also capable of making value judgements about the impact of technology and economic growth. Through C&S we can give students an experience of a different reality, and help them to develop the competencies needed to deal with the contradictions of, for example, the caste system in India and their own views on the inequalities of humankind.

In its 2007 report, the Australian Curriculum Standing Committee of National Education Professional Associations (CSCNEPA) locates its 21st century curriculum in a global context (CSCNEPA, 2007), identifying global features and consequent skills that should be considered when devising a new curriculum:

• globalisation of economies – global outlook and international competencies for entrepreneurs and workers

• increased labour mobility and use of multinational teams – heightened cultural awareness, second language skills and sophisticated interpersonal skills

- global environmental problems – international cooperation, knowledge of local and worldwide environmental issues, and a willingness to change local habits in the interests of global sustainability

- global insecurity – understand the need to build alliances and understand the factors that generate conflict and mistrust between nations

- the knowledge economy as a generator of wealth – the capacity to identify problems, work in transdisciplinary teams to identify solutions, to manage complex tasks, to synthesise ideas, and to communicate effectively.

CSCNEPA encourages students to 'be global in outlook, see themselves as citizens of the world, be culturally aware and sensitive of other societies, and be proficient in a second language' (CSCNEPA, 2007). These competencies are important because social interaction in a flat world requires an appreciation of cultural diversity, and an understanding of complex global trade. We raise this point again later in this chapter.

In the UK the then Qualifications and Curriculum Authority (QCA) identified five areas of change influencing what it means to be educated for life in the 21st century: 'changes in society and the nature of work; the impact of technology; new understanding about learning; the need for greater personalisation and innovation; and the increasing global dimension to life and work.' (QCA, 2005) One of the key elements of their curriculum for the 21st century is that it should be future-oriented and deal with the big issues in young people's lives. The QCA document is forward-looking and stresses many of the concepts we feel are important for students, such as taking responsibility for themselves and their environment, finding sustainable solutions for the planet, and addressing social issues through extending their experience beyond the local to the global through active and diverse participation.

The International Baccalaureate (IB) has developed its own key elements for a 21st century curriculum. Through the IB learner profile, the IB has translated its mission statement into a set of learning outcomes for the 21st century, with the profile making explicit the values of an IB education. The aim of the IB learner profile is to identify attitudes, attributes and behaviours that help develop internationally-minded people who, 'recognizing their common humanity and shared guardianship of the planet, help to create a better and more peaceful world'. With a focus on the 'dynamic combination of knowledge, skills, independent critical and creative thought and international-mindedness, the IB espouses the principle of educating the whole person for a life of active, responsible citizenship' (IB, 2009).

The IB states that these values should permeate all three IB programmes (Primary Years Programme, Middle Years Programme and Diploma Programme) and should be the bedrock of the culture and ethos of all IB schools. The IB believes the profile provides a long-term vision of education, delineating a set of ideals that can inspire and motivate members of the IB community, providing them with a common focus and unifying purpose. The key features of the IB learner profile, related to this chapter's theme of MYP C&S, are that students:

- have a personal commitment to service, and act to make a positive difference to the lives of others and to the environment

- understand and appreciate their own cultures and personal histories, and are open to the perspectives, values and traditions of other individuals and communities

- act with integrity and honesty, with a strong sense of fairness, justice and respect for the dignity of the individual, groups and communities

- explore concepts, ideas and issues that have local and global significance

- make reasoned, ethical decisions

- work effectively and willingly in collaboration with others

- show empathy, compassion and respect towards the needs and feelings of others

- approach unfamiliar situations and uncertainty with courage and forethought, and have the independence of spirit to explore new roles, ideas and strategies

- give thoughtful consideration to their own learning and experience

- are able to assess and understand their strengths and limitations in order to support their learning and personal development.

(Adapted and summarised from the IB learner profile booklet: IB, 2009)

Whilst being in close agreement with the attitudes and attributes espoused in the IB learner profile, we have adapted and extended them appropriately for the unique situation in our school, resulting in the Sotogrande International School (SIS) Values. In particular we have incorporated the concepts of perseverance, resilience and purpose, as well as clarifying some of the IB wording. The resultant *SIS Values* are summarised in Table 2.

The *SIS Values*:

- make an explicit link between our mission statement and what we do in practice;

- identify the attitudes and attributes we are aiming to develop in students, and across our community;

SIS Values: Developing Global Citizens; Striving for Excellence	
Communicator Inquirer Thinker	Balanced Committed Considerate Courageous Knowledgeable Open-minded Principled Reflective

Table 2: Summary of SIS *Values, based on IB learner profile (Sotogrande International School, 2010 and IB, 2009)*

• indicate that we are aiming for excellence in all areas; and

• drive our assessment policy.

The *SIS Values* reflect the different attitudes and attributes that we regard as important to develop in our students as global citizens. We support development of this profile by innovative, active and experiential programmes of PYP action, MYP community and service (C&S) and Diploma Programme creativity, action, service (CAS) (Sotogrande International School, 2010).

Service learning, community service and global citizenship education

We believe that a 21st century curriculum must contain, as a crucial core component, a strong commitment to the concepts of service learning, community service and global citizenship. We will consider now some definitions of these concepts and how they could be implemented through MYP C&S.

Service learning

Coles defines service learning as arising from teaching in which academic subjects, as well as skills, are taught within the context of citizenship through community service (Coles, 1993). A widely accepted definition comes from the US National and Community Service Trust, which defines it as 'a method under which students learn and develop through active participation in thoughtfully organized service experiences that meet actual community needs and that are coordinated in collaboration with the school and the community' (National and Community Service Trust, 1993). An examination of literature by service learning advocates (see, for instance, Sigmon, 1979; Kendall, 1990; Coles, 1993; Furco and Billig, 2002; Butin, 2003) reveals a relatively consistent articulation of service learning criteria and components which are actually a close match with the section on experiential learning in the IB diploma CAS guidelines (IB, 2008a):

• clearly identified learning objectives;

• student involvement in selecting, creating and designing the activities;

• integration of service with the academic curriculum;

• student reflection; and

• respect, reciprocity and relevance.

Service learning has been found to have a significantly beneficial impact on students' academic achievements and in particular on their problem solving abilities (RMC Research Corporation, 2007). Klute and Billig also found that service learning activities were linked with positive academic results. They indicated that students who had engaged in service learning activities were able to make better links across the curriculum and that direct contact with those being served helped students in their class work. (Klute and Billig, 2002) Additionally, Coles cites the transformative nature of service learning on the individual as 'being a consequence of doing' rather than just thinking (Coles, 1993).

Global citizenship

A number of terms are used in the global citizenship education literature such as 'global education', 'world citizenship', 'international education' and 'intercultural education'. However, global citizenship education defies a singular definition: to try and characterise such a diverse collection of ideas, content and pedagogy presents a formidable challenge. The term 'international education' has proved difficult to define and certainly has a long history linked to multicultural education, intercultural education, comparative education, environmental studies and citizenship education – to name but a few. In the context of international education programmes such as those offered by the IB, international education has been defined as 'an ideology of international understanding and peace, responsible world citizenship and service' (Cambridge and Thompson, 2004). When using the term 'international education' the intention of many educationalists is to imply a combination of 'political astuteness, communication skills across languages, elements of multicultural understanding, global awareness and responsibilities involved with national and global citizenship' (Haywood, 2007). Our use of 'international education' in this chapter will be based on these definitions.

Beginning in the 1970s, global education highlighted the knowledge and understanding of people, cultures and the global issues that affect us all and it has grown in response to the effects of globalisation (Hicks, 2008). The Maastricht Global Education Declaration, drafted by the Council of Europe in 2002, includes such elements as development education, human rights education, education for sustainability, education for peace and conflict prevention, and intercultural education as being the global dimension of education for global citizenship. The declaration defines global education as 'education that opens people's eyes and minds to the realities of the world, and awakens them to bring about a world of greater justice, equity and Human Rights for all' (Council of Europe, 2002). Global education has also been defined as education that 'promotes the knowledge, attitudes and skills relevant to living responsibly in a multi-cultural, interdependent world' (Fisher and Hicks, 1985). There appears to be some consensus by researchers on the academic fields that comprise global education. They are described as peace education, development education, environmental education and human rights education (Tye and Tye, 1999; Greig, Pike, and Selby, 1986; Heater, 1980).

A number of common threads have been identified in the theoretical articulations of global education: 'global connectedness and interdependence, global systems, global issues and problems, cross-cultural understanding, human beliefs and values, and awareness and choices for the future.' (Lewin, 2009) Two main trends identified in global citizenship education are described as offering two different 'paradigms of global literacy' (Richardson, 1976; Toh, 1993). One view highlights the universal values that we all share, with an emphasis on commonalities, while the other highlights the cultural differences and the celebration of diversity. As the IB itself puts it: 'Without an understanding of the importance of diversity of culture in human life and an openness to cooperative sharing of knowledge, students are unlikely to develop tolerance and an acceptance that civilised life must be sustained through living together peacefully.' (IB, 2002)

We believe diversity is something to be celebrated and we support Gardner in his view of diversity as a positive aspect of humankind. In *Five Minds for the Future*, Gardner states: 'The respectful mind ... starts with an assumption that diversity is positive and that the world would be a better place if individuals sought to respect one another.' (Gardner, 2010) It is crucial that students learn about why diversity is important and are able to appreciate the diverse backgrounds and cultures of those we encounter in our everyday life. As Walker points out: 'Three inter-related global issues will dominate the 21st century: diversity, complexity and inequality ... all schools are places of learning and all students need to study why diversity matters, how it is linked to human rights and why the biggest threat to the peace of the world is posed by inequality.' (Walker, 2010)

Several commentators argue strongly for the competencies required in a 'global village'. Zhao suggests that to educate global citizens, we need to develop a framework that fosters good relationships with others. He contends that our global village is now so interconnected and interdependent that no individual, organization, or nation should continue to live a privileged lifestyle while their fellow villagers live in poverty. Zhao argues that 'Cross-cultural competency ... means being able to live in different cultures and move across different societies fluently. In the globalized world, it is impossible to be competent in all world cultures, but it is essential to be open to new and different cultures' (Zhao, 2009). Reimers, meanwhile, defines global competency as 'the knowledge and skills that help people understand the flat world in which they live, the skills to integrate across disciplinary domains to comprehend global affairs and events, and the intellect to create possibilities to address them', as well as 'the attitudinal and ethical dispositions that make it possible to interact peacefully, respectfully, and productively with fellow human beings' (Reimers, 2010). A distinction is made by Roberts between global education that is 'about' global issues and global development education that nurtures the traits 'for' global citizenship, stating that 'Global education provides a focus on issues and concerns that affect people and the planet as a whole, notions of systems and interdependence, and a coherent pedagogy; global development education contributes to the development of ethical and moral responsibility towards our fellow planetary inhabitants' (Roberts, 2009). There should be a balance between the development of skills and development of attitudes and attributes. The challenge for educators is how to nurture these competencies through diverse and active curricular and co-curricular experiences.

Many researchers have the concept of a global citizen at the centre of their definitions of global education (see, for example, Ramirez, 1997; Nussbaum, 1997). In international education, the development of a global citizen appears to be a much more explicit process than in some national education systems. Walker emphasises 'intellectual rigour, human compassion and cultural sensitivity' as three qualities that contribute to the making of a global citizen (Walker, 2006) and continues by highlighting the need to link knowledge with action.

Oxfam remains one of the strongest proponents of global citizenship education and expounds it as an essential component of learning for the 21st century, arguing that 'In a fast-changing and interdependent world, education can, and should, help young people to meet the challenges they will confront now and in the future' (Oxfam, 2006). Oxfam defines clearly the key elements of knowledge and understanding, skills, and values and attitudes for responsible global citizenship, as shown in Figure 1.

A global citizen is defined by Oxfam as someone who 'is aware of the wider world and has a sense of their own role as a world citizen; respects and values diversity; has an understanding of how the world works economically, politically, socially, culturally, technologically and environmentally; is outraged by social injustice; participates in and contributes to the community at a range of levels from local to global; is willing to act to make the world a more sustainable place and who takes responsibility for their actions'. Meanwhile,

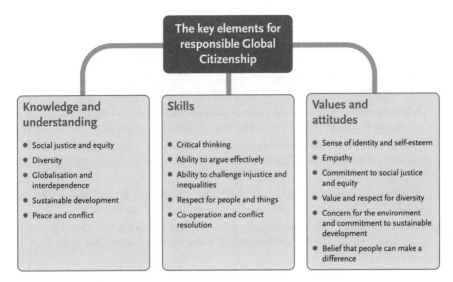

Figure 1: Key elements for responsible Global Citizenship (Oxfam, 2006)

eight characteristics of global citizenship are proposed in useful guidelines from DFID, DfES for those designing 21st century curricula that aim to develop a global dimension (2005): see Figure 2.

Oxfam makes a strong case for 'Education for Global Citizenship' as good general education. Since the lives of our students are increasingly shaped by what happens in other parts of the world, it is essential to nurture elements such as those discussed above if students are to be able look after themselves and others, and make a positive contribution to their local and global communities. Students should become deeply involved in their own learning through a wide range of active and collaborative learning opportunities, which 'engage the learner while developing confidence, self-esteem and skills of critical thinking, communication, co-operation and conflict resolution', thus making an important contribution to improved motivation, behaviour and achievement (Oxfam, 2006).

Bringing it all together

Since the 1990s, global citizenship education and service learning have been linked, and the participatory aspect of social responsibility arising out of social injustice is a growing and significant element. Service learning helps to build a type of 'bridging as well as bonding social capital' (Putnam, 2000) and may also develop capacity building for democratic citizenship within civil society. However, the growth in active global citizenship with an emphasis on participation in local and global communities continues and, more often than not, it is in participation with communities outside one's home country that the growth is most marked (Annette, 2002; Kahne and Westheimer, 2003).

The 8 key concepts for developing a global dimension to the curriculum

- **Global citizenship:** Gaining the knowledge, skills and understanding of concepts and institutions necessary to become informed, active, responsible global citizens

- **Conflict resolution:** Understanding how conflicts are a barrier to development and why there is a need for their resolution and the promotion of harmony

- **Social Justice:** Understanding the importance of social justice as an element in both sustainable development and the improved welfare of all people

- **Values and perceptions:** Developing a critical evaluation of images of other parts of the world and an appreciation of the effect these have on people's attitudes and values

- **Sustainable development:** Understanding the need to maintain and improve the quality of life now without damaging the planet for future generations

- **Interdependence:** Understanding how people, places, economies and environments are all inextricably interrelated, and that events have repercussions on a global scale

- **Human rights:** Knowing about human rights and, in particular, the UN Convention on the Rights of the Child and the United Nations Universal Declaration of Human Rights

- **Diversity:** Understanding and respecting differences, and relating these to our common humanity

---

Figure 2: The 8 key concepts for a global dimension adapted from Developing the global dimension in the school curriculum. *(DFID, DfES, 2005: 12)*

When linking global citizenship education and service learning, a key consideration is the need to develop partnerships with the beneficiaries of the service. Without a conversation involving both partners, the outcomes may serve only to reinforce donor and receiver stereotypes. There should be collaboration and negotiation between partners that involves taking into consideration the needs of both parties and ensuring that the relationship is 'win/win' for both (Porter and Monard, 2001). However, there are a number of examples of global citizenship initiatives that indicate a cultural disconnect between the community and the service providers (DiSpigno, Fallon, and Christen, 2001).

The concept of community service is a common thread running through the three IB programmes ('action' in PYP, 'community and service' in MYP and 'creativity, action, service' in the DP), although it is currently rather discontinuous and even the same word 'action' has different meaning in the PYP and DP. The growth of this concept within the IB can be traced to the late 1940s, when Kurt Hahn proposed the idea of enhancing the prospect of world peace by bringing together students of different cultures and backgrounds to learn together and from each other. In the 1960s, this dream became a more widespread reality when Hahn founded Atlantic College, which went on to become the first of the United World Colleges, and a group of international educators established a syndicate that would later become the International Baccalaureate. In his short biography of Kurt Hahn, James describes the programmes in Hahn's schools as fostering 'world citizenship, an interconnected leadership of people who have experienced a collective life of active dialogue and peacemaking service.' (James, 2000)

Alec Peterson, the first director general of the IB, whose thinking was greatly influenced by Kurt Hahn, was passionately committed to this aspect of international education. Peterson stated, in the seminal final chapter of his book, that the intention of international education is 'not simply to help the next generation to know better their enemies or their rivals, but to understand and collaborate better with their fellow human beings across frontiers' and that 'if you believe in something, you must not just think or talk or write, but must act' (Peterson, 1987).

Peterson's influence can be felt to this day in the IB. The most recent edition of the *Creativity, action, service guide*, for the IB diploma programme, gives an indication of recent IB thinking (IB, 2008a). The guide states that the CAS programme aims to develop students who are:

- 'reflective thinkers – they understand their own strengths and limitations, identify goals and devise strategies for personal growth;

- willing to accept new challenges and new roles;

- aware of themselves as members of communities with responsibilities towards each other and the environment;

- active participants in sustained, collaborative projects; and

- balanced – they enjoy and find significance in a range of activities involving intellectual, physical, creative and emotional experiences.

(IB, 2008a)

These guidelines could clearly apply to C&S within the MYP and, indeed, to any community service programme.

A key belief across IB programmes is that education must 'extend beyond the intellectual to include socially responsible attitudes and also thoughtful and appropriate action'. As shown above, experiential learning is a fundamental feature of IB philosophy. Students are expected to participate in service activities both inside school and beyond the school community. 'Through such service, students are able to grow both personally and socially', say the IB, 'developing skills such as cooperation, problem solving, conflict resolution and creative and critical thinking, as well as developing their own identities. It is also through service that IB students may make the connections between their academic studies and real life.' (IB, 2008b)

The active nature of the global citizen is paramount: participating and serving their community, whether local or global, having gained relevant knowledge and understanding about the members of that community and reflecting on their part in the whole community and service initiative. Students are encouraged to act on their knowledge and understanding and to make an effective contribution to local and global society.

The role of MYP community and service (C&S)

This brings us to the future role of C&S within the MYP. As Boix-Mansilla points out: 'Curriculum developers of the MYP share a commitment to prepare young people for the changing demands of life in the 21st century. They understand the competencies required for students to thrive in today's world as well as in tomorrow's, such as the capacity for lifelong learning, expert thinking, problem solving, effective communication and collaborative work in diverse human groups. They also understand the opportunities for growth and challenges that students encounter between ages 11 and 16.' (2010)

The concepts of service learning, community service and global citizenship are encouraged through MYP C&S as an important area of interaction (AOI) (IB, 2008c). This is a change from the original concept of community service as an additional element of the programme rather than permeating the entire curriculum (IB, 2010a). C&S highlights the importance of global citizenship and also emphasises, and is intimately linked with, the IB learner profile as mentioned above. As Marshman states: 'The constructivist pedagogy of the PYP and MYP is what makes the programmes a vehicle for promoting a sense of global citizenship; it is what turns the three fundamental concepts of the MYP – intercultural awareness, communication and holistic learning – from theory into practice.' (Marshman, 2006)

Let us focus for a moment on holistic learning as a key element of the MYP and C&S. Hare presents a comprehensive view of this aspect of the IB. He contends that holistic education 'prepares a student for lifelong learning in which the educational focus moves towards the life skills, attitudes and personal awareness that the student will need in an increasingly complex world'. He places an emphasis on real-life experience and learning beyond the classroom and describes it as a journey of growth, discovery and a broadening of horizons. He further says that holistic learning encourages a desire to develop understanding and to engage with the world, concluding that 'from their interaction with others, their experiences and learning, [students] take a considered global perspective on international concerns and bring an informed appreciation of the issues relevant to these concerns' (Hare, 2010). C&S plays a crucial role in enabling holistic learning to be applied in practice.

C&S aims to encourage respect and tolerance leading to understanding, empathy, action and reflection. There is an expectation that all students become involved in positive action and are able to engage in a variety of situations and communities that offer new insights and understandings that, in turn, enrich their lives and the lives of others. The emphasis is on the development of the skills, attitudes and knowledge needed to make an effective contribution to the communities of which they are members – locally, nationally and globally – through positive action.

One interpretation of C&S is an attempt, through experiential learning, to merge the classroom and the real world. The MYP guiding questions (*How do I live in relation to others? How can I contribute to the community? How can I help others?*) can be answered as academic questions based on the student's immediate cultural, social and physical contexts and can be applied to the immediate school community in which the students find themselves every day (IB, 2008c). However, the students must undertake an element of real service and engage with current world situations and issues that may affect them directly or indirectly.

C&S must stretch beyond being simply just one of five MYP AOIs grouped under the three broad philosophical foundations of: holistic education, communication and intercultural understanding. Meaningful C&S activities must offer experiential opportunities for schools to address George Walker's suggestion that the default position of our cultural hardwiring is one of suspicion and mistrust (Walker, 2010). We must now forcefully reach out to consolidate, innovate and create long-term sustainable relationships and partnerships, both locally and globally. The MYP C&S programme offers powerful, authentic and meaningful opportunities for all schools to generate a central interdisciplinary focus – a spine – to their curriculum, through which students may develop the key skills necessary to enable the 21st century global society to move forward to a common preferred future.

The three exemplars given in Figures 3, 4 and 5 demonstrate ways in which 21st century skills and global citizenship education can be brought together in active service projects. The first is a programme in our own international school that has allowed the school community to establish its own NGO, choose its own projects to support, and find sustainable ways of supporting those projects, using approaches such as micro-finance and social entrepreneurship. The second is an online newspaper that is a partnership between an international school and a global IT organisation that encourages skills of journalism and global awareness, and encourages taking active steps to make real changes. The third is a new IB website that fosters global citizenship education, provides resource and ideas for active global citizenship activities, and facilitates the development of networks between IB schools, enabling them to engage in projects together.

The way forward

The 21st century skills movement gives us some guidelines as to the requirements of students in this modern era of globalisation and in an inter-connected digital world. Service learning, community service and global citizenship indicate to us a possible structure for developing many of the skills

Exemplar 1: *The Kindred Project,* a school-based NGO

The *Kindred Project* is an NGO created by Sotogrande International School (SIS) to enable all stakeholders to participate in project construction, to help deliver quality services at local, national and international levels, and to build capacities for all to become self-reliant. (Kindred Project, 2010) It is both independent and interdependent on the SIS community, its main source of benefactors, as is the nature of many successful NGO relationships. The *Kindred Project*'s primary goals are to: provide a framework for the nurturing of global citizenship and 21st century skills; support ongoing initiatives within SIS; extend gap-year and volunteer outreach programmes; and develop a young social entrepreneur network to help enrich the lives of disadvantaged children and adults worldwide through a variety of education-related projects. The *Kindred Project* activities extend outward from the school and local community to four communities worldwide: Morocco, India, Uganda and Ecuador.

The Kindred Project's driving imperative is to ensure that all programmes are sustainable, accountable, replicable, inclusive and scaleable, in addition to offering appropriate quality services delivered in cost-effective ways. A Kindred Project trustee recently blogged on the SIS website: 'We too need to get rid of another form of apartheid: educational apartheid. So how can we go about the business of creating a tipping point? We wish to put international education to work by setting up the Kindred Project as an NGO to be run by you. This is your chance to become a social entrepreneur and help create global projects which: extend the learning beyond our international school to a global community; bring the advantaged and disadvantaged together in equal partnership; and help nurture the next generation of global citizens and social entrepreneurs.'

All participants in the *Kindred Project* activities are expected to make informed choices as to how they exercise their own rights and responsibilities, as demonstrated through diverse activities and practical work opportunities from project planning and evaluation, child care, teaching and teacher training, to building, farming and e-learning.

Service learning in action: Uganda example

SIS is currently working with the Williams Hill School situated close to Masaka town in southern Uganda. Williams Hill provides education for 350 AIDS orphans and rudimentary boarding facilities for 80 girls. There is no electricity and no well or running water at the school. Students at the school are encouraged to provide for themselves at the small school farm by learning how to sow and harvest their staple foods. The *Kindred Project*'s goal is raising funds and harnessing expertise to help create a sustainable future for the Williams Hill School and local community by: building a dormitory for girls; creating independent solar-powered sources of electricity; digging a bore-hole and filter system to provide clean water, and extending the school farm.

Staff and students are involved in developing appropriate solar electricity networks, water pumps and sanitation plans in close liaison with the project directors. Young entrepreneur networks will be generated by students from SIS and the Williams Hill School. Current discussions include micro-finance projects for a portable solar electricity generation scheme for rural communities, 'Fair Trade' coffee plantation initiatives, and a bicycle purchase system. Perhaps most importantly, the solar electricity installation will enable the Williams Hill students, through a local internet provider, to connect with peers at SIS and elsewhere, enabling them to contribute to similar projects worldwide.

Figure 3: Exemplar 1: The Kindred Project

Exemplar 2: *The Student News Action Network*: **a website for 21st century skills and action**

Schools with a global perspective, and in particular those with an IB MYP programme, share a common sense of purpose as defined by the IB mission statement: 'to create a better and more peaceful world through intercultural understanding and respect.' (IB, 2004) Collectively, we value collaboration rather than competition and encourage students wherever possible to assume leadership of their own self-defined programme. If our shared goal is to create 'a better and more peaceful world', this clearly demands action. The mission of encouraging and empowering students to make a difference, by working with their peers worldwide to develop solutions through global cooperation for collectively recognised global issues, presents an intense challenge for all schools with global aspirations.

Whilst recognising the power and commitment of the myriad of global initiatives and networks initiated by schools worldwide, one website offers a compelling and successful model – *The Student News Action Network* (2010). *The Student News Action Network* was created, and is maintained, by students and teachers at Washington International School in collaboration with *TakingITGlobal* (2010) and 'bureau' schools worldwide.

The Student News Action Network takes the concept of the school newspaper into the digital world, allowing students 'to work collaboratively on a global level to create an interactive, multimedia-rich student-driven online newspaper. It brings together a network of students in an online, peer-driven environment to address issues of local and global significance, such as poverty, the environment, and human rights, in a creative and constructive format that culminates in meaningful efforts to make a positive impact on their world. Contributors bring their unique voices to the discussion, representing their regions and their cultural histories'. Members of the network 'have a commitment to addressing global issues through exploring ways to make meaningful change in their communities. The action component distinguishes the network from a conventional journalism outlet. Members are not just reporters; they are also seriously engaged in work that seeks to effect local change with global impact!' (The Student News Action Network, 2010).

This highly effective website, which brings together the concepts of 21st century skills and community and service, gets a ringing endorsement from none other than Daniel Pink, author of *A Whole New Mind* and *Drive*: '*The Student News Action Network* is one of the most exciting new ventures I've seen in a long while. It will help students sharpen some of the 21st century's most important skills – communication, collaboration, and conceptual thinking. But equally important, it offers young people a meaningful way to engage with the world, direct their own work, and shape the public conversation. This one-of-a-kind program has the potential to remake journalism and reinvigorate education.' (Pink, 2010)

Figure 4: Exemplar 2: The Student News Action Network

Exemplar 3: *Global Engage* – a website to provide a focus for IB community and service

Finding ways to share projects effectively – failures, successes and dreams – given the plethora of conferences, workshops and internet networks available becomes increasingly problematic. How can we best discover and share innovative ways to encourage our students to investigate the world, recognise perspectives, communicate ideas, take appropriate action and reflect? Keynote speakers and discussions at international conferences and MYP workshops consistently recognise our shared imperative, a powerful call to action, to make 'poverty history' and 'education for all' a reality.

Many experts agree that education is perhaps the best long-term solution to poverty and inequality, with the internet potentially offering the most powerful tool and way forward for learners of all ages, regardless of age or social background (Anup Shah, 2010). A decade ago, the then UN Secretary-General Kofi Annan called for 'a bridge that spans the digital divide' between the 'haves' and 'have-nots' (Annan, 2001). Today the divide has become a chasm, not only economically but also technologically (Internet World Statistics, 2009). While past statistics reflect a grim reality, remarkable progress has been made in recent years to improve conditions for disadvantaged communities through MYP community and service projects worldwide.

How can we effectively identify and share common needs, and develop focused training programmes? How can we encourage independent grass-roots projects within all IB schools and stakeholders, whilst also networking more effectively within our exponentially expanding virtual universe? Given the mountains of networks available, but with a paucity of potent, forward-looking community and service resources available for students and teachers, how can the MYP community join forces to provide a common springboard for future success? How can we collectively best consolidate, construct and monitor work done to date, beyond the rather cumbersome and lacking-in-focus IB Online Curriculum Centre (OCC), to create a singular media-rich virtual environment?

A powerful communications tool and networking solution has now arrived in the form of the IB website *Global Engage* (IB, 2010b). The website encourages IB schools to learn more about important global issues, and links knowledge and understanding about a particular global issue with action ideas to address it. It includes details of online professional development activities, specific issues (overseas trips, teaching controversial issues, school links and partnerships, information technology and global dimensions in the classroom) and related resources. The website has the potential to become a powerful unifying networking force within the IB.

Figure 5: Exemplar 3: Global Engage

needed for this new age. If the IB, and in particular the MYP, are to make a contribution to learning in the 21st century, they should be cognisant of the possibilities of using C&S as the vehicle for developing the competencies that students require for this new global world.

Perhaps the strongest messages coming through in the literature are that students must be partners in designing their pathways towards the future, and that the 21st century and global citizenship skills must be put into action. The Asia Society describes what it means to be a globally competent student: 'Alone or with others, ethically and creatively, globally competent students can envision and weigh options for action based on evidence and insight; they can assess their potential impact, taking into account varied perspectives and potential consequences for others; and they show courage to act and reflect on their actions.' (Jackson, 2009) Hargreaves, meanwhile, argues eloquently for his notion of learning 'beyond the knowledge society', urging us 'to help build a strong and vigorous civil society, developing the character that promotes involvement in the community, and cultivating dispositions of sympathy and care for people in other nations and cultures that are at the heart of a cosmopolitan identity' (Hargreaves, 2003). This concept of 'cosmopolitan identity' requires that a 'mindful' learner should experience a curriculum that includes opportunities for developing international-mindedness and intercultural understanding. We contend that this curriculum should have at its core a structured programme of C&S that allows students to choose and devise their own progressive and coherent pathways and experiences towards active global citizenship.

Concluding her report on interdisciplinary learning in the MYP, Boix-Mansilla paints a vivid picture of the MYP in the 21st century:

> At the dawn of the 21st century the quality of an educational programme is to be judged not only by the professionalism of its instruction and the deep understanding it instils in its students but, quite importantly, by the relevance of what students learn. To meet the demands of contemporary societies wisely, young people of today must become able to navigate growing international interdependence, participate actively in the local and global sphere, understand the environment and its sustainability, care for mind, body and well-being and become reflective learners in dynamic knowledge societies. Responding to these demands the MYP curricular model articulates a much needed bridge between what is typically learned in schools and the most pressing questions that concern our societies. Attentive to adolescents' development, the programme emphasizes rigorous learning in the disciplines and interdisciplinary synergy, inviting students to tackle relevant issues – from climate change to globalization – thus preparing them for the work of the next generation. (Boix-Mansilla, 2010)

A curriculum with a strong core of C&S focusing on global citizenship education will enable students to make those essential connections between school and wider communities, to focus on key global issues that affect them, and to develop the key competencies in a manner that takes account of the developmental stage of emergent young adults.

IB recently gathered ideas from a forum of educators from across the IB community, including one of the authors of this chapter, to consider ways forward for the IB in the 21st century. The ideas from that forum are tentative and not yet formalised at this stage, but the most promising proposal emerging is for the IB to consider developing, as part of its long term continuum planning, a fourth programme for the age range 3-19 years. The forum suggested that the basis for this possible new programme would be an *IB learning profile* in addition to the IB learner profile, which would consist of a set of learning characteristics and competencies, using common language and defining age-specific expectations, and which would include fundamental common threads connecting profoundly across the full age-range of the programme. The common threads would include:

- **the IB values and principles** enshrined in the mission statement and IB learner profile, *eg* international-mindedness, caring, respect, inquiry, thinking, action, reflection;

- **community and service and global citizenship**, using common language and identifying what community and service and global citizenship would mean at age-appropriate stages;

- age-appropriate **personal research project**, culminating events at different stages to celebrate learning, based on the current exhibition, personal project and extended essay;

- **holism**: encouraging 21st century learner skills through trans/inter/multi-disciplinary learning;

- age-appropriate **learning to learn competencies** (ways of thinking), based on the current transdisciplinary approach in PYP, *approaches to learning in MYP* and *theory of knowledge* in DP, leading to self-awareness and self actualization; and

- **communication skills**, based on the ideas of intercultural understanding and using latest research on language learning and cognitive development.

The forum also suggested that a new programme should:

- define and develop a core for the 21st century, serving the needs of all learners, preparing them for life as well as university;

- suit the needs of different groups of learners, enabling whole school implementation;

• be outcomes-driven, with clear progression, coherence and articulation across the age range 3-18; and

• be assessable with clear and flexible pathways.

The forum proposed that development of the programme should be led by an IB think tank with extensive partnerships, involving global innovators and leaders in relevant fields, and from different disciplines, that will shape the 21st century – including educators, researchers, industry leaders, corporations and entrepreneurs. This proposal combines many of the ideas developed in the above discussion, making 21st century skills and community and service key elements of a possible new programme. In the words of Hargreaves and Shirley, 'the Old Ways of educational change in the 20th century are ill suited to the fast, flexible and vulnerable New World of the 21st century' (Hargreaves and Shirley, 2009). If these tentative ideas are developed further, then it could lead to IB initiating a completely new in-house programme, something it has arguably never done completely under the IB banner, using the vast experience and talent at its disposal in the IB community and opening up exciting new horizons for the IB.

We would like to finish with some inspiring words from Hargreaves and Shirley that might guide the next phase of IB development:

> Horizons draw our eyes towards the distance. They define the very edge of our existing vision. Spread all around the compass, they provide points of focus to possible ways forward. Horizons are not destinations. They are places on a journey that offer their own viewpoints and that can motivate travellers to find and forge their path ahead. (Hargreaves and Shirley, 2009)

References

Annan, K (2001): *World Telecommincations Day.* From: www.itu.int/itunews/issue/2001/04/wtd.html [Accessed October 2010]

Annette, J (2002): Service Learning in an International Context, in *Frontiers: The Interdisciplinary Journal of Study Abroad,* 8 (1) pp83-93.

Boix-Mansilla, V (2010): *MYP guide to interdisciplinary teaching and learning.* Cardiff: International Baccalaureate.

Butin, D (2003): Of what use is it? Multiple Conceptualizations of Service Learning within Education, in *Teacher's College Record,* 105 (9) pp1674-1692.

Cambridge, J, and Thompson, J (2004): Internationalism and globalization as contexts for international education, in *Compare,* 32 (2) pp161-175.

Coles, R (1993): *The Call of Service: A Witness to Idealism.* Boston: Houghton Mifflin.

Council of Europe (2002): *Maastricht Global Education Declaration.* Europe-wide Global Education Congress. Maastricht: Council of Europe.

CSCNEPA (2007): *Developing a 21st century school curriculum for all Australian students.* CSCNEPA.

Dede, C (2010): Comparing Frameworks for 21st Century Skills, in J Bellanca and R Brandt (eds), *21st Century Skills: Rethinking How Students Learn* (pp51-75). Bloomington, IN: Solution Tree Press.

DFID, DfES (2005): *Developing the global dimension in the school curriculum.* From: http://publications.education.gov.uk/eOrderingDownload/1409-2005PDF-EN-01.pdf [Accessed November 2010]

DiSpigno, A, Fallon, M, and Christen, R (2001): Combining Volunteer Work and Study Abroad: An international service learning project, in *NSEE Quarterly*, 26 (4) pp7-10.

Fisher, S, and Hicks, D (1985): *World Studies 8-13: A Teacher's Handbook.* Edinburgh: Oliver and Boyd.

Friedman, T (2005): *The World is Flat.* London: Allen Lane.

Furco, A, and Billig, S (2002): *Service Learning: The Essence of Pedagogy.* Greenwich, CT: IAP Press.

Gardner, H (2010): Five Minds for the Future, in J Bellanca and R Brandt (eds), *21st Century Skills: Rethinking How Students Learn* (pp9-31). Bloomington, IN: Solution Tree Press.

Greig, S, Pike, G, and Selby, D (1986): *A Survey of Environment and Development Education in Schools and in Non-Governmental and State Organisations.* York: Centre for Global Education.

Hare, J (2010): *Holistic education: An interpretation for teachers in the IB programmes.* Cardiff: International Baccalaureate.

Hargreaves, A (2003): *Teaching in the knowledge society: Education in the age of insecurity.* New York: Teachers College Press.

Hargreaves, A and Shirley, D (2009): *The Fourth Way: The Inspiring Future for Educational Change.* Thousand Oaks, CA: Corwin.

Haywood, T (2007): A Simple Typology of International-Mindedness and its Implications for Education, in M Hayden, J Levy, and J Thompson (eds), *The SAGE Handbook of Research in International Education* (pp79-89). London: SAGE Publications.

Heater, D (1980): *World Studies: Education for International Understanding In Britain.* London: Harrap.

Hersh, R (2009): A Well-Rounded Education for a Flat World, in *Educational Leadership*, 67 (1) pp51-53.

Hicks, D (2008): *Ways of Seeing: the origins of global education in the UK.* Background paper for the UK ITE inaugural conference on Education for Sustainable Development/Global Citizenship, London: July 2008, Accessed via: www.teaching4abetterworld.co.uk/docs/download2.pdf

IB (2002): *A Continuum of International Education.* Geneva: International Baccalaureate.

IB (2004): *Strategic Plan.* From: www.ibo.org/mission/strategy/documents/sp2004.pdf [Accessed November 2010]

IB (2008a): *Creativity, action, service guide.* Cardiff: International Baccalaureate.

IB (2008b): *Towards a continuum of international education.* Cardiff: International Baccalaureate.

IB (2008c): *MYP: From principles into practice.* Cardiff: International Baccalaureate.

IB (2009): *IB Learner Profile booklet.* Cardiff: International Baccalaureate.

IB (2010a): *History of the Middle Years Programme.* Cardiff: International Baccalaureate.

IB (2010b): *Global Engage.* From *Global Engage:* http://globalengage.ibo.org/ [Accessed November 2010]

Internet World Statistics (2009): *Countries classified by internet penetration rates.* From: www.internetworldstats.com/list4.htm [Accessed November 2010]

Jackson, A (2009): *Global Competence: The Knowledge and Skills Our Students Need.* From: http://asiasociety.org/education-learning/partnership-global-learning/making-case/global-competence-knowledge-and-skills-ou [Accessed December 2010]

Jacobs, H H (2010a): A New Essential Curriculum for a New Time, in H H Jacobs, *Curriculum 21: Essential Education for a Changing World,* (pp7-17). Alexandria, VA: ASCD.

Jacobs, H H (2010b): Introduction, in H H Jacobs, *Curriculum 21: Essential Education for a Changing World,* (pp1-6). Alexandria, VA: ASCD.

James, T (2000): *Kurt Hahn and the Aims of Education.* From: www.kurthahn.org/writings/james.pdf [Accessed March 28, 2010]

Johnson, P (2009): The 21st Century Skills Movement, in *Educational Leadership,* 67 (1) p11.

Kahne, J and Westheimer, J (2003): Teaching Democracy: What Schools Need to Do, in *Phi Delta Kappan,* 85 (1) pp34-40 and 57-66.

Kendall, J (1990): *Principles of Good Practice in Combining Service and Learning.* Raleigh, NC: NSIEE.

Kindred Project (2010): *Kindred Project.* From Sotogrande International School: http://globallearning.sis.ac/blog/bid/50083/Global-Learning-in-action-The-Kindred-Project [Accessed November 2010]

Klute, B and Billig, S (2002): *The impact of service learning on MEAP: A large scale study of Michigan Learn and Serve grantees.* Denver, CO: RMC Research Corporation.

Lewin, R (2009): *The Handbook of Practice and Research in Study Abroad: Higher Education and the Quest for Global Citizenship.* New York: Routledge.

Marshman, R (2006): *Values, Constructivism and the IB Continuum.* Retrieved November 2010, from: www.ibo.org/ibaem/conferences/documents/ValuespaperRMarshman.pdf

National and Community Service Trust (1993): *History and Legislation.* Retrieved November 2010, from: www.nationalservice.gov/pdf/cncs_statute_1993.pdf

National Leadership Council for Liberal Education America's Promise (2008): *College Learning for the New Global Century.* Washington, DC: Association of American Colleges and Universities.

Nussbaum, M (1997): *Cultivating Humanity: A classical defense of reform in liberal education.* Cambridge, MA: Harvard University Press.

Oxfam (2006): *Global Citizenship.* From: www.oxfam.org.uk/education/gc/files/education_for_global_citizenship_a_guide_for_schools.pdf [Accessed November 2010]

Partnership for 21st Century Skills (2009): *Framework for 21st Century Learning.* From: www.p21.org/ [Accessed November 2010]

Peterson, A (1987): *Schools Across Frontiers.* La Salle, IL: Open Court.

Pink, D (2010): From *The Student News Action Network:* www.studentnewsaction.net/ [Accessed November 2010]

Porter, M and Monard, K (2001): 'Ayni' in the Global Village: Building Relationships of Reciprocity through International Service-Learning, in *Michigan Journal of Community Service Learning*, 8 (1) pp5-17.

Putnam, R (2000): *Bowling Alone: The Collapse and Revival of American Community.* New York: Simon and Schuster.

QCA (2005): *A curriculum for the future: Subjects consider the challenge.* London: Qualifications and Curriculum Authority

Ramirez, F (1997): The Nation State, Citizenship and Educational Change: Institutionalization and Globalization, in W Cummings and N McGinn, *International Handbook of Education and Development: Preparing Schools, Students and Nations for the Twenty First Century* (pp47-62). New York: Pergamon Press.

Reimers, F (2010): Educating for Global Competency, in J Cohen and M Malin, *International Perspectives on the Goals of Universal Basic and Secondary Education* (pp183-202). New York: Routledge.

Richardson, R (1976): *Learning for Change in World Society.* London: World Studies Project.

RMC Research Corporation (2007): *Impacts of Service-Learning on Participating K-12 Students.* From: www.servicelearning.org/instant_info/fact_sheets/k-12_facts/impacts [Accessed November 2010]

Roberts, B (2009): *Educating for Global Citizenship: A Practical Guide for Schools.* Cardiff: International Baccalaureate.

Salganik, D and Rychen, L (2005): *The Definition and Selection of Key Competencies (DeSeCo).* From: www.oecd.org/dataoecd/47/61/35070367.pdf [Accessed October 2010]

Shah A (2010): *Causes of Poverty.* From *Global Issues*: www.globalissues.org/issue/2/causes-of-poverty [Accessed November 2010]

Sigmon, R (1979): Service Learning: Three Principles, in *ACTION*, 8 (1) pp9-11.

Sotogrande International School (2010): *SIS Values.* From: www.sis.ac/page/?title=SIS+Values&pid=206 [Accessed November 2010]

TakingITGlobal (2010): From: www.tigweb.org/ [Accessed November 2010]

The Student News Action Network (2010): From: www.studentnewsaction.net/ [Accessed November 2010]

Toh, S H (1993): Bringing the world into the classroom: Global literacy and the question of paradigms, in *Global Education*, 1 (1) pp9-17.

Tye, B and Tye, K (1999): *Global Education: A study of School Change.* Albany, NY: State University of New York Press.

Walker, G (2006): *Educating the Global Citizen.* Suffolk: John Catt Educational Ltd.

Walker, G (2010, Autumn): Reaping the benefits of plural schools: exploiting the cultural breadth of a school, in *is – International School Magazine*, 13 (1) pp5-7.

Zhao, Y (2009): Needed: Global Villagers, in *Educational Leadership*, 67 (1) pp60-65.

Chapter 8

Language and the MYP

Adam Brown, Maggie Dickson and Sally Smitheram

Introduction

This chapter has been written by three educational leaders at the International School of Milan (ISM) who are all involved, at various levels, in the coordination of the MYP. As a team, we have been directly involved in the implementation of MYP – through initial authorization to programme evaluation. Our experience also includes MYP language A curriculum planning and mapping, standardization of assessment, language across the curriculum, English as a second language (ESL), the role of mother tongue, the central role of language across the curriculum, the centrality of the writing process across all subject areas, the promotion of reading and related reflection activities, the development of inter/trans-disciplinary units of work, and reflective portfolios.

The main focus of this chapter is what we see as being the (not always overtly) fundamental role of language within the IB Middle Years Programme. We come at the issue in three distinct sections, beginning with a discussion of the social constructivist underpinnings of the IB programmes, taking, as a starting point, Bruner's definition of constructivism according to which 'there is no unique real world that pre-exists and is independent of human mental activity and human symbolic language' (Bruner, 1986). The aim of this section is to provide a theoretical foundation for the sections that follow. The second section deals with the specific role of language A English in the MYP, and ways in which language A English teachers can help to raise standards of literacy across the curriculum. Here, particularly in light of the MYP fundamental concept of *communication*, we look at language-related objectives within each of the subject groups and consider ways in which the profile of language can be raised in every MYP classroom. In the third section we deal specifically with the place of ESL, inseparable from mother tongue development, in the MYP.

Social constructivism, language and the MYP

Constructivism, and in particular *social* constructivism, emphasizes the fundamental role of collaborative, language-based processes in making sense of the ideas of others (Roth, 1999). As is also the case for the IB Primary Years and Diploma Programmes, the MYP promotes a collaborative learning model (the learner at the centre) based largely on social constructivist principles. As Marshman contends, 'the MYP fulfills quite explicitly many accepted criteria of constructivist approaches to curriculum, approaches widely held to be vital for middle schooling if our pupils are to be truly engaged in their learning' (Marshman, 2006). Indeed, as a point of departure, it will be useful to view the MYP fundamental concepts of communication and holistic education through a social constructivist lens, in which 'knowledge is not passively received but actively built up by the cognizing subject' (Von Glasersfeld, 1989), and where the student is seen as an actively constructing agent in the learning process.

In many ways, and at many levels, *communication* permeates all MYP principles and practices. Through teacher/student communication the written curriculum becomes the taught and then the learned curriculum; students communicate their understanding of significant concepts and areas of interaction when assessed, formatively or summatively. Meaningful and constructive student communication, through collaborative group work, is one of the key approaches to learning (ATL) skills in MYP that learners must develop if they are successfully to complete the five year programme. Level-specific learning objectives are developed for these ATL skills, with *student expected outcomes* steadily becoming more demanding as students progress through the programme. In terms of communicative skills, this progression can be approximately mirrored by a developmental progression through the learning objectives of Bloom's Taxonomy (1956) – from basic remembering to analyzing, evaluating and creating.

The fundamental concept of holistic education emphasises the 'links between disciplines, providing a global view of situations and issues' (IB, 2008a). IB students should be flexible and adaptable, with the 'knowledge, attitudes and skills they need to participate actively and responsibly in a changing and increasingly interrelated world' (IB, 2008b). The MYP places particular emphasis on *trans-disciplinary skills* – skills that enable students 'to apply what has been learned in new situations' (IB, 2009a) – and it is often through these (rather than through content) that learning becomes truly holistic, and truly enduring: lifelong learning. Again, the constructivist perspective is evident. Within the MYP, meaning is actively constructed by the learner, the holistic programme model recognizing and valuing students' efforts to construct meaning when exploring the world around them. 'The MYP requires teachers to provide learning experiences that draw on students' prior knowledge and provide the time and opportunity for reflection and consolidation. This constructivist approach respects students' ongoing development of ideas and their understanding of the wider world.' (IB, 2008a)

Language, for Bruner (1986) is 'our most powerful tool for organizing experience ... and constituting realities'. The centrality of language in the MYP (underpinned by the fundamental concepts and by ATL) is further buttressed by the deeper pedagogical implications of social constructivism, where 'knowledge is a product of social processes and not solely an individual construction' (Roth, 1999). Within this model it is useful to consider Mercer's description of language as a 'social mode of thinking' that cannot be considered in isolation from the 'occasions and activities of which it is the product' (Mercer, 1995). The MYP classroom, in this social constructivist model, aspires to become a 'discourse village', a socio-cultural learning environment where 'exploratory talk' (Mercer, 1995), or 'transactive discourse... negotiation and co-construction' (Azmitia, 1998), become the principal modes of social constructivist learning. The exploratory nature of the MYP – with its emphasis on student debate and discussion, generated by open-ended guiding questions – 'fosters flexibility' in its emphasis on the 'interpretative, meaning-making side of human thought' (Bruner, 1999). Students create their own meanings in the guided construction of collaborative knowledge, a notion supported by Roth (1999) who suggests that 'expertise can be developed and employed for cognitive growth in collaborative peer groups' and by Baker-Sennet *et al* (1998) for whom socio-cultural classrooms 'provide fertile ground for the development of new ideas'.

It is important to underline, however, the point made by Mercer that learner talk and collaboration are not necessarily useful in the active construction of knowledge. For student discourse to be meaningful and constructive, certain ground rules for communication must be developed and followed, with teachers in effect serving as 'discourse guides', scaffolding students' construction of 'educated discourse' (Mercer, 1995). Mercer uses the term 'exploratory talk' to describe such communication, while for Azmitia such discourse is 'transactive' ... involving 'negotiation and co-construction'. (Azmitia, 1998) As Mercer asks: simply sitting students down 'with a shared task may stimulate talk, but of what quality?' (Mercer, 1995) The teacher (no longer omniscient) orchestrates the proceedings, emphasising social interaction, and acting as a 'discourse guide', needs to develop and reinforce ground rules that will facilitate 'exploratory talk'. These ground rules (adapted from Mercer, 1995) can be as simple as the following:

• Give reasons for your opinions.

• Listen to others and respond appropriately.

• Respect everyone's opinion.

• If you contradict someone, explain why.

• Everyone contributes equally.

ATL learning expectations for collaborative skills include: delegating and taking responsibility, accepting and analyzing others' ideas, respecting others' points of view, using ideas critically (IB, 2008a), demonstrating, as can be seen, a close correspondence to Mercer's ground rules.

The MYP is an example of a 'framework that is both context-sensitive, but is also recognisably consistent with universally recognised values and principles' (Woodhead, 1999). Among these universally recognised values is the ATL strand of reflection, whereby underlying all MYP learning and understanding is the student's ability to reflect meaningfully on areas of perceived limitation, reflecting at different stages in the learning process (IB, 2008a). This process of reflection, clearly linguistic in its articulation, is hardwired into the MYP unit planner to assessment criteria across several of the subject groups and, in particular, the personal project. Such reflective thought processes require the kind of metacognitive self-monitoring defined by Glaser as 'the ability to observe and, if necessary, reshape one's performance' (Glaser, 1999), with the MYP student becoming steadily 'more independent, more engaged and more inclined to challenge assumptions' (Marshman, 2006).

The role of language A English in the MYP: raising standards of literacy

This section focuses upon how provision can be made, across the curriculum, to enhance the literacy skills of all students studying in MYP language A English in order to enable them to access the curriculum equally, whilst still maintaining the tenets of learning through inquiry and interdisciplinary learning espoused by the MYP. 'Literacy' in this context is used in its widest application, including 'cognitive academic language proficiency' (Cummins, 1979). An examination of the MYP assessment criteria for language A English, as well as the communication-related assessment objectives within different subject groups, will attempt to demonstrate the necessity of a drive towards structured literacy (or language) across the curriculum.

Language A is the language of instruction and communication within MYP schools, and language A departments must play a dominant role in raising standards of literacy within the student body. Planning the language A curriculum in order to develop the core language skills of reading, writing, speaking, listening, viewing and presenting, through the use of language and literature texts, is the responsibility of language A teachers who have been professionally trained in this area. It is vital that these skills are taught and learned in context, at word, sentence and text level, and that prior learning is taken into account. Learning needs to be active and teaching needs to be explicit. This is especially true if, as is recognised by the IB, 'many students must access an IB programme curriculum in a language other than their mother tongue' (IB, 2008c). Moreover, explicit teaching of the objectives outlined in the MYP language A guide is imperative even for mother tongue learners, as very few students learn by osmosis – even if they do have an 'intuitive unconscious sense of how their language works'. Evidence of this can be found when asking students when they might use commas in a sentence, eliciting a response such as "when you need to take a breath", rather than "to demarcate sub-ordinate from main clauses".

Initiatives to extend language through reading are often devised, developed and implemented by language A departments, in conjunction with the school library. At ISM, half a language A lesson per week (half an hour) and one homework task is allocated for personal reading – known as PRISM. Linked to this are the reading awards where students document the books they have read, and complete an activity on every book, in a series of journals labelled from bronze to platinum level. Each level is increasingly challenging in terms of texts prescribed, and the students are awarded certificates after completing each one. In addition, every year the whole school takes part in Reading Together Week where students are sponsored for the amount they read. Fun activities take place throughout the week, culminating in a literary character fancy dress competition, and guest authors are often invited to speak to the students in an attempt to raise the reading profile, to develop in students a love of reading and to highlight the importance of literature. This event is linked to the community and service area of interaction as the money raised from sponsorship is donated to a local charity.

Teaching and developing literacy is not, however, the sole responsibility of the language A department. It is not only the language-heavy subjects such as the humanities, with their range of text types, that benefit from developing literacy through explicit teaching. Each curriculum area has its own literacy requirements or 'curriculum literacies' (Cumming *et al*, 1998) that need to be taught explicitly. Learning and understanding subject-specific terminology (vocabulary) is the basic literacy requirement relating to all subjects. In addition, it is through the medium of language that knowledge and understanding are acquired and expressed in all teaching and learning contexts. The Middle Years Programme not only promotes the fundamental concept of communication to foster the attributes of the IB learner profile; communication is also one of the key components of approaches to learning, the area of interaction 'at the core of all curriculum development and of all teaching' (IB, 2008a). Consequently, 'all teachers are, in practice, language teachers with responsibilities in facilitating communication', (IB, 2008d) a point further illustrated by Table 1, which outlines the communication component within each subject area's assessment criteria. Words in italics, directly quoted from subject guides, clearly refer to effective language use.

Many teachers, in our experience, feel that they are ill-equipped to teach language skills explicitly; that, having to cover a lot of content, there is no time to focus on the communication aspects of their curricula. In relation to the latter point, the MYP is not content-prescriptive as many national programmes are, and therefore time can be built into every unit in which to address language development. The first point is an understandable concern, but can be alleviated by in-house professional development delivered by language A teachers. There is also a wealth of support material on language teaching in every subject on the website, in England, of the Department for Education (DfE, 2011). A strategy as simple as writing key vocabulary and phrases on the

MYP Subject Area	Descriptor (top level)
Arts	'There is evidence of *purposeful expression* and *effective communication* of artistic intentions.' Criterion B, Application (IB, 2008f)
Humanities	'The *language, style* and visual representation used are *always appropriate to the audience* and purpose.' Criterion D, Organization and presentation (IB, 2005a)
Mathematics	'The student ... provides a *detailed explanation* of the importance of his or her findings in connection to real life.' Criterion D, Reflection in Mathematics (IB, 2009b)
Physical Education	'The student *reflects critically* on their own achievements, sets appropriate goals.' Criterion D: social skills and personal engagement (IB, 2007)
Sciences	'The student *communicates scientific information effectively* using *scientific language correctly.*' Criterion B: Communication in Science (IB, 2005b)
Technology	'The student *explains* the problem, *discussing* its relevance.' Criterion A: Investigate (IB, 2008g)
Language B	'The student's *vocabulary is varied, appropriate and idiomatic.* The student uses *basic and complex grammar* with a *good degree of accuracy.*' Criterion A: Oral communication - message and interaction (IB, 2008e)
Personal Project	'Ideas are *sequenced in a consistently logical manner* with appropriate transitions.' Criterion E: Organization of the written work (IB, 2009c)

Table 1: Communication components in assessment criteria of each MYP subject area

board at the beginning of the lesson, combined with a word wall displaying subject specific words and phrases and connectives that will be used throughout the particular unit, would be a step in the right direction. The communication components within each subject area's assessment criteria also need to be clarified in terms of the specific language objectives implicitly contained within them, to ensure that marking of language is consistent.

When creating unit-specific rubrics, based on the generic rubric, in order to assess students' language skills appropriately – particularly within criteria B and C – it seems to be the responsibility of the language A department to clarify what each objective entails, as they can appear ambiguous. The phrases used in 'Criterion B: organization', for example ('rarely employs organisational structures', 'sometimes employs organisational structures', 'usually employs organisational structures') can be open to arbitrary interpretation. In contrast, our own interpretation of the same intention ('Your ideas are organised simply by clustering related points in a generally logical sequence', 'Your sentences are clearly organised into appropriate paragraphs ... perhaps using topics sentences', 'Your writing is clearly controlled and sequenced and you have used a range of features that signal direction') are considerably clearer. Not only does this practice aid consistent departmental marking; it is also crucial for students who need specific criteria in order to peer-assess or self-assess assignments. MYP course leaders have stated that these criteria deliberately avoid being prescriptive and may be amended to suit the needs of each school.

The correlation between literacy levels and academic achievement is well documented: low literacy skills lead to underachievement across the board (Dykes, 2007). All teachers, therefore, have a vested interest in developing language skills as a means of improving attainment within their subjects. The role of the language A department is to lead the way in bringing all students to language proficiency for academic purposes. Language A teachers can help to facilitate literacy across the curriculum by supporting teachers from other subject areas in explicitly teaching the necessary language skills appropriate to their literacy requirements. The added advantages here are that students are given many opportunities to practise these skills in real contexts, thus embedding learning, while the transferability of language skills also allows them to realise the links between subjects sought by all IB programme curricula.

The place of ESL in the Middle Years Programme

The place of ESL in the Middle Years Programme has been much discussed since the early years of its implementation, not least because the eight subject-group curriculum model at the centre of student learning refers to language A and to language B, neither of which fully serve the linguistic needs of the ESL student. Language A is a rigorous course that 'equips students with linguistic, communicative and analytical skills' (IB, 2009a) and has been written for mother tongue learners, while language B emphasizes the importance of 'practical communication' (IB, 2008e) and of gaining competence in a modern language other than the student's mother tongue. Faced with the challenge of accessing an entire curriculum in a language that is not his/her mother tongue, the ESL learner must be offered more. In this context, through the determined efforts of the European Council of International Schools (ECIS) ESL and Mother Tongue Committee (originally known as the ESL Committee) and subsequent ECIS ESL and Mother Tongue conferences organized by passionate ESL educators and attended by illustrious speakers in the field of language cognition and mother tongue development such as Jim Cummins (2000), Virginia Collier and Wayne Thomas, it was formally established and documented in 2000 that the continued teaching of the student's mother tongue should form an inseparable part of an ESL language learning programme (Gallagher, 2008). As a direct result, in 2004 the IB published *Second-language Acquisition and Mother-tongue Development: a guide for schools* (IB, 2004), a document that states that additive bilingualism takes place in programmes that promote the development of language cognition and literacy skills in the mother tongue while English is being learned as a second language.

The guidelines suggested in *Second-language Acquisition and Mother-tongue Development* are more about good practice than about a prescribed approach, though practical examples of courses are included, as are differentiated subject-specific coursework exemplars and suggested supported-learning strategies. A range of best-fit assessments are also suggested which may then be interpreted according to school language policies. These include the use of teacher-generated ESL benchmarks, the evaluation of student cross-curricular portfolios, to the use of modified grades using language A or B interim objectives that are aligned with modified interim assessment criteria. Another example is the practice of commenting on student work rather than giving grades while learning is taking place, thus contributing to a message that inspires learning rather than penalizes ESL students in their progression towards grade-level proficiency. In this way, the ESL student fulfills the requirements for MYP certification, which are to demonstrate competence in two or more languages, including the language of school instruction, the student's mother tongue and the language of the host country in which the school is located (IB, 2008a). The school may offer the latter as a language A and as a language B course; a distinct advantage in the case of the ESL student who is a citizen of the host country.

The MYP, as part of the IB continuum of three programmes including the Primary Years Programme and the Diploma Programme, strives in its documentation – beginning with its mission statement – to address the notion of the multilingual communicator. In the context of the continuum (IB, 2008b) the language learning environment is referred to as one in which 'students feel able to take risks'. A clear connection between intercultural understanding and learning in more than one language is presented both in this document and in other IB publications. The IB learner profile describes the student who can 'express ideas and information confidently and creatively in more than one language'. The question is, how may this be achieved? In accordance with guidelines suggested in *Second-language Acquisition and Mother-tongue Development* (IB, 2004), a school's language policy should ensure that good English language learning practice takes place in an inclusive, supportive and non-threatening environment. Assessment of student language needs should be thoughtfully administered before placement at an appropriate level of a well-planned programme of study. Its delivery should consider student prior knowledge (whether declarative or procedural) in their mother tongue and embrace teaching strategies that enable the student to gain competence such that full integration into the mainstream classroom takes place. Complete access to the extracurricular, cultural and social aspects of school life should also be part of the inclusive climate of the school. Awareness must also be given to the variety of cultural and linguistic histories of the student's language learning profile, which may differ as a result of factors such as family mobility or the student having grown up in multilingual backgrounds of two or more languages with different levels of proficiency in each. Such students can only add richness to the fabric of the school community.

The MYP's guidelines for second language learning differ from those for subjects uniformly outlined in the other MYP guides. There are no stipulated lists of aims and objectives; neither are there related assessment criteria. Instead, generic descriptors suggest the elements of an effective second-language programme, such as the ability to use language confidently and to develop the communicative skills required by the whole curriculum. Some language B objectives at foundation level may apply as the student begins to learn English, as may some language A objectives as the student reaches a proficiency that enables them to access more of the mainstream curriculum with its subject specific language, at first supported by a differentiated approach. As aforementioned, ESL lies between these two sets of subject objectives. It is the responsibility of each school's management and ESL educators to craft a written curriculum with clear entrance and exit requirements that determine appropriate courses for students according to levels of proficiency. At the same time, appropriate assessment should be based around the suggested principles of MYP second-language acquisition that best serve the linguistic and social needs of the student while considering their cultural identities.

The overall important role played by subject teachers as embedded language specialists who promote knowledge through various academic linguistic genres is emphasized by the three programmes comprising the IB continuum. The significance of this claim is supported in the IB document *Learning in a Language other than Mother Tongue in IB programmes* (IB, 2008c), considered essential reading for all educators who teach ESL students in their mainstream classes. The publication explains the theoretical principles of language acquisition and formal learning, as well as the importance of maintaining the mother tongue as a cognitive asset to further language learning. It describes the lengthy process required in order to achieve full grade-level proficiency. This begins by activating prior knowledge in the student's mother tongue, then nurtures new language understanding through a range of supportive strategies and finally leads to the extended use of sophisticated written academic discourse.

One final aspect of the MYP model may be considered as a tool for ESL course planning. The MYP encourages the concept of learning as an integrated whole; it is the five areas of interaction that allow the planning of meaningful links between subjects to forge that whole, one of which is approaches to learning with its thesis based on learning how to learn. There is much relevance here for the ESL student as well as for the ESL teacher. Largely generic in its address to language learning, ATL promotes good learning skills and encourages a range of learning tools, of which learning through language forms a central part. Thus, the concept referred to by Krashen as 'comprehensible input' (Krashen, 1996) allows the student, through teacher guidance, to know how to activate their current level of language understanding in order to acquire a deeper level of proficiency. Similarly, ATL enables the inclusion of invaluable strategies which ESL learners and planners of language programmes can use for the development of reading; ATL encourages the use of supportive skills for emerging writers such as frames that impose a structure on writing as proficiency progresses, and graphic organizers that help learner planning. It allows for the planning of ESL courses that encourage the understanding of and relationship between common underlying elements in student mother tongue languages such that the transfer of oral and literacy skills can take place. 'Learning how to learn' can form the framework of the type of ESL course students entering schools offering the MYP need in order to make meaningful connections between their past and their present learning environments.

Conclusion

Throughout its programmes the IB places particular emphasis on language acquisition as crucial for 'exploring and sustaining cultural identity, personal development and intercultural understanding' (IB, 2008b). This chapter has attempted to show the multifaceted centrality of language acquisition to the MYP, as an essentially social constructivist curriculum model, implying 'a pedagogy that leads to the most substantial and enduring learning' (IB, 2008a). For learning to be truly 'substantial and enduring' our contentions are twofold:

(i) with the help of language A teachers, all teachers need to be aware of the language objectives explicitly outlined within the published rubrics in every subject guide; and

(ii) ESL students, lying as they do between two sets of not wholly appropriate objectives, must be given access to the curriculum, as well as to meaningful (and encouraging) assessment, in a way that best serves their linguistic needs.

References

Azmitia, M (1998): Peer interactive minds. Developmental, theoretical, and methodical issues, in Faulkner, D, Littleton, K and Woodhead, M (eds), *Learning Relationships in the classroom*, London: Routledge.

Baker-Sennet, J, Matusov, E and Rogoff, R (1998): Sociocultural processes of creative planning in children's playcrafting, in Faulkner, D; Littleton, K and Woodhead, M (eds), *Learning Relationships in the classroom*, London: Routledge.

Bloom B (ed) (1956): *Taxonomy of educational objectives: the classification of educational goals.* London: Longman.

Bruner, J (1986): *Actual Minds, Possible Worlds.* Cambridge, MA: Harvard University Press.

Bruner, J (1999): Culture, mind and education, in Moon, B and Murphy, P (ed), *Curriculum in Context*, London: Paul Chapman Publishing.

Cumming, J J, Wyatt Smith, C M, Ryan J and Doig, S (1998): *The Literacy Demands of the Curriculum in Post Compulsory Schooling.* Griffiths University Brisbane.

Cummins J (1979): Linguistic interdependence and the educational development of bilingual children, in *Review of Educational Research*, 49, pp222-251.

Cummins J (2000): *Language, Power and Pedagogy: Bilingual Children in the Crossfire.* Clevedon: Multilingual Matters.

Department for Education (2011): Available at: http://nationalstrategies.standards.dcsf.gov.uk/ [Accessed 13 January 2011]

Dykes, B (2007): *Grammar for Everyone: Practical tools for learning and teaching Grammar.* Melbourne: Australian Council for Educational Research.

Gallagher E (2008): *Equal Rights to the Curriculum: Many Languages, One Message.* Clevedon: Multilingual Matters.

Glaser, R (1999): Expert Knowledge and Processes of Thinking, in McCormick, R and Paechter, C (eds), *Learning and Knowledge.* London: Paul Chapman Publishing.

IB (2004): *Second-language Acquisition and Mother-tongue Development: a guide for schools.* Cardiff: International Baccalaureate.

IB (2005a): *Middle Years Programme: Humanities Guide.* Cardiff: International Baccalaureate.

IB (2005b): *Middle Years Programme: Sciences Guide.* Cardiff: International Baccalaureate.

IB (2007): *Middle Years Programme: Physical Education Guide.* Cardiff: International Baccalaureate.

IB (2008a): *Middle Years Programme: From Principles into Practice.* Cardiff: International Baccalaureate.

IB (2008b): *A continuum of international education: the Primary Years Programme, the Middle Years Programme, and the Diploma Programme.* Cardiff: International Baccalaureate.

IB (2008c): *Learning in a Language other than Mother Tongue in IB Programmes.* Cardiff: International Baccalaureate.

IB (2008d): *Guidelines for Developing a School Language Policy.* Cardiff: International Baccalaureate.

IB (2008e): *Middle Years Programme: Language B Guide.* Cardiff: International Baccalaureate.

IB (2008f): *Middle Years Programme: Arts Guide.* Cardiff: International Baccalaureate.

IB (2008g): *Middle Years Programme: Technology Guide.* Cardiff: International Baccalaureate.

IB (2009a): *Middle Years Programme: Language A Guide.* Cardiff: International Baccalaureate.

IB (2009b): *Middle Years Programme: Mathematics Guide.* Cardiff: International Baccalaureate.

IB (2009c): *Middle Years Programme: Personal Project Guide.* Cardiff: International Baccalaureate.

Krashen S (1996): *The Natural Approach: Language Acquisition in the Classroom.* Highgreen, Northumberland: Bloodaxe Books Ltd.

Marshman, R (2006): Available at: www.ibo.org/ibaem/conferences/documents/ValuespaperRMarshman.pdf [Accessed 13 January 2011]

Mercer, N (1995): *The Guided Construction of Knowledge: Talk amongst Teachers and Learners.* Clevedon: Multilingual Matters.

Roth, W (1999): Authentic School Science: Intellectual Traditions, in McCormick, R and Paechter, C (eds), *Learning and Knowledge.* London: Paul Chapman Publishing.

Von Glasersfeld, E (1989): Facts and the Self from a Constructivist Point of View, in *Poetics*, 18 (4-5) pp435-448.

Woodhead, M (1999): 'Quality' in Early Childhood Programmes – a Contextually Appropriate Approach, in Moon, B and Murphy, P (eds), *Curriculum in Context*. London: Paul Chapman Publishing.

Chapter 9

The learner profile and the MYP areas of interaction: a relationship explored

Lesley Snowball

The International Baccalaureate (IB) learner profile, initially a core component of the Primary Years Programme (PYP), was extended in 2006 to all three programmes to 'express the values inherent to the IB continuum of international education' and to 'help develop coherence within and across the three programmes' (IB, 2006). In practice, in most PYP schools the learner profile is visibly central to the school's practical implementation of the programme, but it appears to be less central and/or less visible within the other two IB programmes. While the IB MYP and Diploma Programme schools may display the learner profile attributes on classroom walls or use them as the focus for assemblies, it is clearly important that they should also be reflected in every aspect of school life, from mission statements and codes of conduct to classroom activities and assessments. In keeping with the title of this book, the learner profile has great potential for 'taking the MYP forward', both within the MYP programme itself and by creating smoother transitions between the three programmes.

This chapter will focus specifically on the learner profile attributes within the MYP areas of interaction. It will consider how they are already included implicitly, and suggest how they might be emphasised more explicitly in order to be better developed in each student, thereby facilitating a smoother transition from PYP to MYP.

What are the learner profile attributes?

It is widely accepted within the literature on school effectiveness (for example, Sammons 1995) that effective schools identify and articulate long-term aims for their students, in terms not only of academic achievement, but also of personal, social and physical development. Often expressed through mission statements, guiding philosophies, core values or overall outcomes, such aims are articulated for the benefit of school leaders, staff, students and parents in order to define the essence of what the school stands for and strives for. 'They can help give a clear focus to learning and teaching, providing a benchmark for overall evaluation, both of the students themselves and of the programme.' (Snowball, 1998) These aims should drive the whole programme and their influence should be apparent throughout the entire planning, teaching and assessment process; for example, when planning cross-curricular units of inquiry, defining grade level objectives for specific subject areas, or creating student portfolios and progress report cards.

Common feature: both ...	areas of interaction	learner profile
are transdisciplinary	'Emphasize the links between the disciplines' so that 'students see the cohesion and the complementarity of various fields of study'.	Emphasizes 'intellectual, personal, emotional and social growth through all domains of knowledge'.
aim to synthesise knowledge, skills and attitudes learned	'Address all aspects of learning including knowledge, understanding, skills and attitudes.'	Focuses 'on the dynamic combination of knowledge, skills, independent critical and creative thought and international-mindedness'.
place the learner centrally in the educational process	'Connect the development of the individual at the centre of the MYP curriculum model'.	'Places the learner firmly at the heart of IB programmes.'
provide a long-term focus	Can be described as 'interactive organizing themes which facilitate long-term learning'.	'Can be considered as a map of a lifelong journey in pursuit of international-mindedness.'
establish a context for teaching and learning	Provide 'perspectives through which teachers and students consider teaching and learning, approach the different disciplines and establish effective connections'.	'Provides a clear and explicit statement of what is expected of students, teachers and school administrators in terms of learning, and what is expected of parents in terms of support for that learning.'
emphasize the value of inquiry and reflection	Act as 'a guide for inquiry and reflection for the students'.	Includes 'inquirers' and 'reflective' as two of its ten attributes.
act as a common focus for collaborative planning	Are 'a point of reference for team planning on the part of all teachers'.	'Provides a focus and reference point for teacher collaboration.'
provide a common language within and across schools	Are described as 'a common language used by educators and students across the curriculum'.	Acts as 'a common language for teachers and administrators across the IB programmes'.
act as a common base for all age levels and all subject areas	Act as 'an anchor for learning'.	Becomes 'the central tenet of each IB programme'... providing 'a tool for whole-school reflection and analysis'.
are key elements in the MYP personal project	Act as 'the starting point for the personal project'.	Should be monitored 'in as many ways as possible, by engaging students and teachers in reflection, self-assessment and conferencing'.

Table 1: Common features of areas of interaction and learner profile

For IB World Schools the learner profile serves this purpose, uniting the schools as part of a worldwide community sharing a culture and ethos of international-mindedness and representing a synthesis of the knowledge, skills and attitudes that students are expected to develop during their time in IB programmes. As IB points out (and as expanded in Chapter 1), IB learners strive to be:

Inquirers
Knowledgeable
Thinkers
Communicators
Principled
Open-minded
Caring
Risk-takers
Balanced
Reflective

(IB, 2006)

Optimising the relationship between the learner profile attributes and the MYP areas of interaction

Initial examination of two key IB documents reveals that the five areas of interaction (AOI) (approaches to learning, community and service, environment, health and social education, and human ingenuity) (IB, 2002) and the learner profile (IB, 2006) are highly complementary. Table 1 (previous page) shows the comparative descriptions synthesised from the two documents.

Cross-referencing the areas of interaction with the learner profile

Having demonstrated that a broad, implicit relationship exists between the areas of interaction and the learner profile attributes, it seems likely that each learner profile attribute will have a close relationship with each area of interaction, as represented by the graphic in Figure 1. The remainder of this section will highlight those relationships more explicitly, by cross-referencing the two components to show how each of the five areas of interaction can contribute to developing each of the ten learner profile attributes.

Approaches to learning

The main goal of approaches to learning (ATL) is for students to take responsibility for their own learning, reflecting on the key questions of 'How do I learn best?', 'How do I know?' and 'How do I communicate my understanding?'. ATL is about helping students to become better learners within individual subjects and across subject groups, and it should therefore lie at the core of every school's programme, playing a crucial role in the development of all the learner profile attributes.

Figure 1: The dynamic relationship between the MYP areas of interaction and the learner profile

Inquirers: Students' natural inquisitiveness will be sustained by understanding and managing their own learning; for example, by teachers supporting them in planning and carrying out their own inquiries within the context of their subject objectives.

Knowledgeable: Students can deepen their knowledge and extend connections by appreciating and comparing the nature and methodology of different disciplines. Teachers can help to make these connections more explicit by, for example, planning interdisciplinary units to integrate complementary content knowledge.

Thinkers: Students can more readily tackle complex problems and make reasoned decisions by developing and articulating a range of higher level thinking skills. Teachers can explicitly focus on thinking skills by, for example, incorporating Bloom's *Taxonomy of Educational Objectives* (Bloom, 1956) or De Bono's *Thinking Hats* (De Bono, 2000) into their planning, teaching and assessing.

Communicators: Students can become confident and creative communicators by expressing and accessing information and ideas in different formats.

Teachers can encourage this by, for example, varying the modes they use in teaching and that they require students to use for assessment purposes.

Principled: Students can take responsibility for their own actions and decisions by becoming independent and ethical learners. Teachers can hold students accountable for their own learning by, for example, insisting that sources are always cited or by requiring students to keep individual participation logs when working as part of a group.

Open-minded: Students can enrich their understanding with a wider range of perspectives by appreciating different learning styles, tools and techniques. Teachers can act as role models of open-mindedness by, for example, using new technological teaching platforms such as Moodle or Blackboard.

Caring: Students can learn to work effectively with others by demonstrating empathy, compassion and respect. Teachers can nurture an ethos of respect by, for example, openly discussing diversity and differentiation and enlisting students' support for one another.

Risk-takers: Students can approach uncertainty with courage and prudence by developing independence of thought and action. Teachers can facilitate this by, for example, welcoming non-conformist ideas and divergent thinking, and recognising them when creating assessment tools.

Balanced: Students can better manage their intellectual, physical and emotional development by acquiring a wide repertoire of skills and strategies. Teachers can help students to balance their lives by, for example, teaching them time management and stress management techniques.

Reflective: Students can better understand their strengths and limitations and therefore optimise their learning by systematically self-evaluating. Teachers can explicitly enhance students' self-awareness by, for example, presenting tools such as Multiple Intelligences profiles (Armstrong, 1994).

Community and service

The main goal of community and service is for students to develop a sense of responsible citizenship, reflecting on the key questions of 'How do we live in relation to each other?', 'How can I contribute to the community?' and 'How can I help others?' As with the learner profile, this AOI aims to extend student learning 'beyond intellectual achievement', helping each of them to 'develop a personal value system through which to guide their own lives as thoughtful members of local communities and the larger world' (IB, 2002).

Inquirers: Students develop their skills of observing, questioning and interpreting by exploring roles and relationships within their own and other community(ies). Teachers can nurture a spirit of inquiry by, for example, encouraging students to investigate the unfamiliar as well as the familiar.

Knowledgeable: Students acquire in-depth knowledge about different communities and the differences and similarities amongst them. Teachers can push students beyond surface level information by, for example, using compare/contrast and cause/effect organisers to uncover deeper understandings.

Thinkers: Students critically evaluate the characteristics of communities in order to develop their understanding of the concept of community. Teachers can provoke the use of different levels of thinking skills by, for example, planning a range of activities that require students to list, define, explain, analyse, recreate, evaluate and reflect.

Communicators: Students develop their ability to express and receive ideas and information in different ways by working with and for others. Teachers can provide opportunities for students to take on different roles within different groupings such as leader, scribe, timekeeper, mediator.

Principled: Students can better understand the values of fairness and justice and their importance to mutually respectful relationships amongst individuals and groups by developing their sense of community in both a local and global context. Teachers can explicitly teach relationship skills by, for example, using discussion circles focused on concepts such as fairness in different contexts, and using personal, class, local and global examples.

Open-minded: Students can become accustomed to seeking, evaluating and learning from a range of perspectives by developing enhanced insight into different social patterns and ways of life. Teachers can encourage students to value difference by, for example, having them record and share observations from holiday destinations.

Caring: Students can show empathy, compassion and respect for the needs and feelings of others by contributing intellectually and socially to the community. Teachers can provide opportunities for students to demonstrate their caring by, for example, establishing local links for community and service projects.

Risk-takers: Students are courageous in acknowledging and defending the rights of others and in being active members of their communities. Teachers can encourage students to interact with different cultural groups within the school and the local community by, for example, organising cross-cultural activities during and after school.

Balanced: Students balance their own personal wellbeing with that of others, being neither overly selfish nor selfless. Teachers can help students achieve such balance by, for example, discussing personal, class and community needs and wants in order to establish priorities.

Reflective: Students can assess and understand the impact of their contributions and involvement by reflecting through journals, discussions and presentations. Teachers can help students internalise the reflective process by, for example, explicitly emphasising the stages identified for this AOI – community awareness, community involvement and service, and reflection – which equate closely to the PYP action component cycle: 'choose, act, reflect' (IB, 2007).

Environments

The main goal of environments is for students to be able to deal with issues of both local and global environments, reflecting on the key questions of 'Where do we live?', 'What resources do we have or need?' and 'What are my responsibilities?' Focusing on five stages – awareness, responsibility, action, reflection and implementation – this AOI contributes to the development of the learner profile attributes through exploration of a variety of environments, their characteristics and their interconnectedness.

Inquirers: Students' enjoyment of and long-term commitment to learning can be stimulated and sustained by investigating issues of personal relevance and concern. Teachers can provoke students' natural curiosity by, for example, exposing them to a diverse range of significant environmental issues.

Knowledgeable: Students' knowledge can be extended across a broad range of disciplines through exploration of a range of local, regional, national and global environments, both natural and man-made. Teachers can help students to see connections by, for example, cross-curricular content mapping in order to plan meaningful interdisciplinary units.

Thinkers: Students' ability to think critically and creatively will be extended by analysing complex environmental issues and seeking to identify potential solutions. Teachers can nurture a problem-solving mindset in students by, for example, explicitly including in their assessment criteria higher level thinking skills such as analysing, synthesising and evaluating.

Communicators: Students' ability to communicate effectively and work collaboratively with others will be extended by working through different modes of communication and evaluating their relative effectiveness in conveying ideas and information. Teachers can encourage the development of critical communication skills by, for example, helping students to identify bias in information they receive and by offering choices in modes of presentation.

Principled: Students' sense of fairness, justice and respect can be developed through interaction with local and global issues and the complex economic, political, social and cultural considerations that often surround them. Teachers can encourage students to form, explain and sustain their own opinions by, for example, holding structured debates.

Open-minded: Students will extend their own perspectives through exposure to the perspectives of others, appreciating how the impact of different issues and solutions are dependent on individual values, roles and cultures. Teachers can encourage open-mindedness by, for example, teaching dialectical thinking skills that require students to argue from perspectives with which they do not necessarily agree.

Caring: Students can develop the desire to make a positive difference by building on their knowledge of different environments and awareness of associated issues. Teachers can nurture students' altruistic attitudes by, for example, supporting student-initiated action such as poster campaigns, bake sales, and sponsored events.

Risk-takers: Students can exercise their independence of spirit by making personal commitments to action which may not be popular or widely understood by their peers. Teachers can support such independence by, for example, highlighting historical and contemporary individuals who have fought for unpopular causes.

Balanced: Students can strive for balance by recognising and addressing bias in the information they receive and by routinely seeking and considering multiple perspectives before forming their own opinions. Teachers can formalise this need for balance by, for example, structuring tasks in ways that require inclusion of adequate justification and the citing of sources.

Reflective: Students can give thoughtful consideration to their own learning and experience by considering the balance between local and global perspectives and between personal and social responsibilities. Teachers can help students to internalise the reflective process by, for example, explicitly focusing on the five stages identified for this AOI: awareness, responsibility, action, reflection and implementation.

Health and social education

The main goal of health and social education is for students to take responsibility for their own physical, social and emotional wellbeing, reflecting on the key questions of 'How do I think and act?', 'How am I changing?' and 'How can I look after myself?' This AOI focuses on students' acquisition of knowledge and skills, and the development of attitudes and values, complemented by the ability to choose and take appropriate action, especially in regard to making choices and decisions about health and related issues.

Inquirers: Students can acquire inquiry skills and independence of thought by examining different aspects of health throughout the curriculum. Teachers can encourage students to be actively inquisitive about health-related issues at personal, local and global levels by, for example, investigating incidence, cause and prevention of different diseases.

Knowledgeable: Students can explore concepts, ideas and issues relating to medical, psychological, sociological, economic and legal aspects of health. Teachers can provide opportunities for students to become better informed by, for example, looking at one particular issue in depth in order to consider all the different aspects involved.

Thinkers: Students can develop their ability to make reasoned, ethical decisions by becoming better informed about health issues that might affect them, their communities and the wider world. Teachers can extend students' thinking skills by, for example, using De Bono's *Thinking Hats* (De Bono, 2000) to examine issues from factual, emotional, optimistic, pessimistic, creative and reflective perspectives.

Communicators: Students can increase their confidence as communicators by developing both their receptive and expressive communication skills within the relationships they form with others. Teachers can support this by, for example, teaching specific language to help students to be appropriately assertive, tolerant, empathetic and so on.

Principled: Students can learn to take responsibility for their own actions and associated consequences by developing a strong set of values. Teachers can nurture this by, for example, presenting students with moral dilemma scenarios within problem-solving activities.

Open-minded: Students are able to learn from the opinions and experience of others by appreciating the range of perspectives and factors relating to issues of health and wellbeing. Teachers can model this by, for example, being genuinely willing to listen to students' own perspectives.

Caring: Students can show empathy, compassion and respect for others by taking seriously their relationships with friends, family and the wider community. Teachers can encourage such caring attitudes by, for example, explicitly focusing on difficult aspects of relationships through role-play activities and discussion.

Risk-takers: Students can take reasoned, independent decisions by being well-informed about health issues that might confront them. Teachers can support such decisions by, for example, providing information on the issues and modelling decision-making protocols.

Balanced: Students can deepen their understanding of intellectual, physical and emotional balance by examining the effects of different health-related issues. Teachers can emphasise the need for balance by, for example, focusing on a combination of knowledge, skills, attitudes, values and action.

Reflective: Students can better appreciate their strengths and limitations by critically examining health issues that might affect them, their peers and communities, and the wider world. Teachers can encourage such self-assessment by, for example, providing regular opportunities and a variety of formats for reasoned reflection.

Human ingenuity

The main goal of human ingenuity is to develop students' ability to inquire and create, reflecting on the key questions of 'Why and how do we create?' and 'What are the consequences?' This AOI encourages students not only to engage in being creative themselves but also to examine the concept of creativity, following a protocol that considers origin, process, product, context, impact and development.

Inquirers: Students can develop their natural curiosity and develop the skills needed to conduct inquiry and research by engaging in, and analysing, the process of creating. Teachers across the subject areas can apply this by, for example, helping students to generate potential ideas for their personal project.

Knowledgeable: Students can broaden their knowledge by learning about inventors and creators from different disciplines, eras and cultures. Teachers can contribute to this by, for example, ensuring that the human ingenuity inherent in their particular discipline is explicitly examined as part of the course content.

Thinkers: Students can apply thinking skills critically and creatively by examining the fundamental nature of creativity in humans and considering the positive and negative impacts of this. Teachers can facilitate this process by, for example, presenting a range of graphic organisers that promote different kinds of thinking such as compare and contrast, cause and effect, or SWOT analysis.

Communicators: Students can use their communication skills creatively by exploring different communication systems and modes. Teachers can raise students' awareness of the effectiveness of different methods by, for example, offering choices for presentations and assessment tasks.

Principled: Students can demonstrate integrity and honesty by acknowledging the origins of ideas and information. Teachers can value such attitudes by, for example, explicitly including such acknowledgement as a key assessment criterion.

Open-minded: Students can enhance their creativity by absorbing ideas from a wide range of origins. Teachers can provide encouragement by, for example, teaching them to recognise and appreciate creativity in their peers, family members, local and global communities.

Caring: Students can show they are caring both by appreciating the creativity of others and by using their own creativity for the good of others. Teachers can provide opportunities by, for example, encouraging students to explore specific needs-based projects.

Risk-takers: Students can show courage by pursuing their own ideas. Teachers can help them develop the necessary resilience for this by, for example, sharing the processes, successes and failures of well-known inventors and creators.

Balanced: Students can maintain balance by appreciating the rewards and challenges of the creative force. Teachers can help students to optimise their creativity by, for example, teaching them how to plan using different processes and protocols.

Reflective: Students can support their learning and development by reflecting on their own creativity. Teachers can encourage students to look critically at the motivations and impacts of creativity by, for example, choosing a specific historical or contemporary invention to analyse and evaluate.

Summary

This chapter began by demonstrating a general and implicit relationship between the MYP areas of interaction and the learner profile, two key components of the Middle Years Programme. It continued by detailing a more specific relationship between the individual learner profile attributes and the five areas of interaction including, albeit briefly, practical suggestions for how teachers might make these more explicit. Given the complementarity shown in the relatively short space of this chapter, it seems fair to conclude that the areas of interaction are a potentially powerful vehicle for developing the learner profile attributes. The practical suggestions made here for integrating these two components could be further developed and could also be applied more widely to other components such as assessment criteria, in order to make a significant contribution to 'taking the MYP forward'.

References

Armstrong, T (1994): *Multiple Intelligences in the Classroom.* Alexandria VA: Association for Supervision and Curriculum Development.

Bloom B (ed) (1956): *Taxonomy of educational objectives: the classification of educational goals.* London: Longman.

De Bono, E (2000): *Six Thinking Hats.* London: Penguin.

IB (2002): *Middle Years Programme: areas of interaction.* Cardiff: International Baccalaureate.

IB (2006): *IB Learner Profile booklet.* Cardiff: International Baccalaureate.

IB (2007): *Making the PYP Happen.* Cardiff: International Baccalaureate.

Sammons, P (1995): *Key Characteristics of Effective Schools.* Ringwood: B and MBC Distribution Services.

Snowball, L F (1998): *Teacher's Guide to Curriculum Implementation.* Amsterdam: Putting it into Practice.

Part C

Implementing the MYP

Chapter 10

The role of the MYP coordinator

J Eric Robertson

Introduction

Arguably the most important element for a school in ensuring some degree of success with the MYP is senior management's appointment of an effective MYP coordinator. The MYP coordinator is charged with 'oversee[ing] the implementation and delivery of the MYP' and is to act as the central link between all stakeholders: senior management, teachers, students, and parents, as well as the IB (IB, 2000: 14-15). Certainly, as someone who has been an MYP coordinator in both Europe and Canada and is currently involved for the third time in leading a school through the implementation process, I remain humbled by the challenges MYP coordination poses.

It is more than 15 years since the MYP became an IB programme. To this point, however, little accompanying research has emerged about MYP practice; particularly its implementation and coordination. This chapter seeks to shed light on the experience of coordination from the perspectives of my fellow coordinators. It is largely based on a doctoral thesis involving two stages of empirical research. The first stage comprised semi-structured interviews with eight experienced and highly-engaged MYP coordinators, with interviews undertaken primarily by telephone. The second stage included case studies of three schools, in Canada and the USA: an international private school, a national private school, and a national public school.

Each case study involved semi-structured interviews with the MYP coordinator and a number of others involved in MYP leadership at the school. The incorporation of case studies provided the opportunity to apply the lens of distributed leadership, in which leadership is viewed to be best understood by exploring the 'interaction of [multiple] leaders, followers and their situation in the execution of particular leadership tasks' (Spillane *et al*, 2004). This approach was particularly apt, given that the IB organization recommends shared leadership of MYP implementation in the form of an education team (such as a steering committee), typically including a senior manager (Head of school or Principal), the MYP coordinator, subject leaders, and areas of interaction leaders (IB, 2000:16). This second stage of the study allowed also for triangulation, *ie*, the validation of data through cross-verification (Bogdan and Biklen, 2006). While the origins of interviewees and the school settings were diverse, the Canadian context figured most prominently, with both the American and European contexts slightly less so. Most of the schools of the coordinators involved in the study offered all three IB programmes (Primary Years Programme, Middle Years Programme and Diploma Programme). Contextual decisions were based, to some extent, on my ease of access to interviewees; more importantly, they were made with the aim of tapping a depth and breadth of relevant experience.

In the following summary of the study, I present my findings about the role of MYP coordinator in four sections. First, I present some of the main opportunities and challenges for MYP coordinators, according to my interviewees. Second, I identify key functions these coordinators have taken in response to such opportunities and challenges. Third, I examine several underlying issues that emerged from interviews as integral to understanding this role; I do so in relation to relevant MYP and education leadership literature. Finally, I consider ways forward for coordinators, schools, as well as the IB organization. In all cases, individuals and schools have been anonymised; interviewees are referred to by number.

Opportunities and challenges

The PYP and its planner fit within the boxes of the elementary school. The diploma provides a (curriculum) package for each senior subject specialist. The MYP, on the other hand, is everything to everyone. But it has to be flexible. It straddles the middle school and the high school, where teachers have very different views. It's hard to tell them to do the exact same thing. And the programme offers a solution – a big framework and an impetus for schools to bridge the two' (interviewee no. 4)

Coordinators appreciated how ambitious the MYP framework is in seeking to balance seemingly divergent elements. In incorporating both disciplinary and interdisciplinary elements, this 'cross-bred' curriculum serves as a bridge between the PYP and the DP. For coordinators, the need to ensure that the programme prepares students for the academic rigour of the DP figured prominently. The aim of holistic learning was also deemed important for the early adolescent coming from a largely singular experience at the primary school and integrated approach of the PYP.

In the implementation process, coordinators found the middle school much more compatible with the primary school than with the high school both structurally (*ie*, smaller and often with teachers teaching several subjects) and culturally (with the constructivist and collaborative dimensions of the programme). Often coordinators took advantage of the subject-based organization of high schools by implementing the disciplinary aspects of MYP first. The high school's dominant subject-based organization and accompanying norms of professional autonomy sometimes, however, appeared difficult to overcome. Interviewees felt that much resistance to the MYP constructivist approach from high school teachers was about 'being uncomfortable without a prescribed curriculum', and 'being forced to be [collaborative] curriculum developers themselves' (interviewee no. 4). As subject specialists, '[Teachers] preferred to focus on disciplinary-based diploma preparations exclusively' (interviewee no. 5). One coordinator recognized the dilemma as follows:

If MYP were more prescriptive [like DP], would collaboration [between teachers] be lost? Yes, and that's the frustrating part of this programme. It's a Catch-22. (interviewee no. 5)

One former coordinator asserted that:

The MYP is difficult to implement, not because it hasn't been thought through, but because it requires a lot of work, more than just in your subject. It requires lots of communication, experimentation. Once teachers overcome fears [and] the initial difficulty, many like the freedom – moving away from textbooks, setting curriculum, the freedom to construct something which they own. (interviewee no. 6)

Facilitating interdisciplinary work

Without natural structures (*eg*, physical organization) that lend themselves to cross-subject, grade, and divisional interaction, and, thus, to a collaborative culture, well-articulated curriculum planning had been a struggle for all schools in this study. The schools of many of the interviewees sought to overcome such challenges and to facilitate interdisciplinary collaboration through the establishment of areas of interaction (AOI) leader positions. Areas of interaction leaders are charged with the coordination of the integration of areas of interaction into the curriculum. Based on interviewees' as well as my own experience, these positions seem usually to be allocated according to area, across the grades, *eg*, MYP environments leader. These positions can also be allocated according to grade, across the areas, *eg*, grade six areas of interaction leader. MYP teachers usually take up these roles as an extra responsibility. While the roles are recommended in MYP guides (IB, 2000: 16), they were not always employed in interviewees' schools. When the roles were employed, they were not viewed as a very successful vehicle for promoting AOI, for integrating them into the student learning experience, or for facilitating interdisciplinary work between teachers, as intended. According to a number of coordinators these positions, in practice, did not usually come with release time or a natural forum for regular collaboration with staff or students, and so were not of major value to MYP implementation.

For coordinators interviewed, initial success with the interdisciplinary elements, including AOI, appears to have come by utilizing clearly defined structures, whether these were pre-existing or purpose-built, and by investing ample resources. For example, most schools had successfully implemented AOI within subject teachers' curricula. A second example of such success had been in the form of co-curricular initiatives such as excursions and off-timetable projects, which were found to be more common in private school than public school settings. As a third example, one national private school's leadership team appeared to have had the most success with AOI leaders. The school provided modest release time as well as substantive, and sometimes discrete, roles, venues, and programmes, including a timetabled classroom resource person, a course for approaches to learning, and a Duke of Edinburgh's Award programme for community service. A fourth example, also from a national private school, illustrates larger scale staff collaboration. While the MYP leadership team floundered with such work initially, they eventually decided to take a more structured approach, with a specific goal – one interdisciplinary connection between two teachers – with designated time, support, and accountability mechanisms.

Organizational barriers may make particularly difficult, if not preclude, many of these interdisciplinary initiatives for national public schools in which the MYP operates as a 'school within a school' and straddles partnering middle and high schools. Successful implementation of the interdisciplinary elements, however, appears to require more than the absence of such barriers or even the creation of new structures. The data from this study indicates that success also requires changing cultural norms. In turn, such changes require coordinators and their leadership teams' agency, *eg*, innovation. Progress, according to several interviewees, occurred by experimenting, and sometimes by learning from failures. By modeling this approach, coordinators were able to establish respect and build trust with staff. Requests for this extra work, trying new things, and fulfilling the accompanying accountability measures were then received more constructively. It was evident, nonetheless, that all interviewees struggled in trying to change mind-sets, when staff could easily retreat to what was safe, predictable, and stable – their subject-based habitats.

All interviewees agreed that, at best, this type of curriculum development was a long term goal, which would require significant resources and creative leadership – not only in changing structures but also in changing norms.

Key functions of coordinators

While the role of MYP coordinator is identified as a 'leadership position', I could not determine very well from the guides either the specific priorities of the role or its essential nature (IB, 2000: 14). The current MYP guide for implementation, *From principles into practice* (IB, 2008a), provides less detailed direction in this regard than did the preceding guide, *Implementation and development of the programme* (IB, 2000). The latter guide includes the broad summary of the coordinator's primary role referred to in this chapter's introductory section. The description of the coordinator's responsibilities, however, reads like a laundry list of administrative duties. So I now turn to the experienced coordinators as well as to their fellow school leaders, and describe and analyse these interviewees' perceptions of the coordinator's role and key functions. As a preface, I present a profile of these coordinators.

Pioneering spirit

The coordinators I interviewed can be typified as embodying a pioneering spirit. There were two constituent characteristics that clearly emerged from interviews: innovativeness and dedication. Coordinators often described themselves in ways that reflected an innovativeness: as seekers of new challenges, and as risk-takers, who enjoyed experimenting and were willing to push boundaries. Many coordinators also expressed a dedication to the ideological and pedagogical values of the MYP, despite the difficulties of implementation. The profile of coordinators seems to be one of self-selection. Those who take on this position do so because they are attracted by the opportunity to implement an innovative, idealistic programme such as the MYP; this is particularly so in the case of my interviewees, who were chosen by me for their rich, vast experience with the programme.

Key functions taken up by interviewees, from both stages of my empirical research, in coordinating the MYP will now be discussed, including what I have described as 'guide alongside', 'administrator', and 'orchestrator'. In addition, the role of senior manager and its prevalent function of 'amiable authority' will be examined.

Coordinator as 'guide alongside'

One important function of the coordinators in this study was being a guide alongside. While most coordinators whom I interviewed promptly embraced the MYP framework, many reported that their teachers sometimes struggled. This struggle had practical as well as political, social, and emotional dimensions, which the guide alongside function sought to address. I inferred from interviews that effective coordination involved a sensitive political framing of the role, in order to provide avenues for ongoing communication, support and collaboration. Accordingly, the role of MYP coordinator was usually more closely aligned with the teaching staff than with senior management. Not only did most coordinators have teaching responsibilities, they also rarely had responsibilities for evaluating teachers. Being a teacher provided coordinators with opportunities to lead by example: they could model inquiry in their own classrooms and thereby provide exemplars for teaching colleagues. By establishing their credibility and showing the value and 'do-ability' of the MYP approach, coordinators were often able to move from provider to co-constructor. Models could then be developed with (*ie* alongside) their teaching colleagues. Many of the coordinators interviewed recognized that their most important responsibility was for supporting teachers, but also noted the importance of being seen by teachers as 'one of the gang', *ie*, in partnership and solidarity with the teaching staff. This perception helped to establish trust and foster risk-taking in teachers.

There was one outstanding case in the study, which speaks well to this point. One interviewee (no. 6) reflected that, while she had exemplified the 'right' (*ie*, collaborative) spirit and approach – such as I described above – in her first implementation experience, she was not well-received in her second MYP school. Staff did not accept her as guide alongside even though she offered many exemplars and offered much support. The interviewee conceded that this second implementation experience was more of an exercise in providing expertise than an exploratory venture with colleagues. Her credibility did not appear to be based on wisdom or efficiency. Perhaps ironically, her credibility depended on whether she appeared to be willing to take risks and show her own fallibility in finding her way alongside teaching colleagues. What looked on a rational level to be an advantage was on a social and emotional level a disadvantage. This interviewee acknowledged a major structural barrier: she was not only MYP coordinator but also Principal and, as such, acted as teachers' 'boss' and evaluator. This political divide appeared to compound the social and emotional disconnect.

This example appears to reinforce prevalent views from interviewees of what is essential for a coordinator's profile and role – shedding light on the social, emotional, and political aspects, above and beyond the pedagogical and cognitive aspects, of educational change. It is evident that coordinators' contributions were better-received when emerging within a genuine collaborative process. Such contributions were less well-received when they were presented as a prescribed set of ingredients of a 'change recipe' – something that school effectiveness literature was often criticized for promoting. I suggest this lesson is important when considering both leadership and teamwork within this curriculum framework. The study suggests that while 'finding one's way' with the constructivist elements of this curriculum was a constant source of anxiety for many teachers, and even coordinators, it was also essential to meaningful change.

I note that this function of being a guide alongside, or essential aspects thereof, are not featured much in MYP literature or middle management literature more generally. Fullan (2001, 2007) suggests that in most processes of 'reculturing' (*ie*, changing culture) actions precede beliefs. The decision to commit to the external accountability mechanism becomes the lever for action. The process, however, requires someone to take initial steps in the new direction and show others the way. According to interviewees, guide alongside is a prominent function of coordination in MYP implementation. Reference to such a function, however, is brief, partial, and found only in a more technical MYP document, the *Coordinator's Handbook*, which states that coordinators should have 'a proven teaching ability and [the ability] to act as a pedagogical leader' (IB, 2007: 6). Even then, the denotation only implies political aspects and neglects completely social and emotional aspects. Both of these latter aspects have been deemed in this study as essential to the MYP coordinator role.

Coordinator as administrator

The function of administrator presented coordinators with much difficulty. Having the responsibility for asking teaching colleagues to attend meetings and produce curriculum documents meant that coordinators were sometimes perceived unfavourably. Some teachers, presumably those subscribing to a view of teachers as 'autonomous professionals', perceived such tasks as disconnected from the student experience and classroom efficacy. Other teachers, presumably those more inclined to perceive the teacher as 'collaborative professional', perceived them sometimes as disconnected from genuine school improvement. Even if such curriculum documents are intended to be the product of collaborative planning I can attest, as an experienced MYP coordinator, to their burdensome volume and length. Such administrative work is dictated by accountability mechanisms, *eg*, authorization, evaluation, and moderation. These mechanisms, then, can exert a controlling presence in the work of coordinators and, in turn, in the work of teachers.

Administrator versus guide alongside

Coordinators implied that acting as administrator was only tolerable if they were primarily perceived by teachers as guide alongside, willing to produce the same documents and support their colleagues' efforts. This balance, however, is not only dependent on agency but also on structural support such as resources. If coordinators were provided with generous release time and encountered minimal organizational barriers, there was much opportunity to strike the desired balance. If, however, coordinators were provided with only limited release time and presented with many organizational barriers, the position of MYP coordinator became narrowly defined, even controlled, by these administrative requirements. Such was especially the case in the national public schools studied. Most coordinators interviewed found their situation to be somewhere in between the worst case and best case scenarios. These coordinators had some time and opportunities for both planned and spontaneous meetings for support when teachers needed it, and not just when documents were needed. All coordinators, nevertheless, wished they could be working more with teachers in their classrooms, providing additional support and constructive feedback.

Senior manager as 'amiable authority'

I discerned from coordinators that they were dependent on their senior managers' (*ie*, Principal's or Head of school's) structural support (*eg*, staffing, meeting time, course timetabling, funding). More importantly, coordinators were dependent on their senior managers' authority in order to execute the functions of guide alongside and orchestrator effectively and to manage the many attendant responsibilities. With such essential, though unpopular, administrative responsibilities to fulfil, coordinators possessed little formal authority to ensure compliance. Coordinators were held to account by the IB as their school's lead representatives. Coordinators were, however, reliant on teachers to produce the majority of the work. As much as they sometimes 'nagged' and tried to 'chase down' non-compliant teachers, coordinators were ultimately reliant on their senior managers to call these teachers to account. Fortunately for the coordinators I interviewed, they were mainly content with the support they received from their senior managers, particularly in acting as the 'authority figure'. These coordinators certainly preferred not to have to 'play the heavy', in calling teachers to account. Several coordinators expressed frustration with lack of effective support from their senior managers. These coordinators realized, however, that any attempt to take on such authority themselves would undermine their credibility as guide alongside.

Many interviewees depicted their senior managers as 'amiable authorities'. It became evident in the case studies that those senior managers who were well respected by staff exercised the art of persuasive dialogue rather than applied coercive tactics. Such senior managers also offered ample support – resource and moral – for implementing teachers. In such cases management did not need to resort to 'playing the bad cop' in enforcing compliance by resisters. Senior managers who were not involved sufficiently in MYP implementation and were not effective 'authority figures' appeared to leave coordinators vulnerable to staff resistance.

Coordinator as orchestrator

As dependent as coordination is on the support of senior management, it is clear from the MYP literature as well as from the empirical evidence of this study that the main responsibility for this complex undertaking resides with the coordinator. I describe this function of overseeing the implementation process as 'orchestration' in which, I discerned from interviews, there were three components: chef (of curriculum elements), pace-setter (of implementation process), and connector (of people, *ie*, staff and other stakeholders). It is particularly challenging for the MYP coordinator to act as 'orchestrator'. The strategic planning and execution of such an ambitious curriculum is particularly hard for someone who holds a position of middle leadership. Such responsibilities are particularly difficult without direct control of resources (financial or otherwise) or authority over personnel. There is a sort of 'double bind' for this '[wo]man in the middle'. When problems crop up, the orchestrator usually does not have the jurisdiction to solve them but somehow must ensure, as the person to be held most accountable, that they get solved.

Literature on the general role of coordination (*eg*, Mintzberg, 1989) points to the challenge of bringing together multiple parts in complex organizations, where directive supervision is not always possible or appropriate. On the other hand, according to middle management literature (*eg*, Edwards, 1993), the '[wo]man in the middle' is particularly well positioned to mediate as honest broker the organizational dilemmas that schools must try to address. Being situated in between the senior management and the teaching faculty provides opportunities to bridge the two distinctive viewpoints. Indeed, this study indicated that orchestration was more interactive than directive. This function involved negotiation, improvisation, and recalibration according to where staff members were in their own development. There was a delicate balance between sometimes advocating for teachers to the senior management (*eg,* for time or other resources) and at other times trying to persuade senior management to demand more of teachers (*eg,* documentation submission, incorporating MYP expectations into teacher evaluations). I infer that coordinators must be politically aware, dialogically oriented, and personally persuasive in order to succeed in this function. This assessment of important traits is consistent with those found in much of the middle management literature (*eg,* Busher, 2006).

Underlying issues

I now examine several underlying issues that emerged from interviews as integral to understanding the role of the MYP coordinator. I seek to make sense of these issues through the aid of literature relating to both MYP and education leadership more widely.

Collaboration and teams

The MYP emphasizes collaboration in a number of forms: foremost, through interdisciplinary planning (as discussed earlier) as well as in the form of shared leadership of implementation (*eg,* an MYP education team or steering committee) (also discussed earlier). There is certainly an emphasis in education policy and research on 'collaboration and teams' in the implementation of school reform, generally defined as 'joint work for joint purposes' (Hall and Wallace, 1993: 103). In this context middle managers are often expected to play the role of facilitator. While education leadership literature commonly extols the virtues of collaboration, it sometimes tends to present an idealized picture. In one prominent model of collaboration, Lave and Wenger's 'communities of practice' (1991), participation is voluntary and based on professional interest. Members come motivated, with a shared goal; they participate in a process that is inclusive and arrive at a decision by consensus, with the experience improving the overall working culture (O'Neill, 1997: 79). It is more often the case, according to much education leadership literature and to MYP schools' contexts, that collaboration stems from a pre-existing, formal, often external-initiated, commitment. Furthermore, while secondary school departmental teams in many ways offer the best hope for effective collaboration, their sub-cultural nature can present a major barrier to whole school teamwork. Siskin suggests that to be more than the sum of its departmental parts, there is a need for a school to:

> ...start building bridges, supporting strong leadership within departments, but also creating a variety of committees, task forces and exchange programmes that will span them. (1997: 613)

Even so, cross-curricular collaboration is inherently more challenging than subject-based collaboration since its areas of responsibility and accountability are less defined for both teachers and facilitator, and less ownership is taken outside of teachers' immediate professional homes, *ie,* subject departments (O'Neill, 1997).

In analysing the spectrum of relevant literature, a particular approach emerges for establishing a strong, healthy collaborative process. This approach – which I will call 'constructive discourse' – not only addresses problems and conflicts but also encourages divergence as a means of achieving eventual convergence (*eg,* Heifetz and Laurie, 1997). '*Good to great*' organizations (Collins, 2001) were observed as communicative workplaces with a penchant for intense dialogue. Collins (2001) reports that 'phrases like "loud debate", "heated discussions" and "healthy conflict" peppered the articles and interview transcripts' from such organizations. As Tuckman's developmental model of teamwork (1965) suggests, 'storming' (*ie,* different ideas competing for consideration) must precede (re)-norming. By inviting different points of view, underlying issues can be examined critically (Dalin *et al,* 1993: 28). Such an approach helps to make assumptions explicit, confront entrenched professional positions, air differences, pinpoint key impediments, generate alternatives, and arrive at creative solutions (Wallace and Huckman, 1999: 207-208). Senge *et al* (1994) suggest, however, that in order for such conversations to be effective, raw debate as much as polite discussion must be transcended. According to Senge *et al* (1994), authentic dialogue fosters inquiry and shared meaning, which, in turn, can lead to skilled discussion in which consensual decisions are made. There may, occasionally, be a winning solution. More often, however, this approach is dialectical in nature – resulting in compromise which seeks to incorporate, if not completely reconcile, different perspectives. This approach may also frequently be dialogic; *ie,* different solutions may coexist, with each being applied to a different situation or setting. Constructive discourse may be particularly valuable in schools since their cultures 'are traditionally characterized more by compliance than by engagement and ownership' (Wagner *et al,* 2006, in Helsing *et al,* 2008: 461).

There are several additional though important underlying attributes of this approach, which literature suggests are important for effectiveness. First, and not surprisingly, trust and respect emerge as core values underpinning this process, especially when teachers may be particularly cynical about the extent to which the intent and outcomes of such collaboration are externally prescribed. Second, mutual reflection is recommended throughout this collaboration process of school improvement – not only reflection about where the team assesses itself to be collectively, and where it seeks to develop, but also in terms of the collaborative process itself (James, 2007). Such an honest and open approach can also serve as an emotional container for teachers within which anxieties and difficult emotions can be held (Aubrey-Hopkins and James, 2002: 316-317). As will be discussed below, the IB emphasizes self-evaluation and reflection as integral to its programmes.

I propose several caveats to this approach to collaboration. Several coordinators noted how challenging such constructive discourse can be – particularly in challenging norms of the primacy of the disciplinary curriculum as well as of professional autonomy – and recommended initiating such a process through an external facilitator. Many coordinators found the consultant assigned by the IB in the pre-authorization phase of MYP implementation helpful in this regard. There is much emergent literature on facilitating difficult conversations and fostering learning focused relationships (*eg*, Lipton and Wellman, 2003). One should not overlook that, while some such interaction takes the form of formal meetings:

> ...often much more important is the informal learning activity consisting of unscheduled discussions, debate and conversation about strategic questions that goes on continuously at all levels in the organization. (Davies, 2007: 4)

Moreover, as alluded to earlier, research on attitudinal change has long found that most of us change our behaviours somewhat before we get insights into new beliefs (Fullan, 2001, 2007). Perhaps this is why the coordinators I interviewed were so enthusiastic about MYP moderation – it is a well-defined external commitment that requires joint work. Constructive discourse appears to be more powerful during and after phases of implementation, than before. Initially giving teachers new experiences with the support of the MYP coordinator (*eg*, acting as guide alongside, as described earlier), area of interaction leader, subject leader, librarian or technology support staff provides a low-risk context. Interaction with trusted peers may come next. Eventually, however, an effective mentor provides not only increasing levels of support but also increasing levels of challenge (Daloz, 1986). Effective mentoring has a positive impact socially and emotionally, reducing professional isolation and anxiety (Bush *et al*, 1996: 140). I would contend that, if this relationship fosters trust and respect, it is here, perhaps more so than in larger group settings, that difficult conversations about norms of belief and practice might stand the best chance of being constructive (see McIntyre and Hagger, 1996: 146). In such cases, it is not only a middle manager's teaching expertise that is critical, but also their interpersonal skills of listening and feedback with their mentee (*eg*, Bush *et al*, 1996: 132; Daloz, 1986: 215-220).

Accountability and professional development

According to both MYP guides and interviewees' reported practice, the MYP emphasizes 'collaborative partnership' and 'creative professionalism'. The IB not only expects MYP schools to find unique pathways for adapting the MYP to their local settings (IB, 2000: 18). It also expects MYP practitioners to generate and share ideas and practices with others in the larger IB community and, most importantly, with the IB organization in the evolutionary development of its curriculum framework. This sharing may occur through, for example, professional development workshops, sub-regional associations, and the online curriculum centre. The IB expects MYP practitioners to consider becoming workshop leaders, guide-writers, school consultants, and evaluators (IB, 2000: 5). Thus, the emphasis on 'collaborative partnership' provides MYP practitioners with the opportunity to act as 'creative professionals' (IB, 2008b: 7).

The MYP's approaches to professional development and accountability were viewed by those involved in this study as complementary and constructive. It is apparent from interviewees that the MYP emphasis has been on presenting opportunities for school improvement and professional development, rather than on compliance and control. This perception is consistent with IB literature that depicts the organization as a supportive change agent, offering constructive feedback through authorization and evaluation visits, as well as through subject-based moderation reports. For example, the programme evaluation visit aims to be:

> ...diagnostic and constructively critical, supporting the school's self evaluation processes, informing the school's curriculum development activities, and assisting effective management and allocation of resources. (IB, 2005: 1)

Coordinators in this study appeared to have much faith in MYP accountability. On the one hand, they appreciated the pressure of such mechanisms for inducing staff to take steps towards fulfilling such expectations. On the other, coordinators felt the approach did, indeed, reflect a positive emphasis on aiding schools' self-evaluation and improvement.

Interviewees gave MYP professional development mixed reviews. There appeared, however, to be an honest, albeit sometimes critical, ultimately healthy relationship between the IB organization, MYP schools and their coordinators, which served to underpin the larger process of school implementation, improvement, and curriculum development. Interviewees certainly expressed some frustration with the limitations of IB workshops (to which all MYP schools must send at least one teacher per subject) (IB, 2007: 35). Some reservations were also expressed about other forms of guidance for school implementation of this open-ended curricular framework – for example, in terms of consistent messaging and clear, specific, and practical direction. There was, nonetheless, a realization by and eventual appreciation from coordinators that MYP professional development is a work in progress, as is the programme itself. I observed that this process seemed to have a generative, iterative quality. Many interviewees cited, for example, MYP's strength in facilitating a sophisticated network of professional exchange, not only between schools and the MYP but also between schools' coordinators, colleagues within schools, and even between the MYP and other institutions and resources. This approach positions workshops offered by the IB regional offices merely as one professional development input. As Fullan (2008) reports, successful capacity-building is accomplished when the school's culture supports day-to-day learning of teachers engaged in improving what they do in the classroom and school.

Coordinator as 'creative professional'

The impact of MYP on teachers and students is unclear, and, indeed, was not the focus of this study. MYP implementation, however, appears to have been a transformative experience for the coordinators I interviewed. In many ways, these coordinators have taken a lead in this curriculum development process in embodying creative professionalism. Those I interviewed have risen to the challenge – both in finding creative professional development solutions for their own schools and in taking the initiative to lead professional development, as well as other activities, on behalf of the IB organization (as, *eg*, workshop leader, school consultant, evaluator). It is readily evident that these coordinators have benefited immensely from such opportunities, in terms both of skills and of social and emotional fulfillment. One interviewee remarked that 'IB surprised me with the faith they put in me' (interviewee no. 5). The MYP organization and coordinators' schools have quite clearly benefited as well.

Ways forward

The framing of the role of MYP coordinator evidently provides better opportunity for promoting interdisciplinary collaboration and a more holistic school focus than does that of subject leader, whose interest is vested in pre-existing disciplinary structures. Indeed, some have proposed replacing the subject-based organization of schools with a trans-disciplinary framework (*eg*, Hargreaves, 1997). Others have proposed at least abolishing the role of subject leader as primary middle manager, in order to overcome subject-based fragmentation and resistance to collaboratively-based change (*eg*, Hannay and Ross, 1999). I suggest the middle school model of core teachers teaching multiple subjects as a worthy option to consider in MYP high schools. I remind the reader that such proposals are based on a major assumption: that interdisciplinary learning and cross-curricular collaboration are inherently worthwhile goals, a topic examined in other chapters of the present book. For the participants in this study, there was an appreciation for the value of both subject-based and interdisciplinary work. The former was considered much more practical. The latter produced mixed results, at best. Certainly the ambitious aim of implementing this cross-breed curriculum, linking middle and high schools, makes MYP coordination a difficult enterprise involving much 'messy' negotiation and delicate compromise. I find it confounding that, as effectively as interviewees appeared to mitigate such organizational challenges, there was a noticeable lack of explicit guidance from MYP guides or its professional development workshops in terms of such pedagogical leadership, change management, and collaboration. As for the difficult interdisciplinary work, a recent MYP publication (Boix-Mansilla, 2010) may provide more detailed, and thus helpful, guidance than has heretofore existed.

This study has prompted interesting questions: will this conceptualization of creative professionalism and collaborative (and evolutionary) partnership remain and become enshrined as fundamental principles of the MYP? Or were these simply opportune values at this particular stage of this nascent programme's development? While there was mainly congruence between interviewees' experiences and MYP literature in this domain of accountability and professional development, there was little explicit emphasis on the principles of creative professionalism and collaborative partnership in either the guides or professional development training. Perhaps, as the IB organization continues its rapid expansion, it will seek greater quality control according to a more neo-liberal form of managerial accountability. Certainly the IB has identified the improvement of its quality assurance mechanisms as a major strategic goal. The current IB leadership has also articulated an organizational priority of enhancing service and performance management (Beard, 2006). Whether such plans cast either educators or students and parents as clients, the above-noted principles and their emphasis on curriculum as process may be compromised. These findings suggest, however, that a more business-like relationship and more prescribed, quantifiable product might be appreciated by many educators, and particularly subject teachers. It appears to be highly engaged coordinators, such as those interviewed, who have prospered most with the MYP's open-ended, evolutionary framework. The IB Diploma Programme, a much more prescribed, neo-liberal-oriented product, is certainly more financially viable for the organization than is the MYP (IB, 2004) and arguably more popular with practitioners and other school constituents.

On the other hand, another of the IB's major strategic goals is to widen access to its programmes, particularly for national public schools (IB, 2004). In this study, I discovered that variation in school settings can only be accommodated by a flexible curricular framework. Indeed I wonder, on the basis of these findings, if the ambitious aims and the resource support required to implement the MYP make it an unrealistic fit for many national public, especially high, schools. Regardless, I suggest that the IB must manage this organizational dilemma carefully, in seeking to balance the desire for quality control and access with its inherent need for flexibility.

I certainly learned much from this study, by examining and articulating core MYP principles, strengths, and challenges of implementation as well as functions of coordination in relation to school setting, senior management, and teaching faculty. Through the process of research and reporting I could not help but reflect on my own experiences as MYP coordinator. As I am both an MYP researcher and practitioner, this study is my contribution to the on-going constructive discourse within the IB community about the role, responsibilities, opportunities, and challenges associated with leading IB programmes.

With the dearth of research relating to the IB, and particularly the MYP, I hope further studies will follow. A large scale survey of MYP coordinators on a core issue such as professional development or key functions, a comparative study of the three IB programme coordination roles, or an analysis of MYP implementation from the perspectives of teachers or senior managers – all are examples of likely valuable additions to the discussion initiated by this study, as well as potentially helpful sources of information for the IB. Indeed, I hope that this study could be a basis for related 'knowledge for action' projects, particularly in collaboration with the IB organization, which could draw on and inform MYP practitioners and researchers in the wider IB community.

References

Aubrey-Hopkins, J and James, C (2002): Improving Practice in Subject Departments: the experience of secondary school subject leaders in Wales, in *School Leadership & Management*, 22 (3) pp305-320.

Beard, J (2006): *Sharing the Vision.* Keynote address to IBNA Regional Conference, Bahamas, July 14th 2006. Available at: www.ibo.org/ibna/documents/SharingTheVision_000.ppt, [Accessed 28 July 2009]

Bogdan, R and Biklen, S (2006): *Qualitative research for education: An introduction to theories and methods.* Fifth Ed. Boston: Allyn and Bacon.

Boix-Mansilla, V (2010): *MYP guide to interdisciplinary teaching and learning.* Cardiff: International Baccalaureate.

Bush, T, Coleman, M, Wall, D, and West-Burnham, J (1996): Mentoring and continuing professional development, in D McIntyre and H Hagger, (eds), *Mentors in schools: developing the profession of teaching.* London: David Fulton, pp121-143.

Busher, H (2006): *Understanding Educational Leadership: People, Power and Culture.* Maidenhead: Open University Press.

Collins, J (2001): *Good to Great: Why Some Companies Make the Leap... and Others Don't.* New York: HarperBusiness.

Dalin, P, Rolff, H, and Kottkamp, R (1993): *Changing the School Culture.* London: Cassell.

Daloz, L (1986): *Effective Teaching and Mentoring.* San Francisco: Jossey-Bass.

Davies, B (2007): Developing sustainable leadership, in *Management in Education*, 21(3) pp4-9.

Edwards, A (1993): Curriculum Co-ordination: a lost opportunity for primary school development? in *School Leadership & Management*, 13 (1) pp51-59.

Fullan, M (2001): *Leading in a Culture of Change.* San Francisco: Jossey-Bass.

Fullan, M (2007): *New Meaning of Educational Change.* 4th Ed. New York: Teachers College Press.

Fullan, M (2008): *The Six Secrets of Change: What the best leaders do to help their organizations survive and thrive.* San Francisco: Jossey-Bass.

Hall, V and Wallace, M (1993): Collaboration as a subversive activity: a professional response to externally imposed competition between schools? in *School Leadership & Management*, 13 (2) pp101-117.

Hannay, L and Ross, J (1999): Department Heads as Middle Managers? Questioning the Black Box, in *School Leadership & Management*, 19 (3) pp345-358.

Hargreaves, A (1997): Restructuring Restructuring: Postmodernity and the Prospects for Educational Change, in A H Halsey, H Lauder, P Brown and A Stuart Wells, (eds), *Education: Culture, Economy, and Society.* Oxford: Oxford University Press, pp338-353.

Heifetz, R A, and Laurie, D L (1997): The work of leadership, in *Harvard Business Review,* 75(1) pp124-134.

Helsing, D, Howell, A, Kegan, R, and Lahey, L (2008): Putting the 'Development' in Professional Development: Understanding and Overturning Educational Leaders' Immunities to Change, in *Harvard Educational Review,* 78 (3) pp437-465.

IB (2000): *Middle Years Programme: Implementation and development of the programme.* Geneva: International Baccalaureate.

IB (2004): *Strategic Plan of the International Baccalaureate Organization.* April, 2004. Geneva: International Baccalaureate.

IB (2005): *IBO Guide to programme evaluation.* Cardiff: International Baccalaureate.

IB (2007): *Middle Years Programme: MYP coordinator's handbook 2007-2008.* Cardiff: International Baccalaureate.

IB (2008a): *Middle Years Programme MYP: From principles into practice.* Cardiff: International Baccalaureate.

IB (2008b): *Towards a continuum of international education.* Cardiff: International Baccalaureate.

James, C (2007): Collaborative practice: the basis of good educational work, in *Management in Education,* 21 (4) pp32-37.

Lave, J and Wenger, E (1991): *Situated learning: legitimate peripheral participation.* Cambridge: Cambridge University Press.

Lipton, L and Wellman, B (2003): *Mentoring matters.* Sherman, CT: MiraVia.

McIntyre, D and Hagger, H (1996): Mentoring: Challenges for the Future, in D McIntyre and H Hagger (eds), *Mentors in schools: developing the profession of teaching.* London: David Fulton, pp144-164.

Mintzberg, H (1989): *Mintzberg on management: inside our strange world of organizations.* New York: The Free Press.

O'Neill, J (1997): Managing through teams, in T Bush and D Middlewood (eds), *Managing People in Education.* London: Paul Chapman Publishing, pp76-90.

Senge, P, Kleiner, A, Roberts, C, Ross, R, and Smith, B (1994): *The Fifth Discipline Fieldbook: Strategies and Tools for Building a Learning Organization.* New York: Doubleday.

Siskin L (1997): The challenge of leadership in comprehensive high schools: school vision and departmental divisions, in *Educational Administration Quarterly,* 33 (1 suppl) pp604-623.

Spillane, J P, Halverson, R and Diamond, J B (2004): Towards a theory of leadership practice: a distributed perspective, in *Journal of Curriculum Studies,* 36 (1) pp3-34.

Tuckman, B (1965): Developmental sequence in small groups, in *Psychological Bulletin,* 63 (6) pp384-99.

Wagner, T, Kegan, R, Lahey, L, Lemons, R, Garnier, J, Helsing, D, Howell, A, Rasmussen, H T and Vander Ark, T (2006): *Change leadership: A practical guide to transforming our schools.* San Francisco: Jossey-Bass.

Wallace, M and Huckman, L (1999): *Senior Management Teams in Primary Schools: the quest for synergy.* London: Paul Chapman.

Chapter 11

The MYP: a wider stakeholder context

Dominic Currer

The nature of middle years schooling

I write this chapter not as a seasoned academic, or International Baccalaureate (IB) aficionado, but as a teacher, Headteacher and parent: one who has learned from sometimes painful experience, and sought to understand his role in the creation of a high quality learning environment for teenagers. It is in this context that I believe it is worth dwelling briefly on the aims of education in general, how they relate to the IB, and how our schools choose to pursue them. School mission statements often include phrases such as 'global citizens', 'creative problem solvers', or 'lifelong learners'. Rarely do they allude to a need for science, mathematics or English. The IB mission strives to develop 'intercultural understanding and respect', and to help schools create 'compassionate life-long learners' (IB, 2011), yet nowhere does it state that this might best be achieved through mastery of core sets of skills in independent subject areas (though this is implicit in the frameworks proposed thereafter). As places of learning, most schools choose and are guided to pursue their missions through a time-honoured, traditional approach to curriculum and learning: one that emphasises the importance of discrete subject areas, and the acquisition of subject skills – sometimes attempting to demonstrate links across them in the hope of implying connectivity.

Such a framework or approach, born of a Victorian desire to educate a growing middle class in a way that was different from either the working or upper class, has remained almost constant for more than the last 100 years (White, 2007). We stick rigidly to it, perhaps because nobody has come up with a better or more widely accepted alternative, but additionally because the demands of university entrance processes in most countries the world over are subject to demonstration of subject specific proficiency. Do the subject disciplines as we know them really lend themselves effectively to creating global citizens, promoting intercultural respect or instilling a lifelong love of learning? Or should we perhaps consider a significant shift in our pedagogy, programmes and policies at school – one which more effectively empowers us to achieve the lofty goals our missions set out for us? Time perhaps to rethink not only the MYP, but education in schools in its entirety?

Aims-based alternatives have been suggested. A curriculum based on 'personal fulfilment, social and civic involvement, contribution to the economy, and practical wisdom' (White, 2007) might more adequately help us to address our missions and achieve the aims set out by the IB. Business leaders have regularly remarked that the core skills with which our students exit school and university might no longer provide adequate or even appropriate foundations for them to be successful in later life (Neville-Rolfe, 2010). I suggest, then, that there is a fundamental disconnect between mission and practice that, in taking the MYP and all IB programmes forward, we very genuinely need to address. If the MYP is to progress in a meaningful way, then a thorough overhaul and re-think is necessary. Not one that bases change in the context of its current paradigm, but rather one that revisits the fundamental purpose upon which our schools and programmes are founded, and one that through the tools of its parent organisation (the IB) helps bodies such as the UK's universities to see the folly of outdated methods for the selection of students for university entrance.

For the purposes of this chapter, however, we must assume that the MYP, with no fundamental change in philosophy, will move forward in a relatively unchanged format, and that such a radical review of the programme is unlikely. I will therefore seek to address the wider context within which we are attempting to implement the MYP in our schools, and will assume continuity of the present system for the immediate future. In this regard, the underlying principle behind addressing the school and developmental context of the students we serve is that it should frame the development of curriculum programmes we choose to adopt and deliver if we are effectively to meet the very specific needs of learners at this age.

Regardless of curriculum programme, it is critical to give careful consideration to some of the underlying factors that contribute toward schools' success in achieving the goals of their missions. Namely, the broader context of the home-school relationship, key elements of communication, the timetable and daily schedule within which the curriculum is delivered and, perhaps most importantly, the significant development that adolescents and pre-adolescents go through as they attempt to succeed in the goals we lay down for them through the MYP. If we attempt to optimise all of these factors, then surely we cannot help but be successful. But at times we should also reflect carefully on the appropriateness and adequacy of the MYP as a programme that not only effectively prepares our students for later life, but also critically optimises their chances of success within the IB's Diploma Programme. Is the curriculum programme for 12-13 year-olds also the one that will be most successful for pre-diploma students needing a skills- and content-heavy preparation for a demanding set of examinations? Indeed are there grounds to suggest that a programme covering the gap from the IB Primary Years Programme (PYP) through to the IB diploma really does serve the needs of all students?

I start off every academic year by making a careful and clear point to staff that we are not employed simply to teach mathematics, English or science; or to deliver the MYP, PYP or DP. We are employed to teach students, and this has a variety of ramifications:

1. Whilst we might be passionate about our subjects, our priority is to engage, enthuse, motivate and inspire others to share that passion, not just to deliver content in a bland and forthright presentation.

2. Whilst we might be passionate about any one of the IB programmes, the students come first, and should not be squeezed into frameworks so that authorisation teams can tick boxes.

3. Educating students goes beyond delivering subject skills or content; it involves creating and maintaining programmes that offer social and personal opportunities for growth outside the classroom.

4. Establishing a personal rapport and relationship with the students we teach and their parents is paramount in helping us to understand those students and consequently to guide and assist them with their work and decisions.

With the above in mind, middle level education must take a holistic focus; an approach that is not simply subject-orientated, but that takes account of the personal and social needs, and development, of learners at this key stage of development. The teenage years are difficult to say the least: for educators, parents and indeed for the students themselves. Ongoing issues of brain and hormonal development, body changes, peer pressure and social insecurity constantly play on the minds and bodies of our children. They are often as confused and concerned about their futures as are their parents and teachers. The modern world places significant demands and pressures on them that have not existed in previous generations: instant access to information, media dominance of role-modelling, personal increases in screen time (leading to less physical interaction), and changing family structures and traditions. It is critical therefore that schools and curriculum developers devote enough time at this age level to understanding the social and developmental context within which learning will take place, in order to ensure that we effectively engage students and their support networks in meaningful, relevant and connected partnerships.

The developmental context

Teenage brain development has been increasingly well-documented and discussed (see, for instance, Willis, 2007; Wolfe, 2010) academically and in the media. The more we learn each year, the more we understand teenage behaviour and therefore understand how we might adjust our schools and education in order best to support the children whose needs we aim to serve. During early adolescence there is a clear spurt of brain growth (around Grade 6: age 12, approximately), so much so that it is the second most prolific time of brain growth since birth. There is an explosion of connective activity going on between neurons in the brain as new skills are learned. This is the time when our children want to know it all. They learn the names of the planets, and know every player on the football team they support (and most players in the league for that matter). They carefully observe rules and procedures, and actively participate in debate and conversation. Of course these are gross generalisations, but it is a truism that a student's average behaviour, class participation, and eagerness to engage at around Grade 6 stands in stark contrast to the behaviours observed in a large number of those same students only a year or so later. At this stage of their development, they have mastered most of what we have asked them to do. Their brains are wired to repeat, respond and react in a manner that reflects their upbringing and experience to date, and decisions are made based on the expectations and guidelines offered by parents and educators.

However, during adolescence sudden changes happen. As the brain develops from back to front, the decision-making centre changes focus, and the emotional centre of the brain (the amygdala) becomes far more active. The frontal lobe (associated with analytical decision-making) is not yet fully developed – and will not be until perhaps the mid-twenties. Adolescents therefore often make decisions based on emotional interpretation and response rather than on a rational analysis of a situation. This explains the frequent mood swings, monosyllabic conversation, propensity to fall quickly in and out of friendships, and preoccupation with self. Studies show that teenagers often mistake emotions such as fear for sadness, or anger for confusion (Baron-Cohen; 2003). This inability to identify correctly emotional cues can often escalate an argument into a crisis, and might help to explain why teenagers see hostility in a situation where there is none. There is some evidence to suggest that the problem is exacerbated by the increasing amount of screen time to which our children are subjected (Sigman, 2009). Recent studies reveal that whilst television and computers might have clear educative benefits, they fail to help our children to develop empathy – a core skill needed when interacting with others. Put this mix together and witness the emotional powder-keg that is the modern teenager!

At the same time as the brain is undergoing monumental development, the body is also developing at a rapid rate. The adrenal glands pour in chemicals as teenagers mature. These have a direct influence on the regulation of mood, excitability and stress response. Hairs begin to sprout in places previously barren, and bodies begin to adopt an adult form. All of this leaves the majority of our teens feeling confused, insecure, self-conscious and worried about how they are perceived by others. In this regard the tendency of teenage girls to stare endlessly into mirrors, often viewed as narcissistic, is in fact evidence of self-doubt and unease with the changes they are going through, rather than simple vanity. The dominance of emotion in decision-making can lead to teenagers seeking 'highs', or risk-taking. The evolutionary reason for this might lie in the promotion of exploration and independence, but its modern-age consequence can often be teenage high-risk activity, alcohol or drug abuse; certainly it leads to relatively frequent relationship building and breaking among teens. In essence, adolescents are experiencing a desire to experiment, experience and excite before they are yet ready to exercise controls, limits and reasoning – perhaps akin to putting a non-driver behind the wheel of a finely tuned sports car and turning on the ignition! In brief, our teens at this stage are a potentially explosive mix of potential and vulnerability.

The need to sleep so that teenage bodies can regenerate becomes greater (around 9.5 hours per night is average at this age), and motivation at school can take a significant downturn. Teenagers become fiercely independent, question their parents, spend more time with friends and yet at the same time do not want to be different. It stands to reason therefore that in school they are often far more interested in social relationships, exploring their sexuality and taking risks than they are in the finer points of a soliloquy in *Hamlet*. At this stage of their development, again in contrast to the previous year, brain growth progresses at only half the speed of any earlier time in their lives. The explosion of connectivity around Grade 6 is followed by a period of 'pruning down' or 'weeding out' of connections as the brain rejects those that are seldom used, but 'hard-wires' those that are used more frequently. At this age, adolescents engage in behaviours that offer a high excitement factor with low effort. Little surprise then that schoolwork can suffer, and that students at around 13-14 years-old can often seem to regress. So how can schools help?

The home-school partnership

At home and at school the tell-tale signs are obvious: forgotten homework, lethargy, untidiness, a lack of focus, constant daydreaming, rebellion, emotional outbursts, risk-taking and a propensity to challenge previously accepted norms. Parents are often left feeling bewildered, rejected, isolated and angry as they struggle to come to terms with their child's need to seek independence and question their authority. Particularly for international schools, local support structures for parents might be limited by culture and language barriers, compounding parents' feelings of isolation and insecurity. Yet at this stage of development a caring, well-informed and engaged home is critical to ensure that our children receive enough guidance and support to help them make the right choices in order to be successful. It can be overwhelmingly tempting for parents to disengage, and expect more from schools, but the evidence clearly demonstrates that what students at this age need most is structure, consequence, guidance and care at home, supported by a regular and ongoing dialogue with school. Partnership is key.

Effective schools therefore make time to engage parents in meaningful learning about their children's development – to reduce the stress and to help them to see that the 'abnormal' behaviours they witness at home are in fact perfectly understandable in a developmental context. Taking time from our evening programmes or even out of the school day to engage parents in this kind of dialogue has significant benefits for schools, families and consequently for our students. It reduces stress, improves communication, and empowers parents and teachers alike. It promotes shared goals, emphasises partnership, and helps to ensure a consistent approach at home and at school. Further development of the MYP must recognise the importance of giving time and thought to such activities in schools. Regular opportunities for parents to engage with teachers in dialogue about their son's or daughter's progress provide the support that both parties need to help middle level students keep focused and organised: this might mean days where the timetable is collapsed, and families all come in to school to discuss progress – either with class teachers or with tutors. It might mean more evenings, or it might involve more informal opportunities to meet on an *ad hoc* basis. Either way, schools must work hard to bring parents in and to inform and engage them in their child's learning.

Investment in technology that provides regular and updated information on homework assignments and deadlines can help even busy, travelling parents to keep tabs on their monosyllabic, uncommunicative teens' ability to cope with the demands of schoolwork and balance increasing numbers of assignments. If we know that students at this age can be forgetful, disorganised and disengaged, then why would we not want to help them and their parents to set targets, oversee progress and monitor timelines? But this requires time and commitment from teachers to regularly update homepages or software programmes – difficult if a curriculum programme is already over-burdened with subject expectations, and teachers feel pressed to deliver enough content to prepare students effectively for the demands of the IB diploma or other such programmes. Modern methods of communication can open doors to regular, constructive and supportive dialogue on progress. All of this takes time and investment, thought and care; and a very real school commitment to communication. We so often get caught up with the demands of content and skills delivery that important matters such as these get pushed to the sidelines. But effective home-school partnership is one of the cornerstones of good middle-level education. Any consideration of taking the MYP forward must take into account the time that schools should dedicate to such activities and seek to emphasise their importance.

The learning environment

Teachers of adolescents, for their part, are often left feeling frustrated, challenged and sometimes powerless to help guide their students towards the lofty academic goals that many of our schools set out for them. The sometimes competing priorities of providing academic rigour to prepare students effectively for subject specific demands, and the delivery of an effective pastoral system to care for and support them, make it difficult to find a balance – and of course that balance is different for each child. Our overall school structures can make a significant difference in this regard. It stands to reason that, when teachers teach multi-grade levels such as MYP and DP, their 'dream time' is often with the diploma students and programmes. There is a very real immediacy of these students' needs to pass examinations and to get into a university, while there is more personal accountability as results will be known to the school administration or, in some cases, published to a wider community. For some of our teachers there is more professional pleasure in the dialogue that they can engage in with, and the level of academic response from, older students. Younger non-examination classes often simply take second place. Of course many schools and teachers argue that it is important to have multi-grade involvement so that teachers have an understanding of both where the students 'are coming from' and where they 'are going to'. Nonetheless the problem remains. Surely, however, with our knowledge about the demands of a specific set of developmental characteristics for early adolescence, there are sufficient grounds for dedicating groups of teachers to the specific task of supporting, caring and providing for an academic programme that prioritises their learning and growth?

For many international schools this might mean a review of structure: away from a primary/secondary model and towards a middle school model (Grades 6-8 (ages 12-15) for example). I would suggest that we then go further still – though I accept this is only possible in schools of a certain size – and allocate staff to grade-specific teams. (The Grade 7 team for example might have a mathematics teacher, an English teacher, a science teacher and so on, dedicated specifically to the grade level.) This is not a new idea and was recommended some years ago by institutions such as the National Middle School Association in the United States (NMSA, 2003). The benefits for children are clear: the instant creation of a support structure where teachers have an intimate and shared knowledge of children in a single grade level, the ability to plan cross-disciplinary activities, and a built-in team ready to lay on after-school activities, class trips and so on. Of course many teachers might not like being confined to a specific grade level, but let us not forget that schools are for children after all. For the MYP this might suggest the opportunity to investigate offering a three year programme geared towards the specific needs of middle schools, and the separate development of a pre-IB diploma programme if the diploma is to remain as it is with subject-specific syllabi and demands. Such an approach might provide the IB with an opportunity to develop a completely new approach to middle level education.

Furthermore, the way in which we design the school day – crossing times between classes, length of lessons, sufficient breaks between classes, and down-time in the middle – can make a significant difference. If we know that teenagers are frequently disorganised and forgetful, how does it help to construct a daily timetable with eight different teaching blocks – complicating the amount and type of information students receive in a day and potentially overloading them with homework? Better to reduce the number of periods and create a schedule that rolls over two weeks, I would argue, than try to cram it all in at once. Better to create time and space for dialogue or exploration of ideas than rush from one class to another in a panicked attempt to get as much in as possible.

The creation of an appropriate system for pastoral care (tutor groups/advisory programmes, opportunities to deliver a personal, social and health education (PSHE) programme, morning homerooms) is critical to support our teens, help them understand themselves, and guide them through these difficult years. Small groups of students with teacher advocates who serve as the first point of contact for parents, and develop a clear picture of the whole child, can help to reinforce home-school communication and even communication within schools – providing effective support networks for our students. Homeroom teacher comments on reports help parents to collate and understand a bigger picture and offer a 'point-person' for contact and communication. Yet so many schools relegate such systems to the sidelines in favour of cramming in yet more subject teaching time, as we are forced to chase an outdated dream of subject proficiency. If the MYP is to move forward in a way that supports and understands the developmental needs of middle level students, time and thought must be given to the broader context in which schools must deliver the curriculum framework.

Clearly we are functioning within an educational paradigm (centred on the traditional subject specific disciplines) that has not shifted significantly for the last 100 years or so. There is a drive from some schools, backed by business, to reassess the aims of our curriculum and move towards a model that not only supports what we now know about development, but additionally takes into account the need for a 21st century skill set, and the desire to nurture responsible contributions towards a local and global community. Additionally the plethora of new courses, developing work-specific skills at universities, demonstrates a strong desire for review and change on the part of tertiary education. Unfortunately, there is no way that both sets of institutions can effectively come together to manage this change and create school-university-business skills continuity when the method by which students are selected and approved for university entrance relies so heavily on the demonstration of the mastery of subject-specific skill sets through an outdated end of course assessment such as the IB diploma, Advanced Placement (AP) or A level. Without a thorough review of university entrance requirements and processes, there will be no (needed) overhaul of the DP or other programmes like it, and consequently a fair degree of impotence on the part of curriculum planners when it comes to appropriate re-invention of education at the middle level. Whilst we aim to help our students to become global citizens and lifelong learners, to develop in them core skills of teamwork, problem solving and communication, the very practical reality is that our students want to get into universities, and we are there to help them. In summary, therefore, until there is a drastic shift in the way universities review applications, and the way in which schools carry out exit assessments, any review of the MYP and all other curriculum programmes will be bound by the limits imposed on it by an anachronistic university entrance selection process, with all that this implies for education earlier on.

We can, however, improve learning opportunities and care for students in our given paradigm by thoroughly reviewing the support structures that we offer in schools. As the MYP is taken forward, a clear understanding that schools should give appropriate time to communication, guidance, care and support in a curricular and extracurricular context must frame the way in which the programme evolves. This might have a significant impact on time expectations for subject areas or indeed on the programme itself – laying out clear guidelines for a pastoral curriculum and sets of support structures to help our students navigate the sea of content and skills we throw at them in a meaningful and relevant way. Such an approach would prepare them not only for success in future examinations, but also to be responsible and effective citizens in an increasingly complicated and interconnected world.

References

Baron-Cohen, S (2003): *The Essential Difference: The Truth about the Male and Female Brain.* New York: Basic Books.

IB (2011): Available at: www.ibo.org/mission/ [Accessed 10 January 2011]

Neville-Rolfe, L (2010): They Can't Read, Can't Write, Keep Time or Be Tidy, in *The Guardian,* 10 March 2010.

NMSA (2003): *This We Believe: Successful Schools for Young Adolescents.* Westerville, Ohio: National Middle School Association (NMSA).

Sigman, A (2009): *The Spoilt Generation.* London: Piatkus.

White, J (2007): What schools are for and why, in *IMPACT Paper No. 14.* Philosophy of Education Society of Great Britain.

Willis, J (2007): *Brain Friendly Strategies for the Inclusion Classroom.* Alexandria, VA: Association for Supervision and Curriculum Development (ASCD).

Wolfe, P (2010): *Brain Matters: Translating Research into Classroom Practice.* (2nd edition). Alexandria, VA: Association for Supervision and Curriculum Development (ASCD).

Chapter 12

Introducing the MYP in a national context: a UK independent school perspective

Matthew Albrighton

The Wellington College context

Wellington College is an independent coeducational boarding school in east Berkshire, England, comprising 1000 students and 140 teachers. The school was founded by Queen Victoria as a memorial to the Duke of Wellington with the first students being admitted in 1859. Students enter Wellington in Year 9 (approximately age 13), which is Year 3 of the MYP. The school is academically strong: for the 2010 intake, for instance, there was a 3:1 ratio of applicants to places. Just over 12% of students are international, with a further 5% being UK nationals living abroad. In total over 30 non-UK nationalities are represented in the community with no one group being significant in number. Wellington has been authorised to offer both the IB diploma, from 2008, and MYP, from 2009. Both programmes currently run in parallel to the national qualifications, A level and the General Certificate of Secondary Education (GCSE) respectively.

Since its first student walked through the gates, Wellington College has focused on developing the whole student. Academic study is only part of the process. The school offers access to education across a range of aptitudes, whether linguistic, logical, musical, bodily-kinaesthetic, spatial, interpersonal or intrapersonal (Gardner, 1999). Together with an appreciation of the spiritual perspective, the aim is to offer entry points for all students and then help develop areas of learning for which a student does not have a natural disposition. In recent years, attitudes amongst teaching staff towards the national qualifications offered have hardened as dialogue relating to the purpose of education has been initiated. Teachers have become disillusioned that the valuable work they do across all other aspects of the education process is devalued by a national system that is perceived to be losing integrity. Measures of success seem to have little to do with the actual quality of the learning and extracurricular experience.

Wellington turned to the IB for the opportunity to help return to what it had always done best and deliver a programme that recognised education of the whole person. The emphasis on the IB learner profile, the maintenance of breadth (especially the need to study a language until the age of 18), a desire for international-mindedness and the pursuit of rigour contribute to an education that is not just about examinations. Positive pedagogy is inherent within IB curricula, and recognition of learning how to learn puts students back in control of their own development. The IB promise is compelling and adoption of the tried and tested IB diploma has been relatively straightforward. Introducing the MYP, however, has been more problematic.

The majority of the discussion that follows explores common responses to the implementation of the MYP at Wellington. This provides a useful framework in which to outline strategies for success and, further, to examine many of the issues that will need to be faced. Anecdotal evidence from students, parents and teachers is drawn upon as a means of demonstrating some key points. The need for the IB to change elements of the MYP is also discussed, alongside systemic concerns relating to university recognition.

Vision, leadership and a culture of change

The MYP puts trust in teachers to design their own courses and assessment within the constraints of an objective and criterion-related framework. This may well be exciting for senior management but can in reality be quite daunting for the subject leaders and teachers. To be given essentially a blank canvas requires a level of engagement within the teaching body that most schools will not have typically experienced. Teachers (in England, as in many other countries) are used to prescribed curricula, course guides and text books. There is a great deal of rhetoric in the wider teaching community about freedom with the taught curriculum, but when the opportunity is actually offered many feel that the proverbial rug has been pulled from under their feet. Tried and tested structures are on the whole removed with the introduction of the MYP and teachers can be left, understandably, feeling quite lost and even disillusioned.

The introduction of the MYP needs strong leadership but also sensitive and thoughtful management. Success is dependent upon creating a clear vision of what is to be achieved in adopting the MYP and following it through a structured plan, while ensuring that all systems are in place to support the programme. The reports process, for example, will need to be robust. At Wellington the vision was to place holistic education in the classroom and put the student at the heart of learning. This was placed alongside a further desire to promote a uniquely exciting and stimulating school. This vision was instilled through a new mission statement long before specific discussion began about the MYP. The most important mechanic for clarifying the vision, alluded to in the introduction, is engaging the faculty in discussion about pedagogy and, more generally, the role of education. This must be supported with professional development centred on areas such as formative assessment, philosophy of teaching and creativity in the classroom. At Wellington leading thinkers in education have become regular visitors to the school. Opportunities for members of the faculty to visit leading schools have also been provided. This has included trips across Europe and to north-east USA.

Further to this it is important to supplement vision with an atmosphere, a corporate culture, where change is seen necessarily as positive irrespective of potential mistakes or emotional swings. Mistakes will be made and confusion periodically arises, so management must accept that members of the faculty may head off down unfruitful paths. This is to be seen as part of the process and should not be met with disdain but with positive and structured guidance. Each member of the faculty will experience different attitudes toward the MYP at different times and this must be understood in context and as part of the process. For many the MYP journey can be emotionally charged, and bullish management can turn off excellent teachers. The IB learner profile is as useful a framework as any for reviewing how to encourage and support members of the school during the introduction and development of the MYP. Adopting the MYP in the UK certainly seems to fulfil the attributes of what it is to be a risk-taker.

Managing collective and personal journeys

Figure 1 shows representations of the three most common attitudes of faculty members towards the MYP, as experienced at Wellington. The curves are intended to be viewed at the individual level but it is possible to transpose them to a department or even whole faculty scale. These representations are based on anecdotal evidence from Wellington in the two years since the first full faculty discussion about MYP implementation. They are merely simplifications of notes from regular conversations with teachers and must only be considered as illustrative. The relative strength of 'positivity' or 'negativity' for each curve is not empirical but merely based on external perceptions of the attitudes conveyed amongst different groups of teachers. The curves are used here to provide a framework for looking at a range of issues and management strategies.

It is tempting to characterise the curves with evocative identities such as crusading zealot, foot solider and conscientious objector, but such characterisation is too simplistic given the range of explanations offered for teachers' particular views.

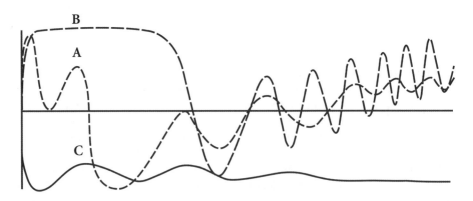

Figure 1: Three common attitudes of faculty members towards the MYP at Wellington College

Response A

Overwhelmingly the most common response in initial discussion of the MYP amongst faculty is positive. Many are drawn by the promise of freedom in the curriculum and the potential to work with students in a more dynamic way. The focus on formative assessment as central to the learning experience can appear as a panacea. In the absence of personal involvement this initial euphoria, however, is all too commonly followed by a period of ambivalence as normal activity carries on. In a few rare cases it will be possible to see a 'head in the sand' approach. The key therefore is to maintain momentum and involve all the faculty in discussion. This can for some be seen as artificial, and even a waste of time, if viewed merely as an academic exercise. Inter-department planning sessions, for example, are essential for the success of implementing the MYP but can be seen in the early stages as irrelevant and a hindrance to day-to-day activity. Restatements of the vision by the management team will need to be frequent and genuine at this time.

When discussion about ideology has passed, and after another flurry of excitement, many will express concern or even despair at the hurdles ahead of them. There is no escaping the fact that introducing the MYP involves work at all levels of the hierarchy, and many members of the faculty will express dismay at the apparent pointlessness of some paperwork. It is this aspect more than any other that can put a stop to the MYP as the organisation as a whole reaches a significant low. My view is that the IB should explore reducing this burden to encourage further growth of the programme. In the meantime it rests upon the shoulders of senior management teams to maintain positive momentum. Emotional support and time need to be provided to help individual faculty members through this low. Whilst some may only need a little cajoling, others may need a greater incentive or an even firmer approach. Difficult conversations are to be expected, but should not necessarily be seen as common. The culture of the school and general attitude to change will become most apparent during this low phase. It is vital that positive habits pervade before the implementation process begins. Derailment at this time could well be permanent if an open and positive culture is not already in place.

After this major downturn, emotions will follow what might be considered a more typical day-to-day pattern. There should however be a long-term upward trajectory, and all constituencies will once again benefit from frequent and genuine restatements of the vision by members of the senior management team. Subject leaders are probably in the best position to take the lead at this time but senior management must not get left behind by the mechanics of the programme. If there is too wide a separation between those who drive the vision and those who need to make it work then failure is imminent. Dialogue must be maintained.

Figure 1 purposefully has no timescale. Two years seems to have been the most appropriate timescale at Wellington; some have taken longer, but others pass through within six months. These phase differences themselves can create anxiety and, in turn, tension amongst colleagues. Whilst some feel that they do not understand the MYP and are in a negative phase others, especially subject leaders, may well have moved on and can become impatient with those apparently dragging their heels. The key to smooth introduction is therefore regular communication, especially concerning changes to systems such as reporting or tracking, and total involvement. An environment must be created where colleagues can safely air their views about the programme. Everybody who goes through the implementation will have swings in their attitude at some stages and these must be respected, not ignored. Nonetheless a culture of continuous change needs to exist and it is vital at these times that leadership is strong and positive. The faculty needs to feel confident that, irrespective of personal concerns, implementation is inevitable.

Response B

In introducing the MYP it is essential to have cultural leaders who believe in the programme. These individuals must also engage with the specific mechanics of the programme introduction. Unit planning, assessment and rubric writing, together with objective box ticking, are as much part of the process as is the classroom experience. The level of paperwork associated with the MYP, as it currently stands, can be questioned but the need to be accountable and rigorous is not. If teachers are to be given greater freedom to write the curriculum then it is vital that an external body offers transparent validation. The IB monitors closely how unit plans fit within an overall scheme of work and the objectives for each subject group. The implementation of the areas of interaction (AOI) including community and service (C&S) activity is reviewed, as well as assessment. The coordinator in any MYP school is not necessarily the most popular person, given the number of grids and charts that are generated in launching the programme. It is important, however, that any school that adopts the MYP understands the need to be accountable and that paperwork will necessarily be part of the process.

There is a danger that some individuals may run away with an idealised dream of the MYP. Details can be ignored and, if not managed, one can expect the visionaries to experience a somewhat cliff-like fall in emotions. Planning how the curriculum and reporting fit together within the IB requirements requires a meticulous eye for detail. Curriculum mapping is a stimulating academic exercise and can indeed be exciting, but it takes time. Prolonged discussions will happen, and mapping out the details and cross checking assessment with objectives is needed if the MYP is to be viewed as a credible educational programme. Checks and measures, however, can stifle creativity, and managing expectations becomes the core job for the coordinator, especially with those initial cultural leaders typified by response B. As the IB continues to reflect on the MYP, the success of harnessing enthusiasm in teachers is predicated upon making the administration process more accessible and manageable.

Response C

There will be opposition to the MYP but in my experience this will rarely be from an educational perspective, as few philosophically argue with the premise of the MYP. There are three distinct non-educational reasons for opposition. The first, already discussed, is workload. The second, what I describe as subject bias, often relates more to the structure of a school's timetable and the threat an individual teacher or department may feel to their position as the balance of lesson allocation shifts (the relative importance of different subjects is open to discussion in all schools, and the MYP brings this issue to the fore). The third, the most difficult to manage and worth discussion here, concerns universities.

Parents and teachers in the UK express most concern about the MYP when relating it to university entrance. There is a perception that higher education institutions do not understand or even know about the MYP, and so look unfavourably upon it during the admissions process. Though there is little, if any, evidence to support this view such concerns present a potential blockage for some schools proceeding with the MYP. The IB has a role to play in raising the profile and understanding of the MYP. Ideology can get in the way of pragmatism in certain areas, and to assume that universities necessarily understand the promise of the MYP would be naïve. Steps need to be taken to get universities engaged with the MYP. This could be an exciting prospect for all parties. One possibility, for instance, would be for university education departments to research the impact of the increased emphasis on inquiry-based learning. The reduced focus on content *per se*, and the drive to uncover knowledge through a skills-based approach, has long been discussed and implementation attempted; the MYP approach explicitly initiates such learning.

A school could independently initiate such research, as responsibility does not rest solely with the IB. Universities themselves should be paying closer attention to what is going on in schools. To my mind there is an unhealthy detachment in university departments from the admissions process and, in turn, a reluctance to engage with what happens in the 14-18 curriculum. The GCSE, the national qualification for 16 year-olds in England, is the most recent incarnation of a school leavers' certificate. With government plans to raise the education participation age to 18 by 2015, the foundation of the GCSE is now shaky and there are calls for a radical review of the curriculum in England. Students who began secondary school in September 2009 should expect to be in some form of education or training until the age of 18. The time of a terminal examination at age 16 seems to have passed, and a progressive approach must be adopted that links educational phases as a continuum. The MYP offers a starting point in the middle school, but universities need to be involved or else the *status quo* will prevail and England could well find itself falling behind on international education rankings.

There are a few signs that debate is on the agenda, and recognition of the MYP on the UCAS form (Universities and Colleges Admissions Service: the centralised university application system operated in the UK) from 2011 is a positive step. This does not, however, offer enough detail about the texture of the MYP qualification, and admissions tutors will not gain much knowledge from a simple final grade. The IB is working with UCAS to develop a tariff rating for the MYP, as a means of assisting admissions tutors in comparing the MYP with other middle school programmes such as GCSE, but sadly this tariff also undervalues the MYP experience. The IB is a recognised brand at diploma level, but less so in the middle school. A tariff based on a few numbers, however well calculated, do not do the MYP justice.

The MYP has the potential to be the qualification of choice but, to help to answer the sceptics represented at the bottom of the curve, the MYP needs to be above reproach. It requires the commitment of all its advocates to deliver exciting, stimulating, rigorous and accountable courses. There is no escaping the work required, but the rewards are worth it. The MYP can deliver an international education driven by the needs of students and guided by the specific talents of the teachers. Personalised learning can be a reality and not just rhetoric. Connections between subjects can help students of the 21st century understand the world they inhabit. Lifelong skills can be nurtured within a formative assessment framework allowing graduates of the MYP to be the adaptable leaders of the future. Existing qualifications at age 16 do not offer this promise. It is the responsibility of all MYP schools to deliver the promise.

Managing student expectations and (re)learning how to learn

The MYP is not easy for students to access in the first instance. Assessment structure and the focus on pupil-centred reflective learning offer two distinct yet connected reasons why the MYP has the potential to be a bewildering experience for students when they first embark upon the programme. The assessment structure of the MYP is an area that the IB is currently looking to improve. There are certain elements, born out of a worthy idealism, that serve only to complicate what at heart is a simple vision. Formative assessment underpins successful delivery of the MYP and must continue to do so, but the assessment criteria seem needlessly complex. Subject groups such as technology and science have six criteria, whilst language A has only three. Faculty members themselves can come to terms with this, even though it does make setting basic tasks and reporting complex, but students and, in turn, parents can get somewhat lost amongst a whole range of mystifying language and numbers. The premise is good but the reality is currently unwieldy. As the IB actively seeks to reduce this complexity it is important to educate students and parents alike about why there is a need to break down assessment in the way the MYP does. There is great value in the formative approach that is sought. There is no better way of communicating this to parents and students than through small group discussion forums. It is through these that the minutiae can be effectively communicated. We should not assume that a written document will suffice. The AOI are another feature of the MYP that take time to absorb and these forums can once again be helpful.

Reflective learning is somewhat daunting for students who have commonly come from an environment where learning has been distinctly teacher-led. Schools looking to implement the MYP will have an appreciation of formative assessment and the role of teacher as facilitator rather than instructor. It can be disappointing therefore in such schools if new students do not seem to sympathise with the vision as they clamour for the recognisable framework of being a passive recipient of education. It takes time for students new to the programme to get used to the nature of assessment and learning. Anxieties can heighten and tension can be created when the classroom experience is unfamiliar. Exposure over time will be enough for most students to become accustomed, but support needs to be very deliberately provided in the first few months – an immersion course in the first few days of term is a useful mechanism. Learning how to learn may seem pointless to students, who will need confidence that the process works. It may seem to them that there is a lack of content in subjects, a problem some teachers have, and that the true substance of what they previously loved has been removed and replaced by intangibles. Open-ended unit questions can be seen as a step too far.

The early stages of the MYP must be very carefully sequenced. It is vital that approaches to learning (ATL) are clearly planned across the school and explained in context. The coordinator will find this task particularly taxing as it requires persuading subject leaders to relinquish some of their 'usual' content in favour of a skills-based approach. The involvement of the whole faculty is vital if this is to work. Should the student experience be inconsistent, the coherence of the process will be compromised and greater confusion result. The faculty must be regularly engaged in discussion about ATL and the framework for implementation must be clear and easy to use. It is worth noting that a pupil-centred approach to learning does not advocate removing content from courses. If anything it allows lessons to be focused more on the content and its nature. It is important that formative assessment and reflective learning are not pushed at the expense of content. The best lessons allow participants unconsciously to develop skills alongside content.

Final reflections on successfully taking the MYP forward

It is my experience that the MYP positively transforms schools but, as with any whole school change, implementation requires strong leadership and careful management. The following strategies have helped with ensuring success at Wellington:

State a clear vision   Engage the faculty in pedagogical discussion and develop a vision for the MYP in the school. Encapsulate the vision with a clear mission statement. Regularly restate the mission statement with confidence. Strong leadership is vital.

Plan the detail	This is best done by a small team who are willing and able to make strong decisions. The school database, timetable and reports procedures will need to be clear and easy to use. The MYP is complex and the school structures will need to offer consistency and comfort to the faculty throughout. Significant financial investment may be needed.
Invest in staff	Training with the IB is important but personalised professional development plans for all teachers need to take this further. The faculty appraisal system should be designed to assist in identifying specific MYP training needs and encourage faculty members to act accordingly. Some will need explicit training in pupil-centred approaches and using assessment in a formative fashion.
Allocate time	The best way to introduce the MYP is systematically up through a school. This will reduce the day-to-day burden on individual teachers. Even after introduction, faculty will need time to develop units of work and teaching strategies. The MYP is not simply a syllabus change.
Listen to students	Regular workshops with students will help decision-making. Provide opportunities for students to be involved in curriculum writing. Students will often have good ideas as to how to make a topic interesting.
Educate parents	Open forums allow parents to understand the vision. The MYP is not always intuitive to people from outside the field of education.
Seek excellence	The MYP has potential to be an outstanding programme in the right environment. The rewards are immeasurable if the vision is followed through. Encourage and seek out excellence. Support the IB in its drive for increased rigour. Faculty members should be given the opportunity to visit beacon schools. Leaders in education should also be welcomed through the door.
Be brave	Above all else follow through on the vision. The national system in England and other countries is, in many respects, at odds with the progressive nature of the MYP. The MYP should allow faculty and students to engage in a creative, stimulating and rigorous programme of learning. Do not compromise by fitting the MYP into, or on top of, an existing system.

A reductionist approach in the school system of England has taken away an emphasis on the development of lifelong skills and the excitement of learning for its own sake. The ranking of schools in league tables according to examination performance has understandably led to a pragmatic approach to teaching. Changes to curricula are typically driven by a desire to improve nominal results rather than to improve the quality of education on offer. The government and, in turn, examination boards and schools alike have inadvertently devalued the role of teachers as educators and students as lifelong learners. Whilst the majority of teachers within the system in England strive to provide quality education, the system conspires against them. The MYP offers a unique opportunity in international education to place the student back at the heart of the learning process and provide the teacher with the freedom to inspire, differentiate and innovate.

Acknowledgements

Personal thanks are due to Dr Anthony Seldon (Master of Wellington College), Dr Justin Garrick (Canberra Grammar School), Helen Forde (Inter-Community School Zurich) and Professor Guy Claxton (Learning Sciences Centre for Real-World Learning, University of Winchester) for their willingness to share ideas which contributed to the writing of this chapter.

Reference

Gardner, H (1999): *Intelligence Reframed: Multiple Intelligences for the 21st Century.* New York: Basic Books.

Related reading

Blanchard, K, Zigarmi P and Zigarmi D (2004): *The One Minute Manager – Leadership and the one minute manager.* London: Harper Collins.

IB (2008): *MYP: From principles into practice.* Cardiff: International Baccalaureate.

Laufenberg, D (2010): *How to Learn? From Mistakes.* Retrieved from TED: Technology, Entertainment and Design. Available from: www.ted.com/talks/diana_laufenberg_3_ways_to_teach.html

Lucas, B and Claxton, G (2010): *New Kinds of Smart: How the science of learnable intelligence is changing education.* Maidenhead: Open University Press.

McRae, H (2010): *What Works: Success in Stressful Times.* London: Harper Press.

Mitra, S (2010): *The child-driven education.* Retrieved from TED: Technology, Entertainment and Design. Available from: www.ted.com/talks/lang/eng/sugata_mitra_the_child_driven_education.html

Robinson, K (2006): *Schools Kill Creativity.* Retrieved from TED: Technology, Entertainment and Design. Available from: www.ted.com/talks/ken_robinson_says_schools_kill_creativity.html

Tobin, L (2010): Slumdog reveals learning treasures. Lucy Tobin meets Sugata Mitra, in *The Guardian.* 16 March 2010.

Chapter 13

The MYP and its cultural context:
a reflection from Dubai

Erika Elkady

What is it like to teach in the Middle East? Colleagues I meet at IB conferences often ask me this question when I mention where I live and work. What they really want to know is: how do you cope as a western woman in the Middle East? What is it like to work in an IB school where the majority of students are from an Arabic speaking country? And how do you uphold the learner profile as you deal with alleged censorship, gender inequality, and issues of race and wealth? – to name but a few.

MYP schools in the Middle East

The number of MYP schools in the Middle East is on the rise. According to data published by the IB in November 2010, there are 130 MYP schools in the IB Africa, Europe and Middle East (AEM) region compared to 92 schools in 2006 (IB, 2010a). Of these 130 schools a total of 14 MYP schools are to be found in the Middle East: Egypt (2), Jordan (3), Kuwait (1), Oman (1), Qatar (2), Saudi Arabia (2) and the United Arab Emirates (3). (IB, 2010b) The make-up of the student population in these 14 schools is not identical, as some schools have a student population of predominantly Arabic speakers and others are communities with a relatively larger percentage of western expatriates. However, the vast majority of these MYP schools consist of students whose first language is Arabic. Even though some of these students hold passports from Australia, the US or Canada, their mother tongue is Arabic and they are raised in the Arabic tradition.

The cultural context

Intercultural awareness and communication are two of the three fundamental concepts of the MYP philosophy. The multicultural classroom in my school very much reflects the same pattern as will be found in many schools with one predominant group of students who share the same mother tongue and culture. The majority of students are non-native English speakers who are taught by mainly monolingual western teachers. The learning styles of these students are often different from those of their teachers, and the teachers' style of instruction is different from what most of these students are used to. Besides interaction with the students, administrators and teaching staff also deal with parents who, on the one hand, want a western education for their children but, on the other hand, find it challenging to deal with certain aspects of the IB philosophy. Due to the absence of a good grasp of each other's languages, the process of educating parents about the MYP philosophy is not always an easy task. This becomes even more challenging when few parents attend information sessions and other school-based activities celebrating aspects of the MYP curriculum. Although not a quick and easy solution, school administrators who recognize these challenges realize that the school will benefit from having amongst its staff bilingual teachers who are familiar with both cultures. Moreover, it is important to train and coach Arabic teachers to become familiar with the MYP philosophy over an extended period of time. This is not only to make sure that the MYP is effectively implemented in all eight subject groups, but also to ensure that the Arabic language A and B departments understand that different learning styles require different teaching styles. This can often involve a cultural change of mind that will require an investment in time and finance on the part of the school.

The well-known metaphor of culture as an iceberg (see Figure 1 for a generalised depiction of the model) shows the visible or 'conscious' aspects of culture above the water's surface, with the 'unconscious' aspects of culture found beneath the water line.

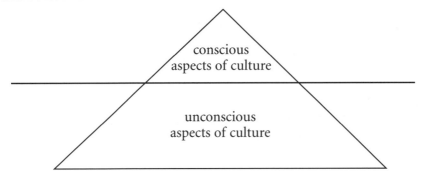

Figure 1: Metaphor of culture as an iceberg

These visible aspects are relatively easy to address within our school community. Rules are put in place and some of the attributes of the IB learner profile are used to explain the reasoning behind them. We have a 'hands-off' policy because we respect the culture of the host country where boys and girls are not expected to display affection in public. This also means that we do not want boys holding hands in the corridors or on the playgrounds, a custom that is not uncommon here. Again, respect for other cultures is the reason why there is no physical contact at all between students, or between students and teachers. A female teacher who put her hand on a local boy's shoulder did not mean to make him feel uncomfortable. She did not even realize that she had done so, as to her this was her way of expressing affection for the student. It is important that staff new to the region receive the appropriate training if they are to become aware of the local customs.

Communication is important in explaining to teachers, parents and students that because we work in a multicultural school and care about each other's values, we have to respect our school culture. It is important to inform staff that local boys, for example, very often feel uneasy when a teacher asks them to sit next to a girl. A male teacher needs to know that he should not extend his hand to a female parent as she may not wish to shake his hand, as would also be the case with a female teacher and male parent. We expect our staff to respect the school's dress code, which states that 'all staff should be sensitive to local cultural norms'. The above mentioned visible aspects of culture are not the real challenge we face, as they can be dealt with under the 'we respect each other's culture' umbrella, which has more or less become our very own school culture.

The MYP model as communication tool

During admission procedures, we use the MYP model to explain to students and parents that the octagonal shape of the model shows that all eight subjects are valued equally, and that visual arts/performing arts and physical education are weighted the same as English, mathematics and science. The latter three are considered the core subjects by most parents, though this assumption is not limited to the Middle East. It is important to explain to potential new parents and students that we expect our students to participate fully in visual arts, music and physical education. Although a very few parents argue that music, especially certain stringed instruments, is not acceptable, they usually change their mind when they learn that the subject is an elective in Years 4 and 5 of the MYP. In order to be culturally sensitive, we do not include a dance unit when assessing criterion B in physical education (movement and composition) as some parents also object to this. All our lessons are coeducational, with the exception of the swimming practice unit in physical education lessons as laid down in the UAE Ministry of Education regulations.

Cultural challenges: the invisible aspects

It is the invisible aspects of culture, those beneath the surface of the water in the iceberg metaphor, that keep us 'on our toes'. Why are these invisible aspects so challenging? One reason is that we are generally not aware of them until we come up against them. In one instance, the school or teacher may unintentionally act in a way that is not understood or in some cases is not even accepted by the student or parents. Students often do not understand that a friendly teacher is still a figure of authority. They are often surprised when the teacher who acted like an equal all of a sudden corrects their behaviour. Teachers new to the region often need to adapt their teaching style in order to obtain respect and to manage their classrooms. In another scenario, a parent or student may upset a teacher. Parents feel that it is the teacher's job to make sure that their children achieve at the highest level. Although there is nothing wrong with this assumption, parents find it hard to understand that in MYP mathematics and science, for example, students will only achieve at the highest level when they are able to solve a problem in unfamiliar situations. Some parents have told teachers that they are not doing their job because they should allow students to practise these unfamiliar situations in class. Many of our teachers are new to the private education sector and are at first bewildered by these expectations. Although most of the time such misunderstandings are not as dramatic as the fate of the *Titanic* – a continuation of the iceberg metaphor – they do surprise us and can make us feel uncomfortable and even insecure.

A second reason why the invisible aspects of culture are so challenging to deal with is that these aspects touch upon the philosophy of the IB in general and that of the MYP in particular. Some topics are classified as 'banned' by the *Guidelines* of the United Arab Emirates (UAE) Ministry of Education (Article no. 16/1), which means that teachers need to be made aware that what is acceptable to discuss in their home country's classroom is not necessarily accepted in this part of the world. As the *Guidelines* are rather broad we do not always know exactly what is acceptable and what is not. Consequently, self-censorship takes place to ensure that we are culturally on the safe side. The often-asked question 'How do you cope as a "real" IB school with censorship issues?' not only implies that there is friction between censorship and the values of the IB but also hints at the impossibility of having both. First, it is important to note that censorship and self-censorship are not only confined to this region. Although some may argue that censorship is not consistent with attributes of the learner profile such as being principled, open-minded and inquisitive, one also needs to recognise that (self) censorship in, for instance, American schools is very common. Sex, profanity, and racism are the primary reasons for banning books in US schools, (American Library Association, 2011) while religious, social and political views contradicting Muslim values are mentioned in the UAE Ministry *Guidelines* (Article no. 16/1) (2004). Interestingly enough, the UAE – unlike the USA – does not have a list of banned books. So, the first step is to acknowledge that (self) censorship is an issue with which many IB schools deal and is not only limited to this part of the world. The second step is to have a closer look at the definitions of the learner profile attributes and to realize that they may be problematic to apply in all international schools.

The IB learner profile in a cultural context

In his IB position paper *East is East and West is West*, George Walker, the former IB Director General, addresses 'the long-standing criticism that the International Baccalaureate (IB) is too closely associated with Western values and, despite its title, does not enable students to see the world from a truly international perspective' (Walker, 2010). Walker acknowledges that the descriptive phrases of the ten learner profile attributes 'resonate with a Western humanist style of learning' (Walker, 2010: 4). Walker's paper was based on discussions during an IB workshop that took place in Singapore (March 2010), and he highlights four major cultural areas in which East and West differ. These areas are interesting to consider in the Middle East context, as some of them seem to be more in agreement with eastern values while others are more consistent with western values. The four areas Walker mentions, which will be discussed here in more detail, are:

- a concern for the group rather than the individual;

- respect for authority;

- a holistic view of the world; and

- aversion to risk.

(Walker, 2010: 7-8)

A concern for the group rather than the individual

Implementing group work in school here has been a much easier task than in my previous school in The Netherlands. We have not had problems with students who find it challenging to divide the workload and argue about who is the leader, although the trend here often seems to be that a western expatriate student takes charge and the others follow. The 'I do not turn in my friends' culture is much more a code of honour here than in the West and, as a Palestinian student once said to me when I was trying to get to the bottom of an incident, 'we will never turn in our brothers even though they did something wrong'. It is useful for administrators here to be familiar with the Islamic religion, as a discussion about local 'tribal values' (you should always support your 'own' people, no matter what) versus the clear religious instructions (*The Holy Qur'an*, Surah 4: Verse 135) helped me to get to the bottom of the above mentioned incident. I was able to convince the students that it was their religious duty to tell me the names of their friends who had acted against school rules, as this was more important than 'protecting' their friends by not 'snitching'. A few parents called me later urging me not to mention their son's name as 'the snitch' as it is against their culture to turn in their 'brothers'. However, they agreed that since school rules were broken the culprits had to face the consequences. So, while our students tend to value the group more than the individual, the learner profile attributes focus more on the individual.

Respect for authority

Walker points out in his position paper that, although the learner profile does not say anything about the student-teacher relationship, another IB document makes clear that IB teachers are expected to 'model themselves on the learner profile' (IB, 2008b: 13). As mentioned earlier, students at first are confused about the friendly teacher who treats them as an equal but who is at the same time a figure of authority. Students who join us after previously attending government schools (schools where the medium of instruction is Arabic and the curriculum is set by the Ministry of Education, with an emphasis on Islamic studies and Arabic language/literature) mention that they were at first surprised that our teachers do not shout at them but listen to their opinions. They also say that it took some time to adjust to being an inquisitive student who is expected to provide constructive support for a personal point of view. Nevertheless, students and parents still expect the teacher to direct the learning as this is believed to allow the student to reach the highest achievement levels. When this is not the case, parents openly question the teacher's ability and in some cases even demand higher grades. One mother stated as the reason for moving her daughter, who was with us for only a few months, that the teachers were not 'good' otherwise her daughter would have top marks. Unlike the East Asian parents Walker refers to, who would not question the teacher's professionalism, 'respect for authority' seems here to be more a mixture of attitudes that might be found in both East and West.

A holistic view of the world

According to Walker, those from eastern cultures 'see the whole picture when confronted with an issue' (2010: 8). This suggests that 'the excuse-driven culture' I have already touched upon earlier leans more toward western values. Moreover, the fundamental concept of holistic learning 'emphasizing the links between the disciplines, providing a global view of situations and issues' that, according to Walker, the East seems better to deal with in shades-of-grey than do their black-or-white western counterparts, shows that the Middle Eastern definition of a holistic view tends to lean toward the west.

Aversion to risk

The learner profile 'risk taker' characteristic might, according to Walker, be more appropriately replaced by 'being courageous'. However, both terms seem to have a western bias. Although people here admire courageous men from the past such as Saladin and Ibn Battuta, as well as current leaders such as His Highness Sheikh Mohamed Bin Rashid Al Maktoum, Prime Minister and Vice President of the United Arab Emirates and Ruler of Dubai, the student in the classroom prefers, as mentioned earlier, a teacher-directed learning environment in which assignments are given that are content-driven. It is common practice in the Arab (Arabic-speaking) world for parents to provide their children with private tuition outside school. As a result, according to Dr Samia Al Farra, chief education officer at Taaleem (an educational organization based in the UAE that governs three IB World Schools: Taaleem, 2011), 'students pay less attention in classrooms, and more frustration builds up among teachers' (El Shammaa, 2010). Although we do not allow our staff to tutor our own students outside school, and discourage parents from hiring tutors for their children, it is difficult to break the habit. A real risk taker in this part of the world may very likely be a student without a tutor. Although many local families and Arab expatriate parents still feel that a teacher-centred, content-driven curriculum is the best way to prepare students for university, it is interesting to see that schools in this region with a long tradition of offering the International General Certificate of Secondary Education (IGCSE) are looking into adapting aspects of, or even implementing, the full MYP.

In the November 2010 *MYP Coordinator's Notes* produced by the IB, the DP results of former MYP students are compared to those of all IB diploma candidates worldwide over a four year period. The numbers indicate that MYP students have a higher pass rate; a higher rate of 40+ points in the diploma (where 45 points is the maximum possible) and a higher pass rate for a bilingual diploma (IB, 2010d). In the 2009 Programme for International Student Assessment (PISA) study, 5,620 15 year-olds of different nationalities who reside in the UAE participated. These students attended schools offering 13 different curricula. The UAE ranked 41st out of 65 countries participating in this study. Remarkably, MYP students scored an average of 540, beating the international average of 500 points (Jones, 2010). These statistics are useful when explaining to parents that, even though their children may be out of their comfort zone for a period of time, being courageous in this way may prepare them better for their future when the long-term goal is to be prepared for study abroad.

The MYP areas of interaction in a cultural context

While Walker concludes that the learner profile may need a multicultural review that will leave 'some space for regional tradition', in the February 2005 issue of *IB World* Michael Allan addressed the fact that the areas of interaction (AOI) are often interpreted from a western point of view (Allan, 2005). So the environments AOI, according to Allan, is seen as separate from humanity while in many cultures man is seen as being one with his environment. Allan points out that the products of *homo faber* are especially valued in the West but that in other parts of the world the community and family, which are also man-made products, are valued much more highly. In 2008, the IB replaced all Latin MYP terminology and, since *homo faber* has become known as 'human ingenuity', the understanding of this AOI in the classroom has become much better. Students do not say anymore that human ingenuity means 'man the maker' and do not automatically assume that this AOI deals with man-made objects only. They know that human ingenuity is about everything that people have thought of, including ideas such as how political systems operate, agreements on how we interact with each other in our school, and whether or not global warming is fact or myth, to name but a few.

Even though there is a better understanding now of what this AOI entails, Allan is right to state that this area, like the others, is addressed from a western point of view, as teachers often approach whichever unit they teach from their own cultural perspective. He hits the nail on the head by stating that the difficulty in delivering an international education does not lie primarily in the curriculum; it lies in the interactions that are taking place in the classroom and the perspectives, or world views, that are presented as orthodox or correct (Allan, 2005: 15). Allan's question 'Can the MYP, with its focus on student-centred, discovery-based learning, be a truly international curriculum and be effectively delivered in a multicultural classroom?' is relevant as the programme claims to be international. Allan argues that in many MYP schools intercultural awareness is an 'add on' to the MYP curriculum rather than a foundation for its delivery. He feels that an international curriculum can only be delivered in the classroom and school environment when it is truly multicultural. Students' own cultures and languages need to be validated by displays, resources and use in the classroom. The importance of students using their own language is that it will enable them to use their existing thinking skills, access prior subject knowledge and relate new concepts to previous experience (Allan, 2005: 14).

Recent developments regarding the importance of the Arabic language and culture

Recent IB publications in the Arabic language that have been made possible by the King Faisal Foundation (KFF) such as *The Middle Years Programme: A basis for practice* (IB, 2009a), *MYP: From Principles into Practice* (IB, 2008a), the *Language A Guide* (IB, 2009b), *Learning in a language other than mother tongue in IB programmes* (IB, 2008c), *Guidelines for developing a school language policy* (IB, 2008d), and the *MYP English-Arabic Glossary* (IB, 2010c) help Arabic staff to gain a deeper understanding of the MYP philosophy. The glossary helps us to be consistent in displaying MYP-specific vocabulary, which benefits the students. The recently published *Guide to interdisciplinary teaching and learning* by Veronica Boix-Mansilla of Harvard Graduate School of Education (Boix-Mansilla, 2010) and the cross-programme publication *Intercultural understanding: Exploring Muslim contexts to extend learning. Sample PYP and MYP planners* (the result of a joint partnership between the IB and The Aga Khan Development Network: IB, 2010e) are also steps in the right direction.

Taaleem (as noted above, a UAE-based educational organization) opened the Jumeira Baccalaureate School in September 2010. This school has a special focus on effective language learning in English and Arabic A and B from the age of four years, which is a development Allan may welcome. Furthermore Taaleem offers MYP workshops for language A and B in cooperation with the IB. The Queen Rania Teacher Academy in Jordan does the same by offering MYP workshops in Arabic. This Academy aims to improve the quality of education 'by boosting teaching standards' (2011). These workshops are conducted by experienced IB-trained workshop leaders who are native Arabic speakers. It is also good news that, as of 2011, Arabic A is a moderated MYP language; hopefully this will also be the case for Arabic B in 2012.

Although many IB practitioners agree that the IB philosophy is embedded in a western humanist tradition of learning, there is also awareness of the importance of, and action aimed at becoming, truly international. Walker's comment that the IB 'cannot be everything to everyone' and that the diploma prepares students for a higher education in the West (Walker, 2010: 8), is exactly why parents and students here choose the MYP as a preparation for the DP. The initiatives by the King Faisal Foundation in Saudi Arabia, the Queen Rania Teacher Academy in Jordan and Taaleem in the UAE indicate that there is action in this part of the world aimed at making the MYP more accessible to Arabic teachers by providing MYP documents in Arabic. Moreover, several initiatives aimed at training Arabic staff to adapt their more traditional teaching style to the needs of the MYP student are very promising. The role of the school is also to educate parents about the programme and to help them to understand that the MYP is a challenging programme, with equal importance assigned to the eight subject groups, which should be external tutor-free. However, while initiatives aimed at supporting teachers in adapting to a more western style of teaching and learning are in place, the MYP philosophy in itself is flexible enough to be culturally sensitive. The taught curriculum is for each school to determine. Units that may be culturally or religiously sensitive for this part of the world do not need to be addressed and can easily be avoided. A school may choose not to offer music or dance as one of the performing arts options, but to offer drama or film instead. Criterion B in physical education, movement and composition, could be a gymnastic routine instead of dance.

Summary

Each international school has its 'own school culture', allowing its members to deal comfortably with the different cultures in their community. However, this school-specific culture mainly addresses the visible aspects of the dominant, often host country, culture. The invisible aspects are much more challenging to deal with as we often come up against them unexpectedly. Moreover, we may tend to feel that some of these invisible aspects may not be in accordance with the IB philosophy. However, we need to ask ourselves if this really is the case as, for instance, the IB learner profile and the AOI are to some extent culturally biased.

The MYP, with intercultural awareness one of its fundamental concepts, allows flexibility in regard to curriculum and assessment. It is this flexibility that makes it not as challenging as one may initially think to make cultural adaptations to the MYP within school. Moreover, an understanding by several regional educational institutions of the need to address change in the educational philosophy of this part of the world has resulted in a willingness to invest in Arabic resources and staff. As a result schools will be better able to offer a challenging Middle Years Programme that prepares students for the IB Diploma Programme and for study overseas.

References

American Library Association (2011): Available at:
www.ala.org/ala/issuesadvocacy/banned/bannedbooksweek/ideasandresources/free_downloads/
index.cfm [Accessed 12 January 2011]

Allan, M (2005): MYP – Where's the awareness?, in *IB World* 42, February, pp14-15.

Boix-Mansilla, V (2010): *MYP guide to interdisciplinary teaching and learning.* Cardiff:
International Baccalaureate.

El Shammaa, D (2010): A vision for the future of the UAE education, in *Gulf News.* 7 October
2010. Available at: http://gulfnews.com/news/gulf/uae/education/a-vision-for-the-future-of-the-
uae-education-1.692849 [Accessed 12 January 2011]

IB (2008a): *MYP: From Principles into Practice.* Cardiff: International Baccalaureate.

IB (2008b): *Towards a continuum of international education.* Cardiff: International
Baccalaureate.

IB (2008c): *Learning in a Language other than Mother Tongue in IB Programmes.* Cardiff:
International Baccalaureate.

IB (2008d): *Guidelines for Developing a School Language Policy.* Cardiff: International
Baccalaureate.

IB (2009a): *The Middle Years Programme: A basis for practice.* Cardiff: International
Baccalaureate.

IB (2009b): *Middle Years Programme: Language A Guide,* Cardiff: International Baccalaureate.

IB (2010a): *The IB Middle Years Programme Statistical Bulletin.* November 2010. Cardiff:
International Baccalaureate.

IB (2010b): *IB World School Statistics.* From: www.ibo.org [Accessed 8 October 2010]

IB (2010c): *MYP English-Arabic Glossary.* Cardiff: International Baccalaureate.

IB (2010d): *MYP Coordinator's Notes.* November 2010. Cardiff: International Baccalaureate.

IB (2010e): *Exploring Muslim contexts to extend learning. Sample PYP and MYP planners.*
Cardiff: International Baccalaureate.

Jones N (2010): Troubling report for Dubai Schools, in *7 Days.* 9 December 2010. Available at:
www.7days.ae/storydetails.php?id=100530&page=localnews&title=Troubling%20report%20for
%20Dubai%20schools [Accessed 12 January 2011]

Taaleem (2011): www.taaleem.ae [Accessed 12 January 2011]

The Holy Qur'an. Surah 4: Verse 135.

The Queen Rania Teacher Academy (2011): Available at:
www.queenrania.jo/education/teachers/teachers-academy [Accessed 12 January 2011]

United Arab Emirates (UAE)(2004): *Ministry of Education Guidelines.* Article no. 16/1.

Walker, G (2010): *East is East and West is West.* IB position paper, Geneva: International
Baccalaureate.

Part D

Futures for Middle Years Schooling

Chapter 14

Evolving the middle years curriculum in practice

Michael Chapman

I think personalised learning is an idea for our time. It's a recognition of human uniqueness – we are not just trying to turn out assembly-line children. It means redesigning our schools to fit the pupils rather than what we do now, which is to take the kids and force them to fit into the existing structures. It means a focus on learning, deep learning, learning for understanding, learning for meaning and giving people time. (Fink, 2005)

The goals of this chapter are to explore how to:

- personalise learning for students in the middle years more effectively by fundamentally re-thinking the curriculum;

- create an ambitious, creative, rigorous, internationalist and inspirational curriculum that will engage and motivate all students;

- directly inform an inspirational, fit-for-purpose curriculum design; and

- ensure robust standards, learner outcomes and planned learner progression.

The later sections of the chapter have been deliberately written to be a practical guide, for school administrators and curriculum leaders undertaking a principled curriculum review of the middle years (within the context of the wider whole-school curriculum where applicable) against clear criteria. Consistent with the attributes promoted by the International Baccalaureate (IB) learner profile, the chapter seeks to pose critical questions as opposed to providing simplistic solutions. What is important is that each school legitimately arrives at a fit-for-purpose curriculum model for 21st century global learners.

There is a strong moral dimension to educational leadership in the 21st century. Too often the relentless pressure for improved learner outcomes places school leaders in a position where they are expecting their teachers/faculty to work ever harder to increase attainment, whilst still broadly doing things the way they have always done them. It cannot, surely, be a sensible strategy to expect people just to work harder and harder to secure incremental school improvement? If it is accepted that such a strategy is not sensible, then fundamental questions are posed for curriculum design.

There must be a different way to innovate in the middle years so that educational experience and learner outcomes are improved, at the same time as the teaching profession is sustained and the staff team is helped to work smarter, not harder. Such a strategy will involve professional courage, informed risk-taking and – above all – the development of a learning-led, not staffing-led, curriculum model. Student and parental voice will also be integral.

Schools must innovate to move forward. Resting on laurels is never an option. Fundamentally, moving school performance to the next level must involve more than incremental tinkering. Sadly, too many schools still blame the learners for not attaining, yet school organisational models in the majority of cases remain essentially 19th century in origin and design.

A number of key questions that pose a challenge for school leaders are as follows:

- Why are so many schools still organised for curriculum and timetable purposes in chronological grade/year groups? What is the educational (learning) rationale for chronological organisation?

- Why do schools retain inflexible curriculum models with a subject focus, even within the cross-disciplinary strategy of many middle years programmes?

- Why do students study so many subjects in every grade? What about depth (deep learning) as well as breadth?

- Why retain timetable models (teaching periods) that often favour staff rather than learners or curriculum content? Is it still tenable to argue for uniform blocks of time in the teaching week, regardless of subject pedagogical requirements?

- Why retain subject grouping and subject leadership? Does this not, often by default, work against a 'whole' learning experience for the student?

- Why in many cases do we offer compensatory learning and not precision teaching?

The need for many schools to conduct an open and robust critical dialogue on curriculum structure is overdue, especially in the middle years. I believe there is wide recognition of the need for further qualitative improvement centred around personalisation of learning with increased rigour, challenge and benchmarking in the middle years curriculum. Pre-requisites of curriculum design, if genuine learner personalisation is to be achieved, are as follows:

- Assessment for learning

• Innovative teaching and learning strategies

• Curriculum entitlement and choice

• Creative approaches to school organisation

• Strong partnerships beyond the classroom

Such a qualitative improvement should have the outcome goal of arriving at a robust international curriculum that stands rigorous external scrutiny, is coherent and challenging, can be securely benchmarked in terms of standards, and into and from which students can integrate and transfer.

Although this chapter seeks to ask fundamental questions about curriculum design in the middle years regardless of the curriculum and accreditation model currently in place, it is perhaps pertinent to start with a brief commentary on the MYP. I understand the present position to be as follows.

As of January 2011, the number of schools worldwide offering IB programmes is 3099. The majority of these schools (2190) offer the IB Diploma Programme (DP). 854 schools offer the MYP and 741 offer the IB Primary Years Programme (PYP). (IB, 2011) Of the 854 schools offering the MYP, 131 are in the IB Africa/Europe/Middle East region, and the majority (558) are in North America and the Caribbean. As these figures indicate, there are very few schools worldwide offering all three IB programmes. The figure cited on the IB website (IB, 2011) is 158 from a total of 3099.

The MYP has no prescribed curriculum content and is only externally moderated at the end of Grade 10. This means that standards are not externally scrutinised until the end of the programme; by that time it is too late to intervene in under-performance. The IB asserts that the MYP in authorised schools is monitored through continuous internal and external evaluation, and ongoing dialogue. MYP co-ordinators on the ground in schools, in conversation, have spoken of their commitment in principle to the programme, but also of the practical and logistical difficulties associated with their role. The IB also recognises that there is a significant issue in planned learning progression and articulation between their three programmes. All three programmes have been developed at different times and in relative isolation. There is no clear learning or pedagogical progression. The strength (or otherwise) of current provision at school level is reliant upon the strengths of the school team. Whilst at one level this degree of freedom and creativity could be welcomed, it is a high-risk strategy for the learner.

In short and in summary:

• Very few schools worldwide offer all three IB programmes. In the context of international education this must inform decisions on transferability and portability for students who move on.

- The lack of rigorous external moderation until Grade 10 could be potentially problematic for learner progression.

- There are significant logistical issues associated with implementing the MYP.

- The absence of prescribed curriculum content by the IB, planned articulation and progression from PYP to MYP to DP means that schools need to develop and plan their own learner progression.

Such arguments lead to the conclusion that the *status quo* is not acceptable and that further qualitative improvements and rigour are desirable.

Taking learning forward in the middle years

The curriculum in the middle years should not be seen as only a preparation for the IB diploma but rather as a coherent part of a pedagogical progression starting in the early years of school. I am therefore very much in favour of a dynamic cross-phase articulation between the phases of learning, however these are identified. What matters most is what goes on in the classroom. By acknowledging the need to address further the academic articulation between learning phases and to develop the inner areas of a curriculum model, it is essential to take a principled stance in any review of the middle years curriculum within the context of the overall learning continuum. Schools require a middle years curriculum that is internationally recognised, is assessed against reliable external benchmarks and is academically rigorous, not only teaching students the necessary skills but also providing them with a firm foundation of knowledge on which to build.

The curriculum, learning and teaching should be the core design drivers for all other aspects of school organisation. Optimal curriculum design must determine timings of the day, period length, staffing, accreditation, assessment methodologies and student grouping strategies. Too often in schools 'the tail wags the dog'. In many schools it is time to revisit fundamental principles of curriculum design. Inevitable incremental change in recent years has often led to some distortion and lack of clarity in aspects of the programme for learning.

As a key design driver, my assertion would be that schools need to move beyond chronology to 'stage not age'. This is important in smaller schools in particular where chronological organisation, small group size and structure of the working week are often hard to defend educationally.

Principles to underpin teaching and learning

As a starting point it is important to articulate the principles that should drive curriculum design and organisation. They may be summarised as follows:

All students:

- have an entitlement to access to a personalised and challenging curriculum, beyond as well as within the classroom;

- have an entitlement to access to teaching and learning of the highest quality that enables them to achieve commensurate with ability and potential; and

- have an entitlement to parity of status.

All faculty/staff:

- have the individual and collective responsibility to manage and deliver a curriculum that facilitates effective learning for all students in all lessons; and

- have an entitlement to professional support and mentorship at whole-school, team and individual levels to empower them to deliver teaching and learning of the highest quality.

Aims of teaching and learning

It is especially important for stakeholders to be specific about the context for a curriculum review. In terms of the aims of teaching and learning, I consider the following to be fundamental to the ethos of any effective school and therefore to be key curriculum design drivers. To empower students to achieve their maximum potential by fostering the knowledge, abilities, skills, attitudes and self-awareness that enable students to work as motivated and increasingly independent learners within a collaborative learning community, learning opportunities should be developed through effective teaching that ensures:

- high and sustained challenge commensurate with ability;

- students acquire knowledge, skills and understanding progressively;

- lessons have clear aims, purpose, content, structure and challenge;

- the learning needs of all students are met;

- full participation and access is achieved at a challenging pace;

- a variety of appropriate teaching methodologies is used embracing visual, auditory, kinaesthetic (VAK) multisensory techniques;

- the conduct of the lesson signals high expectations of teacher and learner;

- regular developmental and motivational feedback to enable progress using assessment for learning;

- positive relationships and the appropriate use of humour to promote motivation; and

- regular extension work and/or homework to continue learning outside the classroom.

This will be achieved by providing learning opportunities that enable students to:

- respond positively and appropriately to challenging tasks;

- concentrate on tasks;

- make high levels of progress commensurate with ability and potential;

- adjust well to the demands of working in different contexts;

- be able to select appropriate learning resources and use them accordingly;

- work with a sustained sense of commitment and enjoyment;

- be sufficiently self-confident to raise questions and to persevere;

- evaluate their work and come to secure judgments about its quality;

- help one another in a collaborative manner when appropriate to do so; and

- benefit from seating plans and classroom arrangements that facilitate optimum learning.

Curriculum and lesson planning will be further developed by facilitating:

- all lessons to have explicit aims and objectives, including a clarification for students as to what progress is expected by the end of the lesson;

- planned opportunities to utilise a variety of differentiated teaching strategies to accommodate all learners;

- an understanding in students of the process of learning in that subject to enable the transfer of learning skills across the curriculum;

- the identification of, and teaching to, the range of VAK preferred learning styles;

- opportunities for praise, celebration and reward, with a ratio of 5:1 reward to criticism;

- the use of students in self-review and wider subject review, using assessment for learning techniques;

- planned use of ICT and extension work across the ability range; and

- targeted internal and external continuing professional development.

Such an approach will require that the effectiveness of teaching and learning will be evaluated in a meaningful manner. This will include the close monitoring of student progress and performance at all levels, regular team review of teacher planning and schemes of work, team-based classroom observation that is developmental, focused team and whole-school *dialogue* about effective teaching and learning, the sharing of professional expertise within and especially between teams, and student feedback and evaluation.

This, in turn, will generate a formal curriculum review process that is identified closely with the notion of an entitlement curriculum model, the characteristics of which will include personalised learning for all students, recognising their needs, interests and talents; an ambitious, creative and inspirational curriculum that will engage and motivate all students, and maximum flexibility and choice in the context of breadth, depth and acceleration. Crucial to this will be stage – not age – learning, with tiered courses in each curriculum area as opposed to grade-based chronological grouping, together with lesson timing that suits the subject, the content and the intended learning style consistent with accreditation that is meaningful and that ensures learner progression.

The review process in summary

When a school embarks on this process everything should be up for review, other than roll-through of existing examination groups. Dialogue should be through pre-determined, cross-disciplinary teams (including students and parents) who will be invited to consider the key questions framed below and to formulate a team response to a pre-determined timescale.

It is essential if a school embarks upon such a highly participative process that team responses are a genuine and accurate composite of the full range of opinions in each team and not solely those of a vocal minority. Stakeholders must be able to voice a constructively dissenting voice and to have it heard, if the process is not to lose legitimacy. Once team feedback has been received, this should be collated and fed back to the school community as a totality. From this the leadership team should design a high-level curriculum model. Planned implementation should begin immediately thereafter, on a pre-determined schedule.

Each multidisciplinary team should be asked to address the following key questions.

How can our school ensure the following?

1. Entitlement to an appropriately challenging curriculum across the age range, incorporating the required support to underpin learning. What will this entitlement look like?

2. Real and informed student choice that encourages high self-esteem, aspiration and expectation. How can such motivational student choice be provided?

3. Secure, verifiable and benchmarked assessment for learning against prior attainment and potential. What do we need to do to really embed assessment for learning?

4. Pathways that are appropriate for the ability of the child and build in appropriate challenge on the basis of ability and aptitude, rather than chronology, in a manner that does not artificially restrict achievement. What will these pathways look like in a 'stage not age' curriculum?

5. Secure, child-centred differentiation that strikes a sensitive balance between acceleration, breadth and depth of study and retains maximum flexibility to innovate with student grouping. When is it right to accelerate, how will we do this and when is greater breadth/depth more desirable than acceleration? How do we ensure high levels of challenge and progression for all students in every subject?

6. Parity of status and outcome for all curriculum areas and cross-curricular dimensions. How do we ensure curriculum parity and how many subjects should students study at any one time?

7. A robust and challenging pre-DP year in Grade 10 (or earlier in the case of some fast-track students). If our Diploma Programme effectively becomes three years with a pre-DP year, what should the pre-DP year look like?

8. Consistency of expectation, rigour and challenge. How do we ensure that every lesson is consistently effective in quality, whilst retaining the individuality of teaching styles and not seeking uniformity to a single teaching model?

9. Reorganisation of the curriculum content so that students can make more sense of their learning. How do we ensure that learners do not compartmentalise their curriculum into narrow subject boxes and, instead, understand the curricular linkages?

10. Organise learning time to enhance the learning experience of our students. Should all teaching periods be the same length or should they vary according to subject/learning need? If they should vary, how could this look in terms of short, fat courses or long, thin courses (for example)?

Whatever the outcomes of this review process in terms of emerging curriculum structure, it is essential to ensure learner progression and to retain the confidence of parents in the standards achieved for such outcomes to be rigorously benchmarked.

To achieve this, schools may wish to consider, *inter alia*:

• Purchasing and implementing appropriate curriculum mapping software to ensure coherent curriculum planning from early years through to Grade 12 (especially all-age international schools): appropriate parental access may be given to this curriculum map via the school website, with clear linkages to graduated assessment and homework.

• Benchmarking their curriculum model for the middle years against broadly comparable schools, wherever possible collaborating over curriculum development and assessment. I believe that many international schools may be interested in such an exercise.

• Creating a new 'leadership of learning outcomes' role to drive forward changes in the rigour and consistency of assessment, recording and reporting of progress to both students and parents.

• Addressing, in parallel with curriculum innovation, the quality of teaching, learning and classroom management in the middle years as a particular focus for classroom observation and student work scrutiny during the appraisal/performance management strategy.

• Developing a whole-school academic council to address planned learner progression, with regard to pedagogical progression, skill progression and, most importantly, the core knowledge base required as an entitlement for curriculum access and achievement. Particular attention should be placed on the Grade 5/Grade 6 interface, with convergence and progression of pedagogy and content expected in both grades.

• Seeking to develop models of planned intervention to address perceived under-achievement by ensuring a professional mentorship model into the middle years, in tandem with the development of a whole-school strategy of accelerated learning for the most able.

• Maintaining a parent curriculum committee to assist with the monitoring of the implementation of curricular innovation, enhancing this with a student curriculum committee made up of representatives from all grades in the middle years. At least once every three months these two curriculum committees might meet together with key members of the faculty to share perspectives on progress.

The focus for this chapter has been on the formal, taught curriculum as it would be too complex to introduce activities, the co-curricular programme and other learning enrichment into the review process in this analysis. Nonetheless, when undertaking such a review, schools should be cognisant of the need to view learning as a totality.

I believe that the successful and rigorous implementation of these recommendations will potentially result in a world-class middle years curriculum in the context of international schools that is of significantly high quality. Furthermore, by using the curriculum audit and design drivers identified in this chapter, schools will be genuinely able to assert that learners are at the heart of their planning for a 21st century global curriculum.

References

Fink D (2005): *Leading Personalised Learning in Schools: Helping individuals grow.* Nottingham: National College for School Leadership.

IB (2011): www.ibo.org [Accessed January 2011]

Chapter 15

The middle years of schooling: some thoughts for the future

Wilf Stout

The school milieu

It is probably safe to say that current practice in school organization – in terms of instructional time according to 'the timetable', subjects taught, and the space and facilities afforded for the middle school years – is fairly standard across the world and has not changed much in 160 years. The old story of Rip Van Winkle is often quoted in support of this perception. On awakening from a long sleep, almost everything that Rip Van Winkle sees is new to him. He sees computers, mobile phones, television, cars, aircraft, and fast food. The only thing he recognizes is the school classroom!

It would also be fairly safe to suggest, based on my experiences visiting schools around the world, that – at best – most middle school youngsters spend a high proportion of the week in a traditional model, 48 square metre classroom, with tables and chairs, Whiteboard (possibly interactive Whiteboard), paper and pen technology (with a couple of computers in the corner), a data projector in the ceiling and a hi-fi set, with a teacher-focused academic-based curriculum delivered in periods of between 30 and 60 minutes: the so-called western-style assembly-line instruction model. At the end of each period it is 'all change': off to another room or specialist facility for another 30-60 minutes 'learning about' something that is likely to be totally unrelated to what has just happened.

Over the years the school environment has not changed much. Most schools still have the same basic structure for a timetable. Nowadays, though, it is developed using a smart piece of software and is produced in colour. As a younger man, I assisted with the timetable using golf tees, which I spent several days filling with Polyfilla before covering them with tiny bits of self-adhesive address labels (a step-up from the paper and glue of my predecessor), which were labelled and stuck into a peg board. Heaven forbid that the peg board should fall off the wall.

Our stereotypic classroom represents a location where one teacher is exposed at any given time to a large group of learners; usually 20-30 in most types of schools. This in turn places a major constraint on the kinds of interactions that are likely to occur between teachers and students, and between students and students. It produces a default pattern of exchange that is focused on the teacher. The teacher addresses a question to a particular student, the student responds and the teacher gives some kind of evaluative feedback. These exchanges are transient, lasting only a few seconds and punctuated with only slightly longer explanations and instructions from the teacher (Sinclair and Coulthard, 1992; Smith and Higgins, 2006). This blend of didactic and dialectic methods of teaching has *four* components: initiation, response, evaluation, feedback (I-R-E-F). It engages the whole class as each student has no idea whom the teacher will choose for a response, which has clear advantages in terms of control as each episode of interaction is started and finished by the teacher (Mehan, 1979). It is therefore an effective way of managing a learning situation with large numbers of students.

Why do we need to change what we do?

There appears to be a global consensus that argues for radical change in educa-tion, expressed as a belief that education is no longer fit for purpose. One strand of this draws on developments in neuroscience and the implications for learn-ing and pedagogy. The chief argument here seems to be based on the thesis that the current design of schooling and the teaching and learning approaches which operate within formal settings are inappropriate or inefficient for chil-dren and young people who are learning. (Goodbourn *et al*, 2009)

Learning in school today, and in the future, is less likely than previously to be focused on the acquisition of knowledge since much of it is immediately redundant, being overtaken by newer, and more immediately relevant, knowledge. As educators today we need to focus on learning to learn rather than on merely learning for purposes of knowledge acquisition. We live in an age characterized by exponential change and global uncertainty where natural disasters, climate change, famine and drought, terrorism, economic meltdowns, increasing longevity, population increase, technological advances and new applications both limit and accelerate the delivery of relevant knowledge in our schools. Interestingly this reality is not a 21st century innovation, as noted by Holt almost half a century ago:

Since we cannot know what knowledge will be needed in the future it is sense-less to try to teach it in advance. Instead our job must be to try to turn out young people who love learning so much, and who learn so well, that they will be able to learn whatever needs to be learnt. (Holt, 1964)

In 2000 the European Union produced the Lisbon Framework for international progress towards shared goals in education, which developed into the European Reference framework of key competences. These competences emerged as a result of a demand from European policymakers for the identification of the individual learning outcomes 'needed for a citizen to contribute to a modern globalized society, both economically and democratically' (Fredriksson and Hoskins, 2007; Hoskins and Fredriksson, 2008).

At the heart of the European concept of learning to learn is the changing nature of knowledge brought about by technological innovation, and the importance of economic competitiveness as an essential component of a student's education. The recently-developed concept of 'glocalization' is not a frivolous concept as we shall see later, since an education based exclusively within a global context without firm roots in both the local community and the home language community will be an impoverished education.

What do we need to change and why?

To 'learn to learn', learners need opportunities to initiate, determine and, to an extent, control the direction and pace of their learning, at least for some of the time, so that they experience self-control and self-determination. As highlighted by research carried out in South Australia, learners learning to learn should be able to:

• exercise choice responsibly;

• use meta-cognitive skills;

• take responsibility for learning;

• accept alternative viewpoints;

• work with greater persistence;

• express greater hope for a future with expanded opportunities;

• experience improved progression in site-based programmes; `

• articulate their learning; and

• self-assess their learning.

(South Australia Department of Education and Children's Services, 2005)

Fox has produced a very informative model of how metacognitive development, the development of home/school links and assessment to improve learning can be integrated in the development of independent learning, as adapted in Figure 1 (Fox, 2009).

The importance of schools having the ability to use self-organizational skills to improve institutional learning cannot be overemphasized in middle school education. To my mind, the time has come for us to become seriously radical in revising, revitalizing and revolutionizing the process of middle school education. 'Schools of the future' may be a buzz phrase, but I believe that is exactly what we need – predicated upon the belief that we need to create authentic learning environments. These will not appear overnight, which

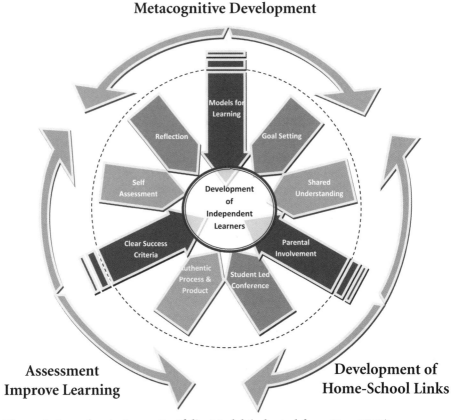

Figure 1: Learning to Learn Portfolio Model (adapted from Fox, 2009)

allows time for evolution and ultimately a better design, but we need to start somewhere. Drawing on metaphors from the context of biology, I argue that an authentic learning environment is the sum total of the influences that mutually impact, interact with, and influence the individual. In terms of applying the model to schools, these include space, time, people and process.

This raises questions such as whether we still need schools and teachers in order for effective learning for the future to occur, and whether students need to interact with each other as part of the learning process. The answer to both questions must be a resounding 'Yes'. So where, when and how does learning occur? I believe that hindsight provides the answer to this question. Change in education is conservative. We are surrounded by innovations with enormous positive implications for learning yet we rely on the established default structures. Only when we see that the impact of an experience has produced a permanent change in behaviour can we be sure that learning has taken place.

The learner needs to be positioned in a *learning space*: a school, the home, the locality and within the community. We need to rethink the way in which the school building is organized and where learning takes place, as it no longer needs to take place within a classroom. That is only part of the story. The learner also needs learning time to be structured effectively. At what time does learning begin in the day and for how long does it last? Is it the same for students of all ages? Should learning time be regimented and broken down into units of time of equal length? Has a 40 minute 'lesson' some magical value in relation to what is learned?

The old African proverb 'It takes a whole village to educate a child' has become a cliché. The origins of the phrase 'It takes a whole village to *raise* a child' seems to be lost in time, but was popularized in a book published in 1994 by Jennifer Cowen-Fletcher. Later, 'raise' was changed to 'educate' by Hillary Rodham Clinton in her 1996 book. I believe this to be true. Creating learning situations is not the sole prerogative of teachers. We need *learning organisers* as facilitators of learning, who can be parents and members of the school community with expertise and passion in different areas of life. Children between 5 and 18 years of age typically spend around 15% of their time in school. Children need to be exposed to different teachers both on a daily and a yearly basis, since each one brings a different personality to influence the students. Somewhere along the line for most of us there will have been at least one teacher who was a powerful role model. We need teachers, but how and when they are deployed requires careful planning. Is there an optimum class size? Is that number 10, 20 or 30 students, and should the number be the same for 5 year-olds and 18 year-olds? John Abbott claims that education today is 'back to front and inside out' (Abbott, 2000). Traditionally we may have class sizes of 35 in primary schools and classes of eight in Year 12. Could there be something wrong here?

Finally, we need to rethink the *learning process* and this is the thrust of my thesis in this chapter. There is a truism that 'if you continue to do what you always did, you'll get what you always got'. The process produced Shakespeare, Newton, Beethoven, Da Vinci, Beckham and the Beatles. It produced you, the reader and me, the writer. So can it be all bad? Of course not, and we should not need to reinvent the wheel. But we do have compelling evidence from extensive research that indicates that, for many children, current education practice is falling short. For example, a recent survey carried out by the Centre for Evaluation and Monitoring (CEM) at Durham University (UK) was published in 2010 (Merrell and Tymms, 2010). It monitored the development of 117,000 children starting primary school in England, aged 4-5 years-old, between 2001 and 2008, and found that basic levels of development in early reading, vocabulary and mathematics have remained largely unchanged during that time. This is despite a raft of costly early years initiatives, such as Sure Start, in the UK.

This example, though from a specific context, highlights the scale of one current problem in education, where even with the investment of significant financial resources the initiative failed. We do not have extensive research evidence of the effectiveness or ineffectiveness of middle years education, be it from the MYP or from national systems. What evidence we have is largely anecdotal and based upon a widespread belief amongst educators of the ineffectiveness of current middle school practices. It is my belief that problems in middle years education begin to appear in Year 7 (first year of secondary school: approximately age 11) and become progressively worse in Years 8 and 9. For many children these are years of intense physiological, psychological and sociological changes (as outlined in other chapters of this book), which require a programme directly linked to their interests and needs.

For these students a five year programme of identical pedagogy in each year is, I believe, inappropriate. Two or three years of, say, the MYP is sufficiently flexible to allow staff (and students collaboratively) to develop a programme of learning that is highly relevant to their current needs and interest while they wrestle their way through early puberty. But by Years 9 or 10 some additional stimulus, in the form of a tangible incentive, is needed to focus students' attention on the rigour and demands that will face them with, for instance, the IB diploma or with any other higher education entry requirement. This was one of the reasons behind the University of Cambridge Local Examinations Syndicate developing the International General Certificate of Secondary Education (IGCSE) in 1985. International schools in Europe, in particular, took the opportunity as England introduced the General Certificate of Secondary Education (GCSE) to demand a two year externally certificated programme that could act as a precursor to the IB Diploma Programme. Prior to the introduction of IGCSE, schools taking the IB diploma relied upon either offering no external assessment and certification or offering the externally-examined O level examinations from England at age 16. Those schools that utilise the IGCSE syllabuses and assessments for the latter two, or preferably three, years of the middle years have some tangible benchmark by which to measure the effectiveness of middle school learning in preparation for the academic programme that is to follow.

Whatever the situation, research suggests that the learner must take centre stage in regulating his/her own learning and in determining the development of his/her own learning history and identity.

A possible model for the future

Curriculum

Curriculum reforms and changes have typically and traditionally arisen from concerns that young people are not being adequately prepared for their future needs in a rapidly changing world. Eva Vass encapsulates, for me, a vision for the future of which I have been dreaming for the last ten years. For this reason, I make no apology for quoting it in full here:

> In terms of possible transformations of school-based learning, thinking and knowing, a central feature is that mediated thought and action will become increasingly collective and interactive. This will have a revolutionary impact

on education, with participation in various online and face-to-face arenas of activity becoming an integral part of on-going classroom practices.

Learning will take place in a complex world of intersecting paths in virtual and real space, blending formal educational contexts, professional practices and more informal arenas of shared activity. Learning will also become essentially mobile, not tied to the physical space of the classroom, with learners and teachers, novices and experts connecting on a global scale. Note that, as a result of these transformations, the boundaries between what is virtual and real, or what is formal and informal, will also shift or possibly break down. Similarly, we will witness the reformulation of the role of the teacher and the student. Educators and teaching professionals will still play a very crucial part in the education process, but their role will be reconceptualised as an expert advisor or moderator. They will monitor students' activities and progress, help students make informed choices about their own learning, and support students on their paths towards collective participation, active agency, self-determination and responsible life-learning. Students will have access to different virtual/real participatory frameworks where they can gain skills and knowledge in diverse subject areas. Students will belong to numerous participatory cultures during their years of education, often simultaneously at one given point in time. A key challenge for students will be to manage such layeredness of collective action in overlapping participatory contexts.

Schools will function as real-life meeting places, entry points to different participatory settings, and points of orientation (like an air traffic control) from where various participatory engagements will be organised, managed and maintained. The assessment framework will shift towards strategies in line with the participatory and interactive nature of mediated learning, including e-assessment, peer assessment, or the assessment features inherent in particular technologies (*eg* instant feedback). (Vass, 2008)

I believe that the determinants of curriculum reform (ancient and modern) have included, and still include, epistemological concerns, societal needs, political expedients, historical perspectives and technological advances. All of these continue to have relevance. Societal needs and political expedients often stand in the way of change for national systems of education. Whilst global societal needs usually call for increased egalitarianism, governments, who traditionally initiate curriculum change, are forced to weigh up the impact such change may have in reducing their control over the nation by devolving more power and control to 'the people'. Usually, attendant financial implications must also be considered, particularly in times of recession.

For those schools that are allowed to operate independently of government control with respect to curriculum, such as international schools and private schools in many parts of the world, all five determinants above support the imperative to change. But change to *what*? Goodbourn *et al* argue that:

The concept of learning to learn is an epistemological one and some of the tensions in the application of the term relate to different understandings of the nature of knowledge and learning. Learning to learn emphasises the process of learning or of coming to know, and implies a difference in the quality of knowledge achieved through purposeful activity on the part of the learner. (Goodbourn *et al*, 2009)

I propose that we consider a move for middle years students from the current emphasis on a subject-based curriculum, to a curriculum based around five central tenets of high relevance to students and to student experience which meets and supports the five determinants listed above. Each of these tenets I will call a *learning domain.*

The 'learning domains' are:

- communication

- cosmology

- civilization

- culture

- community

and they form the backbone or scaffold upon which are based five *learning attributes*: knowledge, concepts, skills, attitudes and values.

Recent proposals produced by the Office for Standards in Education (Ofsted) in England argue that a well-designed curriculum:

- is personalised for learners, focusing on their greatest needs, aspirations and interests;

- uses time, staffing, space, resources and approaches to teaching, learning and assessment in ways most likely to meet the priorities;

- is reviewed regularly to ensure it is having the desired impact on learners; and

- ensures that learning evolves in response to changes in the learners themselves.

The same report suggests that successful, effective curriculum innovation must be disciplined. It must be focused, based on evidence and closely monitored (Ofsted, 2008).

In this chapter, I propose that within the framework of learning domains, and covering the learning attributes listed above, schools should develop *learning topics*. My proposal, outlined here, is unashamedly topic-based, not subject-based. Within each learning domain, areas of knowledge called *learning areas* will form foci upon which topics for study will be developed. These learning areas (see Figure 2) are built upon traditional subject areas; in addition, new areas such as anthropology, sociology and vocation are introduced. English, mathematics, languages and information technology fall within a domain called communication. The traditional sciences become integrated within the broad domain of cosmology, along with related fields of knowledge such as design, mind and spirit. The traditional humanities subjects of geography and history are extended with areas such as phylogeny (the bio-history of human development), ontology (the psycho-social stages of human development) and the roles of politics, sociology and economics into a domain called civilization. The domains of culture and community bring together a range of human arts, sport and leisure endeavours along with the role of relationships, faith and belief and the world of work.

It is not necessary that all learning areas be taught in any given year. At what stage in a three, four or five year programme topics based on the learning areas (of which there are 44) are developed will be a choice made collaboratively by students and staff (see Figure 2).

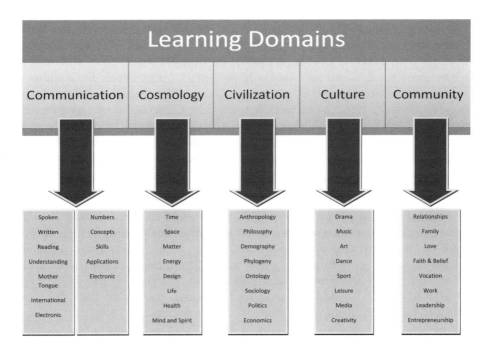

Figure 2: Learning domains

School Organisation

I am convinced that soon we shall see the virtual school become a reality. The visionaries of informal, anytime, anywhere learning already exist. My crystal ball presently confines me to the design of a middle and high school of the future, where learning in formal settings will still be required for social and economic reasons.

I believe that any radical change in curriculum and a pedagogy tending towards *learning to learn* needs a new design for schools in terms of infrastructure, environment, timing, as well as in pedagogy. For this reason I outline here some proposals that I know are already being implemented in a number of schools around the world.

School Buildings

Let us imagine a secondary school offering education from Years 7 through 13 housed in five main, separate, specialised *learning centre* buildings for the teaching of the five *learning domains*, where middle years teaching and learning take place in Years 7 through 11. In Years 12 and 13, teaching and learning of the IB Diploma Programme, A levels or other such programmes would also take place in the specialist areas, but on a more traditional subject basis. The overall building design would support various styles of teaching and learning and be flexible in usage.

School day

The recommended school day would be a minimum of eight hours long including break and lunch. The school would be operational as a school for 180 days per year, which is 1440 hours per year. Students would be in session for seven hours per day, and staff would have contact with students for six hours per day. Each *learning unit* would have a prescribed *learning duration,* which may last from one hour to one week to two weeks; the school would have varied start and finish times, flexible hours for staff and students (offering parent and community opportunities for learning in afternoons and evenings), and students would be encouraged to stay after school for private study with supervision provided by parents and community volunteers.

Timetable

The school week would be broken down for timetabling purposes into flexible units called *learning units,* which may be as short as one hour or as long as five days – with other time periods of two hours, a morning, an afternoon, a day or several days allotted to the learning unit. At the beginning of each term the time allocated for each year group of students to study the learning units would be timetabled for staff and students. This provides maximum flexibility for learning and the efficient use of time, space and resources.

Teaching and learning

The learning programme would be drawn up collaboratively with staff and students in terms of *learning topics,* based on the 44 learning areas of the five learning domains, and offering students opportunities to develop the five learning attributes.

There would be no prescription with regard to which learning areas are addressed in any given year/grade group; nor when they are addressed during the period of the middle years. Neither would there be prescription with respect to the frequency with which they are addressed, or the time allocated for specific learning topics. The subject matter (content) would be learning topic-based, except that in all cases it should be relevant to the needs of students in that school at that time, of broad interest to the majority of students, and based upon local and global issues of concern relevant to the students.

In all cases knowledge should be comprehensive and of sufficient depth to cover the cognitive skills of comprehension, application, synthesis and evaluation. The learning topics should include opportunities to develop the five learning attributes, and the work should be capable of being assessed formatively and summatively using a range of assessment techniques. Full use should be made of technology and the media, and students should be encouraged to create digital learning resources. In terms of encouraging student independence, students should be capable of working from home or elsewhere; trained to lead their own learning and to evaluate their own progress.

The key to successful engagement of students in their learning will depend upon the relevance of the topics selected for study in the learning areas. It is recommended that local and global issues that are topical, and for which information is readily available in the media, should provide the source material for topics that support the generic themes that the school has chosen to develop as its own curriculum. Every week the radio and television, press media and the internet report on recurring themes that can provide source material in all 44 learning areas. Topics areas such as climate change, ecological disasters, natural disasters, terrorist acts, territorial disputes/tensions, violence, disease, epidemics, presidential and national elections, major breakthroughs in science, religious tensions, major sporting events, media events and so on can all provide relevant and immediate sources for topics to study in terms of the 44 learning areas. The school of the future should, I believe, be a 'learning ecosystem' made up of the home, the school and the community – all interconnected by technology.

Summary

I cannot emphasise sufficiently strongly the need to effect change in the design of the curriculum, buildings, the school day and our approach to learning in the middle years. There is something axiomatic about the term 'middle'. In world history the Middle Ages was a time of relative stagnation that ended with the Renaissance and developed into the Age of Enlightenment.

Perhaps we need the same to happen in middle school education.

References

Abbott, J (2000): *The Child is Father of the Man: How Humans Learn and Why.* Stafford: Network Educational Press.

Clinton, H R (1996): *It Takes a Village: And Other Lessons Children Teach Us.* New York: Touchstone.

Cowen-Fletcher, J (1994): *It Takes a Village.* London: Scholastic Press.

Department of Education and Children's Services (DECS) (2005): *Assessing the Impact of Phases l and ll: Learning to Learn 1999-2004.* DECS: Adelaide, South Australia.

Fox, I (2009): http://www.foxedu.co.nz/wp-content/uploads/2009/10/Ian_Fox-ePortfolios-_Personal_Space_for_Learning-Feb2008.pdf

Fredriksson, U and Hoskins, B (2007): The development of learning to learn in a European context, in *The Curriculum Journal,* 18 (2) pp127-134.

Goodbourn, R, Hartley, T, Higgins, S and Wall, K (2009): *Learning to Learn for Life 3: Research and practical examples for Secondary Schools.* London: Continuum International Publishing Group.

Hoskins, B and Fredriksson, U (2008): *Learning to Learn: What is it and can it be measured?* JRC Scientific and Technical Report EUR 23432 EN, Centre for Research on Lifelong Learning (CRELL). Available from: http://crell.jrc.ec.europa.eu/ [Accessed 12 December 2008]

Holt, J (1964): *How Children Fail.* London: Penguin.

Mehan, H (1979): *Learning Lessons: Social Organization in the Classroom.* Cambridge: Cambridge University Press.

Merrell, C and Tymms, P (2010): Changes in children's cognitive development at the start of school in England 2001-2008, in *Oxford Review of Education,* iFirst: pp1-13.

Ofsted (2008): *Curriculum innovation in schools.* London: Ofsted.

Sinclair, J and Coulthard, M (1992): Towards an analysis of discourse, in Coulthard, M (ed), *Advances in Spoken Discourse Analysis,* pp1-34. London: Routledge.

Smith, H and Higgins, S (2006): Opening Classroom Interaction: The Importance of Feedback, in *Cambridge Journal of Education,* 36 (4) pp485-502.

Vass, E (2008): *New technology and habits of mind. Beyond Current Horizons.* Commissioned by Department for Children, Schools and Families' Beyond Current Horizons project, led by Futurelab.

Notes